International Journal on Advances in Security

2016 vol. 9 nr. 1&2

Printed from e-media with permission by:

Curran Associates, Inc.
57 Morehouse Lane
Red Hook, NY 12571

Some format issues inherent in the e-media version may also appear in this print version.

Printed by Curran Associates, Inc. (2018)

International Academy, Research, and Industry Association (IARIA)
412 Derby Way
Wilmington, DE 19810

Phone: (408) 893-6407
Fax: (408) 527-6351

petre@iaria.org

Additional copies of this publication are available from:

Curran Associates, Inc.
57 Morehouse Lane
Red Hook, NY 12571 USA
Phone: 845-758-0400
Fax: 845-758-2633
Email: curran@proceedings.com
Web: www.proceedings.com

The *International Journal on Advances in Security* is published by IARIA.
ISSN: 1942-2636
journals site: http://www.iariajournals.org
contact: petre@iaria.org

International Journal on Advances in Security
Volume 9, Number 1 & 2, 2016

Rivalino Matias Jr ., Federal University of Uberlandia, Brazil
Manuel Mazzara, UNU-IIST, Macau / Newcastle University, UK
Catherine Meadows, Naval Research Laboratory - Washington DC, USA
Carla Merkle Westphall, Federal University of Santa Catarina (UFSC), Brazil
Ajaz H. Mir, National Institute of Technology, Srinagar, India
Jose Manuel Moya, Technical University of Madrid, Spain
Leonardo Mostarda, Middlesex University, UK
Jogesh K. Muppala, The Hong Kong University of Science and Technology, Hong Kong
Syed Naqvi, CETIC (Centre d'Excellence en Technologies de l'Information et de la Communication),Belgium
Sarmistha Neogy, Jadavpur University, India
Mats Neovius, Åbo Akademi University, Finland
Jason R.C. Nurse, University of Oxford, UK
Peter Parycek, Donau-Universität Krems, Austria
Konstantinos Patsakis, Rovira i Virgili University, Spain
João Paulo Barraca, University of Aveiro, Portugal
Sergio Pozo Hidalgo, University of Seville, Spain
Yong Man Ro, KAIST (Korea advanced Institute of Science and Technology), Korea
Rodrigo Roman Castro, Institute for Infocomm Research (Member of A*STAR), Singapore
Heiko Roßnagel, Fraunhofer Institute for Industrial Engineering IAO, Germany
Claus-Peter Rückemann, Leibniz Universität Hannover / Westfälische Wilhelms-Universität Münster / North-German Supercomputing Alliance, Germany
Antonio Ruiz Martinez, University of Murcia, Spain
Paul Sant, University of Bedfordshire, UK
Peter Schartner, University of Klagenfurt, Austria
Alireza Shameli Sendi, Ecole Polytechnique de Montreal, Canada
Dimitrios Serpanos, Univ. of Patras and ISI/RC ATHENA, Greece
Pedro Sousa, University of Minho, Portugal
George Spanoudakis, City University London, UK
Vladimir Stantchev, Institute of Information Systems, SRH University Berlin, Germany
Lars Strand, Nofas, Norway
Young-Joo Suh, Pohang University of Science and Technology (POSTECH), Korea
Jani Suomalainen, VTT Technical Research Centre of Finland, Finland
Enrico Thomae, Ruhr-University Bochum, Germany
Tony Thomas, Indian Institute of Information Technology and Management - Kerala, India
Panagiotis Trimintzios, ENISA, EU
Peter Tröger, Hasso Plattner Institute, University of Potsdam, Germany
Simon Tsang, Applied Communication Sciences, USA
Marco Vallini, Politecnico di Torino, Italy
Bruno Vavala, Carnegie Mellon University, USA
Mthulisi Velempini, North-West University, South Africa
Miroslav Velev, Aries Design Automation, USA
Salvador E. Venegas-Andraca, Tecnológico de Monterrey / Texia, SA de CV, Mexico
Szu-Chi Wang, National Cheng Kung University, Tainan City, Taiwan R.O.C.
Steffen Wendzel, Fraunhofer FKIE, Bonn, Germany
Piyi Yang, University of Shanghai for Science and Technology, P. R. China
Rong Yang, Western Kentucky University , USA
Hee Yong Youn, Sungkyunkwan University, Korea
Bruno Bogaz Zarpelao, State University of Londrina (UEL), Brazil
Wenbing Zhao, Cleveland State University, USA

International Journal on Advances in Security
Volume 9, Numbers 1 & 2, 2016

CONTENTS

The All Seeing Eye and Apate: Bridging the Gap between IDS and Honeypots

Christoph Pohl and Hans-Joachim Hof

MuSe - Munich IT Security Research Group
Munich University of Applied Sciences
Munich, Germany
Email: {christoph.pohl0, hof }@hm.edu

***Abstract*—Timing attacks are a challenge for current intrusion detection solutions. Timing attacks are dangerous for web applications because they may leak information about side channel vulnerabilities. This paper presents a methodology that is especially good at detecting timing attacks. Unlike current solutions, the proposed Intrusion Detection System uses a huge number of sensors for vulnerability detection. Honeypots are used in IT Security to detect and gather information about ongoing intrusions by presenting an interactive system as attractive target to an attacker. The longer an attacker interacts with a honeypot, the more valuable information about the attack can be collected. Honeypots should appear like a valuable target to motivate an attacker. This paper presents, in addition to the possibilities of timing attack vulnerabilities, a novel way to inject honeypot and analysis capabilities in any software based on x64 or i386 architecture. It fulfills two basic requirements: it can be injected into machine code without the need of recompilation and it can be configured during runtime. This means the honeypot is able to change the behavior of any function during runtime. The concept uses sophisticated stealth technologies to provide stealthiness. In conclusion, the research presents a novel way to detect side channel vulnerabilities and an inbuilt hypervisor to provide configurable honeypot capabilities to explore these vulnerabilities to an attacker. The proposed solution in this paper offers a highly configurable injection technology, which can change the behavior of any function without the need of recompilation or even reinstallation. It is able to provide these capabilities in the kernel or userland of actual *Nix systems.**

Keywords*—*intrusion detection; honeypot; virtualisation; sensor; brute force; timing

I. Introduction

This paper is an extended version of [1]. It also extends another research, published by the authors in [2], [3]. Hence, this research paper is based on those publications and extends them with a novel way of honeypot creation.

Intrusion Detection Systems (IDS) in combination with firewalls are the last defense line in security when protecting web applications. The purpose of an IDS is to alert a human operator or an Intrusion Prevention System that an attack is in preparation or currently taking place.

One common challenge for web applications is the detection of timing attacks. A timing attack is an attack, which uses time differences between different actions to gain information. Intrusion Detection Systems typically use sensors to collect data. In this work, a sensor describes a data source that provides data useful for attack detection. Useful in this context means that the data must be linked to actions of a web application. Data of sensors is analyzed by All-Seeing Eye to detect attacks.

Usually, honeypots can be classified into Low- and High Interaction Honeypots. A Low Interaction Honeypot is able to simulate services or system environments. A High Interaction Honeypot provides a real exploitable system.

A common challenge in honeypot creation, is to inject exploits into a High Interaction Honeypot. The provider of such a honeypot needs to install exploitable software or to inject vulnerabilities into a software. This means a high consumption of resources.

The major reasearch question in this research is twofold:

- Is it possible to detect timing attack vulnerabilities and to identify the correct function, reponsible for this leak?
- How to change the behavior of functions to deploy a honeypot (for example to provide timing attack vulnerabilities), but without the need of reinstallation, recompilation or resource expensive development?

The proposed solution in this paper offers a highly configurable injection technology, which can change the behavior of any function without the need of recompilation or even reinstallation. It is able to provide these capabilities in the kernel or userland of actual *Nix systems. This manipulation technology allows the provider to present different environments or behavior depending on current system status. For example: the attacker knows that a system is based on ext4-File system and uses a standard hard drive (SATA based) without any virtualisation. He expects that the system will have a throughput of about 65 MB/s. The real honeypot system, based on ESXI virtualisation with extensive caching has a throughput of 550MB/s (ESXI will cache all IO in RAM). To scale down the system, the provider needs to install the honeypot on the expected system, or to rewrite the syscall for writing and reading. This means a lot of overhead in recompilation the kernel or installation on specific hardware.

The proposed solution is able to hook functions and provide a hypervisor-like technology, which makes it possible to change the behavior without the need of any compilation, nor installation.

Another possibility is to inject a rule engine for function parameter, system parameters and the result generation of any function. The honeypot provider is able to formulate rules which can change the behavior based on those parameters. For example, the provider is able to present a file structure for PID 42 and a completely different file structure for PID 84. This manipulation is able to decoy an attacker or even to suppress harmful actions. A rule just needs to prevent a system call by returning an error code.

For productive usage, the honeypot should not be detectable by an attacker (or just with sophisticated analysis tools). It must also provide a low overhead in time consumption (performance).

The proposed solution fulfills all requirements. Hence, it is a novel way to build easy to configure honeypot systems.

The rest of this paper is structured as follows: Section II presents related work. Section III describes the concept and implementation of the sensors used by All-Seeing Eye. The use of multiple sensors to detect intrusions is described in Section IV. Section V evaluates All-Seeing Eye under different attacks, especially timing attacks. Section VI describes a novel way to inject honeypot technologies in a running system. Section VII evaluates this technology with different settings. Section VIII concludes the paper and gives an outlook on future work.

II. Related Work

Anomaly detection is based on the hypothesis that there are deviations between normal behavior and behavior under intrusion [4], [5], [6], [7]. Many techniques have been researched for the detection like network traffic analysis [8], [9], [10], statistical analysis in records [11] or sequence analysis with system calls [12], [13], [14], [15]. A combination of this research with anomaly detection methods based on multiple sensors allows to find yet unknown attacks. Configuring intrusion detecting systems for one distinct system or one distinct vulnerability needs configuration with current solutions. The solution presented in this paper does not need any configuration.

In [13], [14], it is proved that call chains of system calls show different behavior under normal conditions and under intrusion, hence intrusion detection is possible. However, a normal model must be trained using learning data to detect attacks. In [14], it is shown that normal behavior produces fingerprintable signatures in system call data. A deviation from these signatures is defined as intrusion. This method is restricted to the usage of system calls and does not use more fine granular sensor data. In [16], a way to detect anomalies with information flow analysis is shown. Profiling techniques are used, injecting small sensors in a running application. They propose a model with clusters of allowed information flows and compare this normal model against actual information flow. Similar models are proposed in [17], [18], [19]. This approach is similar to our approach, but [16] focuses on offline audits for penetration testing. The approach presented in this paper is intended to be used online, hence it does not analyze the whole information flow but focuses on the method call chain, and is therefore more efficient.

In [20], it is shown that vulnerability probing can be detected using multiple sensors, especially sensor that calculate the possibility a resource is called by a user. These sensors are called access frequency based sensors. However, the system presented in [20] needs a lot of information about the system to protect (e.g., patterns describing legitimate resource calls), hence is difficult to deploy in the field. The solution presented in this paper does not need any configuration.

A well known honeypot tool, based on LKM for 2.6 Linux Kernel, is Sebek [21][22]. Sebek is primarily used for logging purposes in High Interaction Honeypot. Thus, it provides several possibilities focused on logging (like logging via network or GUI). In [23][24], ways to detect Sebek are described. Sebek does not provide the possibility to manipulate system calls as Apate does.

Another approach for monitoring systems is to use virtual machine introspection and system view reconstruction. This approach is used, e.g., in [25][26][27]. This approach is stealthier then Apate, because the introspection is done by the hardware layer of the virtual machine. However, Apate also provides means to manipulate the behavior of system calls, which is not supported by [25][26][27].

SELinux [28] is a well known tool, which inserts hooks at different locations inside the kernel. This provides the possibility for access control on critical kernel routines. SELinux can be controlled on a very fine granular level with an embedded configuration language. While SELinux is very useful in hardening a kernel, it is not designed for honeypot purposes. Especially, it lacks in the possibility to decoy the attacker with "wrong" information.

Grsecurity [29] with PAX [30] is similar to Apate. However, it greatly differs in ease of deployment and ease of configuration [31]. It also lacks in the possibility to decoy the attacker with "wrong" information.

In conclusion, non of the mentioned related work fulfill all requirements. Apate fulfills all requirements, hence is a useful building block for upcoming High Interaction Honeypots.

III. Sensors for a Massive Multi-Sensor Zero-Configuration Intrusion Detection System

A sensor describes a data source that provides useful data for attack detection. Useful in this context means that the data must be linked to actions of a web application. Data of sensors is analyzed by the proposed Intrusion Detection System All-Seeing Eye to detect attacks. Sensors are:

- Already available data sources like memory consumption of an application.
- Software sensors inserted into a web application or a web application framework.
- Sensors in the underlying operating system p.ex. sensors in the glibc or in system call routines

All-Seeing Eye depends on the availability of a large number of sensors that can be used for attack detection.

A. Sensor Implementation

Software sensors are implemented by injecting hooks at the beginning and end of functions. Hence, hooks are called before and after code execution of a method. With this approach, e.g., it is possible to measure the method execution time for each method used. It is also possible to identify the order of method execution. Hooks are injected directly into bytecode. It is not necessary to recompile any application protected by All-Seeing Eye. It is not necessary to perform any configuration for the web application that should be protected, hence All-Seeing Eye is called "zero configuration". As injection the technology proposed in [1], [2] is used. For the testbed used for the evaluation presented in this paper the sensors are placed in OpenCMS [32]. OpenCMS is a well known and widely used framework for Content Management. All-Seeing Eye takes care that methods used by the protected web application do not clash with method names used by All-Seeing Eye. Sensor data is written to a log file for further analyses.

One way to minimize the output of sensors (and the number of data to write to the log file) is to produce no output for methods that have an execution time lower than the resolution of the timestamps (1 ms). It is suspected that these methods would not generate any interesting output as these methods are usually helper methods or wrappers.

IV. Massive Multi-Sensor Zero-Configuration Intrusion Detection System

This section describes the design of the proposed massive multi-sensor zero-configuration intrusion detection system All-Seeing Eye. All-Seeing Eye uses the software sensors, described in more detail in the last section, to calculate intrusion metrics. The metrics described in the following are focused on detection of outliers in timeline data values to detect brute force attacks. However, the approach presented in this paper is not limited to this attack class, it can be easily adapted to detect various other attacks. Even attacks on the business logic can be detected as the presented approach uses software sensors embedded in the code of an application. This is out of scope of this paper.

An advantage of All-Seeing Eye is that it allows to detect side channel attacks without knowledge of the web application which is to be protected. In the absence of an attack, there is a high correlation between method calls defined in a method chain. As shown in Section V a single call results in correlated calls (method chain) of other methods. The system under load shows the same correlations. These correlations are further called as fingerprint s. Under attack, however, the system shows a different behavior, hence allows to identify attacks, see Section V for details. All-Seeing Eye does not need a preconfigured or constructed normal model. For this approach the normal model is created from history. At time $t = 0$ it is always assumed that there is no attack, hence status c is always $c! = attack$. If there is no attack, the same fingerprint s should show up in each distinct time period T with the same probability. A deviation from the number of fingerprints (written as $|s|$) in a time period T is defined as possible intrusion. This behavior is well known, as stated in Section II. The new approach here is the lack of need to define what a similar request is. The normal model is built using a quantile function, where the result is called α. α uses a floating history time period, which is defined as $n \times T$ and $t \in T$ are in state $c! = attack$.The multiplier n defines how much of the history is used. To control the sensitivity of the system, a configuration parameter p is used. In normal model α, a deviation is detected by:

$$c = \begin{cases} attack & \text{if } |s_{currentT}| \geq \alpha \times p \\ !attack & \text{if } |s_{currentT}| < \alpha \times p \end{cases} \tag{1}$$

This calculation is robust against statistical outliers and can be evaluated fast enough for real time calculation, in combination with structures related to sort optimization. In further researches these calculations will be done (together with other sensor calculations) with a graphical processing unit.

V. Evaluation

For the evaluation of the massive multi-sensor zero-configuration intrusion detection system, two typical attacks on web applications are used: timing attacks and vulnerability probing. Especially timing attacks are hard to detect for common intrusion detection systems. For our test environment OpenCMS version 8.5.1 [32] is used as web application to protect. OpenCMS is a well known and widely used framework for Content Management.

A. Evaluation Environment

For the evaluation of All-Seeing Eye, a paravirtualized, openvz solution [33] is used. This approach has the advantage that is is very realistic compared to simulations. The presented hardware settings are the settings of the corresponding virtual machine. Table I lists hardware and software used for the evaluation.

TABLE I: Experimental setup

Hardware(Server)	
CPU	4 Cores (2.1GHZ on hostsystem)
Memory	6 GB Ram
Ethernet	Bridged at 1 GBit Nic
Software(Server)	
Server Version	Apache Tomcat 7.0.28 [34]
JVM	Sun 1.6.0.27-b27

B. Fingerprints of Normal Behavior

To validate the hypothesis, that requests to the same target have the same fingerprint, the following experiment has been conducted.

First, a baseline is established for all other experiments. To do so, several requests are sent to the server and the server is restarted after each request. No interfering processes are running on this server.

After establishing the baseline, the whole website is crawled in a second step, ensuring that requests are sequential. The crawler is configured to request a single page and all depending images and scripts. To test the software under load in the third step, another crawler requests the server with 20 concurrent users, with a delay of one second between each request/user. Overall, there were in average 20 requests per second for different websites. The second and third step have been repeated 100 times. In each run of the experiment, the

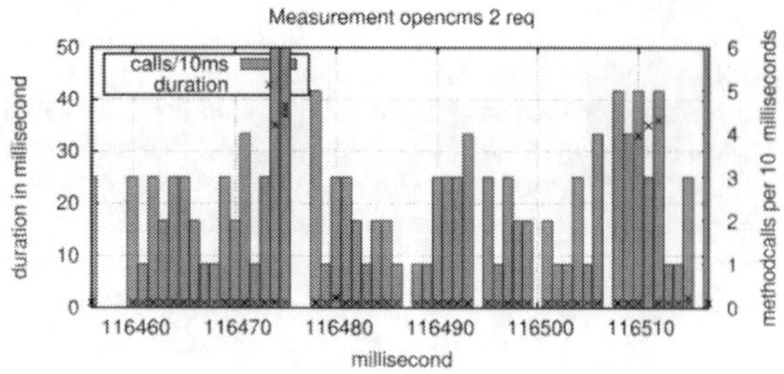

Figure 1: Two fingerprints of different requests

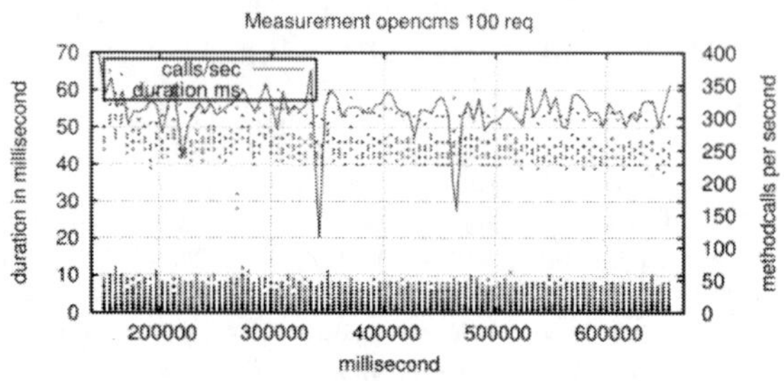

Figure 2: 100 requests on the same page

metrics described above produced unique fingerprints for every requested target. This can be seen in Figure 1. In this figure the fingerprint of the start page and the request to the login page are extracted from the logged data. Under load the signature looks like the picture presented in Figure 2.

The result in Figure 1 shows that there are stable correlations between method calls. For better readability, points that differ less then 3 milliseconds are averaged. The experiments show that it is possible with All-Seeing Eye to identify similar requests using their fingerprint.

C. *Fingerprints of Information Leakage and Probing for Vulnerabilities*

OpenCMS version 8.5.1 has a known information leakage vulnerability, as described in [35]: using the default setting there is no limit for failed logins per time period. Also, a large amount of information is given in error messages, especially the error message "this username is unknown", if the given user name does not exist and "password is wrong", if the given password is wrong for an existing user allow an attacker to find valid user names, by trying possible user names from a dictionary and using error messages to find out if an user name is valid. This attack can be detected with a statistical analysis to detect the brute force analysis II. To do so, a detection technique needs to identify if a single resource is called many times but with different parameter in the request header. A normal model is needed for allowing patterns to test for deviations of the normal model. This needs deep knowledge of the system to protect and the vulnerability itself. All-Seeing Eye is able to detect this attack (and also other probings using brute force attacks), without this knowledge about system and vulnerability.

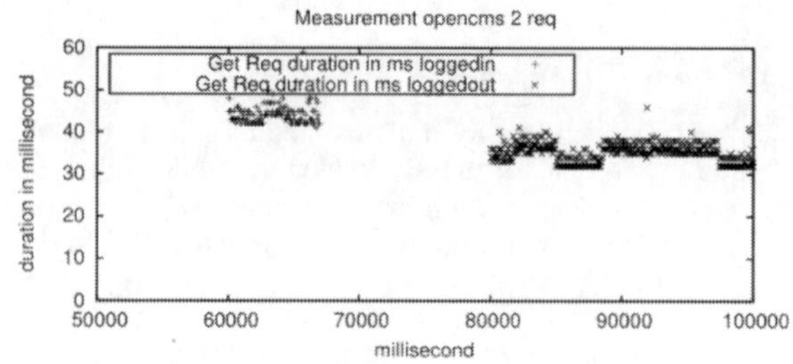

Figure 3: Time difference between logged in users and users not logged in on the start page

To evaluate if All-Seeing Eye can recognize brute-force attacks, an experiment has been conducted where an attacker probes the login page and tries to identify valid user names. The following pattern was used to generate the login requests:

```
http://192.168.2.89:8080/opencms/.../index.html?
    action=login&username=username_1&password=
    passwordnotindb ... snippedEnd
//username_1..username_n in dictionary
http://192.168.2.89:8080/opencms/.../index.html?
    action=login&username=username_n&password=
    passwordnotindb ... snippedEnd
```

The attacker used a dictionary with 1000 names for the brute-force attack. To make detection harder, the attacker uses 50 different user agents as well as 20 different IPs. Only one valid username exists in the database.

Figure 2 shows a subset of 100 requests. From the figure, it is obvious that the probing attempts produce many similar fingerprints. It shows a high correlation between different requests, the sensor values and the order different sensors are called in one requests. This order and the values are stable over all requests. Hence, All-Seeing Eyes can easily detect a probing attack even if someone uses different header data. No a-priory knowledge of the system which is to be protected or the vulnerability itself is necessary.

D. *Fingerprints of Timing attacks*

OpenCMS version 8.5.1 is vulnerable to timing attacks as can be seen in Figure 3. The figure shows the times for loading of the start page for users that are already logged in as well as for users that are not logged in. A significant difference (849 ms to 798 ms) exists.

Using this timing difference an attacker can brute force user names by a dictionary attack. All logged in users can be detected. As with the information leakage and probing attack in Subsection V-C, current intrusion detection solutions need information about the system which is to be protected and the vulnerability to detect this attack.

To test if All-Seeing Eye is able to detect timing attacks without knowledge (zero-Configuration), the following experiment has been conducted: An attacker uses a dictionary of 1000 user names to execute the timing attack. Each request has different header data in the request only in the login name and the password as shown in listing 1.

Listing 1: Header Data

```
//successful login
http://192.168.2.89:8080/opencms/.../index.html?
    action=login&username=admin98&password=admin
    1...snippedEnd
//username not present, pwd not present
http://192.168.2.89:8080/opencms/.../index.html?
    action=login&username=usernamenotpresent&
    password=wrongpwd...snippedEnd
//username present with wrong password
http://192.168.2.89:8080/opencms/.../index.html?
    action=login&username=admin832&password=
    wrongpwd...snippedEnd
```

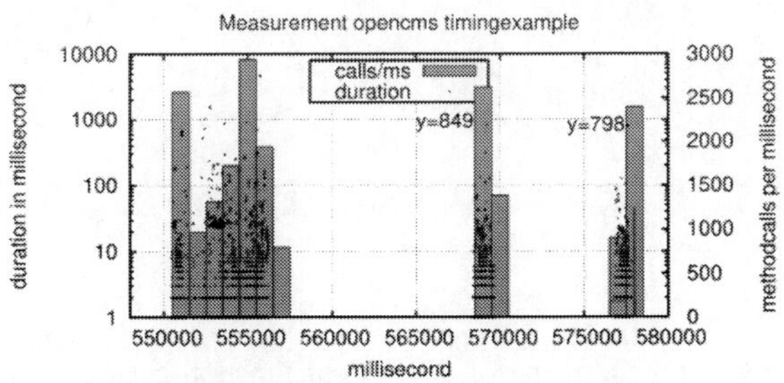

Figure 4: 100 requests on the same page

Figure 4 shows an example of fingerprints of the experiment.

The first fingerprint shows a successful login, the second fingerprint shows a login with no present username and third fingerprint shows a login with present username but wrong password. The results clearly show a correlation of the differences in order, time, and amount of method calls for each request.

VI. Bridging the Gap to Honeypot Deployment

As stated in Section III, it is possible to analyze an application for timing attack vulnerabilities without the need of sophisticated penetrations tests. However, whenever a provider wants to offer a vulnerability, he needs to install this exploitable piece of software. In the proposed example of timing attacks, the provider is able to identify the place where such a vulnerability has to be installed.

More generally, this place can be any function or a set of functions available on the target system. The provider needs to change this function or set of functions to change the behavior of this functionality.

This solution, further called APATE, intercepts functions and allows to execute custom routines in those functions. Figure 5 shows this interception strategy.

Any function call to the hooked function will be intercepted by a preprocessor hook. This hook leads to the hypervisor. Inside the hypervisor some custom code gets processed. The hypervisor and its language is explained in Section VI-E. The result of this routine decides on the action to invoke. Within this hypervisor process, it is possible to manipulate,

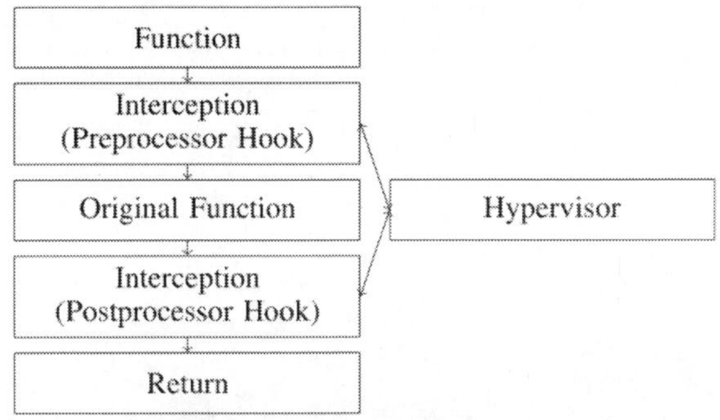

Figure 5: interception strategy of Apate

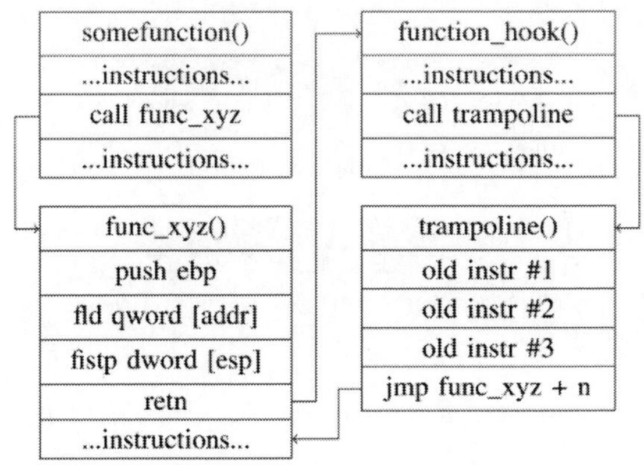

Figure 6: Hooking using a so-called trampoline

block and/or log the original function parameters and the further execution of the original function. The manipulation possibilities are explained in detail in Section VI-A. The postprocessing hook has the same capabilities than the preprocessor. In addition it is able to manipulate the return code of the original function.

To prevent detection, Apate is injected into the original function with a trampoline technology. Figure 6 describes this trampoline.

This technology, well known in rootkits for Windows or Linux, is explained in detail in [2]. The hook injector overwrites original code (located in `func_xyz` in Figure 6) with a jump to the hooking code. The hook will process the hypervisor. At the end of the hook, the trampoline gets called. The trampoline holds the overwritten code from the original code, and returns then back to the original code. This technology makes it hard for rootkit detection tools and is live patchable.

A. Manipulating functions

Apate and, therefore, the manipulation of functions can be configured with the help of a high level language. In detail the configuration high level language and the rule possibilities are explained in [2]. This high level language formulates rules (or any other functionality), which gets process by the hook. A brief overview over this functionality is described in Figure 7.

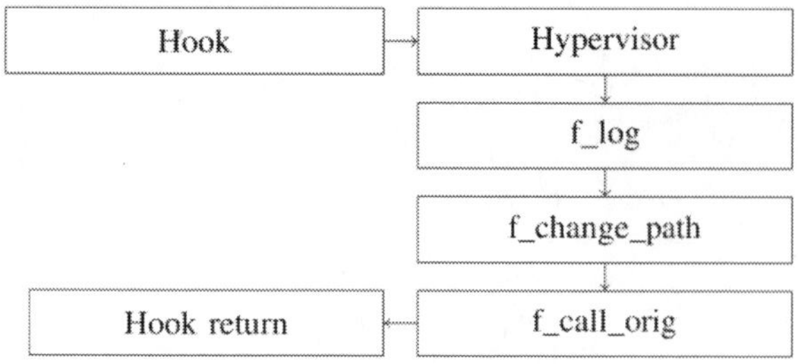

Figure 7: Conceptual Manipulation Strategy

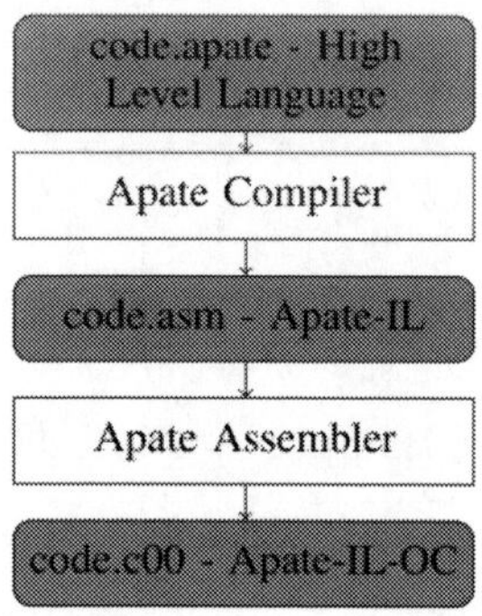

Figure 8: Configuration workflow of Apate

In this case the hypervisor works with three "rules". The first rule logs the function call and its parameter, the second rule manipulates some parameter and the third rule proceeds the original function with the manipulated parameters. Of course, it is possible to write rules which delays the original function or prevent the execution of the original function.

In demarcation to [2] the high level language results in binary machine code like bytecode, which gets processed by the hypervisor. Figure 8 shows the compilation and assembling of the rules. A rule is formulated in a high level language (*code.apate*). This gets compiled over bison and flex to an intermediate Assembler like language (*code.asm*). This language is further called the Apate Intermediate Language or *Apate-IL*. This Apate-IL must be architecture dependent, as it provides addresses. In the assembling step the Assembler like code gets assembled to a machine code like language (*code.c00*, see also Section VI-E). This binary code is processable by the hypervisor and further called the Apate Intermediate Language Operational code or *Apate-IL-OC*.

B. The Apate High Level Language

The language provides a flexible language to build hooks for functions in any x86 or i386 architecture. It is able to define functions, reuse patterns, store variables and basic mathematical computation. With those abilities it is possible to build transparent rulesets for the hooking of functionalities. This section gives a brief overview over some core components of this language. The language is inspired by Haskell[36] and pf [37]. A more detailed description is given in [2].

Listing 9 shows some example source code for the Apate language. In this case, 3 different conditions will be generated.

```
define c1,c2,c3 as condition
define r1,r2 as rule
define a1,a2 as action
define cb1 as conditionblock
define rc1 as rulechain
define sy1 as syscall

let c1 be testforpname
let c2 be testforparam
let c3 be testforuid
let a1 be manipulateparam
let a2 be log
let sy1 be sys_open

let cb1 be {(c1("mysql") && c2(0;"/var/\
   lib/mysql/*"))}

let r1 be {cb1->a1(0;"/var/lib/mysql/*" \
   ;"/honey/mysql/")}
let r2 be {{c3(">",0)}->a2()}
let rc1 be {r2,:r1} // :defines exit

bind rc1 to sy1
```

Figure 9: Example Sourcecode Apate language

`c1` tests the actual process name against a given name. `c2` tests if a parameter of the hooked function is equal to another value. `c3` tests if the uid is equal to a given value. The actions `a1,a2` manipulates a parameter and write some log. The `bind` statement binds the rules to the syscall `open`. This will build a hook in the `open` function. In conclusion, the rulechain rewrites the parameter to any call for `open` and when the param inherits */var/lib/mysql* to the path */honey/mysql*. This redirection of the path gets logged for further analysis.

C. The Apate Intermediate Language

The intermediate language is based on the concept of the Intel i386 assembly language. A command consists of the command and at maximum two parameters. As minimum a command has no parameter. A parameter can be a constant, a register, a value of an register, a pointer or the value of a pointer. The hypervisor has an own stack, registers and memory management. This leads to the basic concept in Listing 2:

Listing 2: Apate-IL Concept

```
labelname:
command <dest> <source>
command <dest>
command
```

Technically, a label gets assembled to a [nop] and all references to the label are transformed to the appropriate address. Apate-IL consists of the basic commands like [nop],[jmp|jz|jnz],[add|sub|mul|div],[cmp|test],[call],[ret],[push|pull] and a few other commands for convenience.

In addition to a standard assembly language, there are commands especially designed for honeypot purposes:

- [sleep] - delay for ticks
- [inwind] - does some sophisticated jumps for anti disassembling

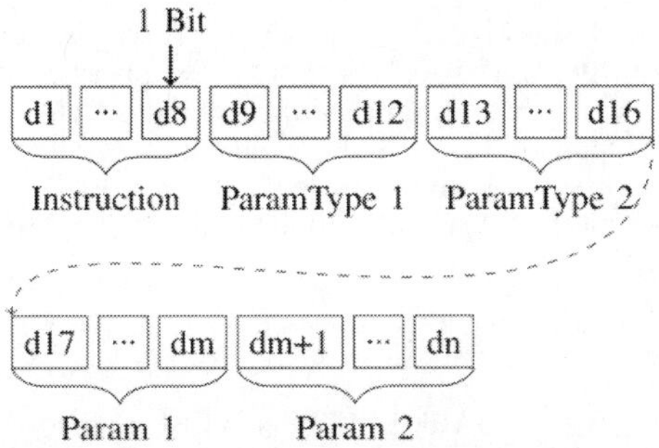

Figure 10: A command in Apate IL-OC

- [adebug] - does some anti debugging techniques
- [asm] - executes real Machine code
- [fcall] - calls "real" functions
- [oops] - provides kernel oops
- [fpush| fpull] - makes it possible to interact with the underlying process (the original function)

The [sleep] command consumes real CPU-Time and provides a sleep functionality. The [inwind] command is just a wrapper for inwind calls. This technology makes it possible to jump into a real command. This means, that whenever a "long" command, like the [move <dest> integer] command uses the constant integer to formulate a new "short" command like [jz 5], which is only four bytes over all and has the size of an integer, the inwind command calculates the jump address to this "obfuscated" command. This is just for convenience to avoid annoying calculations. The command [adebug] provides some, out of scope in this paper, technology against debugging. The command [asm] maps real machine code(provided as shellcode) into RAM and runs it. This makes it possible to optimize some calculations. The [fcall] command is able to call real functions on any given address and is used as a wrapper for the real [call] command. The [oops] command provides in combination with a special kernel system call a real system kernel oops. The [fpush| fpull] commands can interact with a special stack, provided by the hypervisor, to communicate with the hooked function. Both commands are used to read parameters and store them back.

D. The Apate Intermediate Language Operational Code and the Assembler

The Apate-IL-OC is assembled from the Apate Intermediate Language. It is a binary, optimized and preprocessed version of the Apate-IL. A single command is shown in Figure 10. An instruction is a 8 Bit operational code, followed by 2 nibbles, representing the parameter types. This type decides if the param is an address (64 or 32 Bit), an Integer (64 or 32Bit) constant, or a register ($r0 \ldots 9$). The decision for 64 or 32 Bit is architecture dependent and uses the length of size_t. The following parameters can have different sizes, depending on their type. Some commands, like [nop], does not have any parameters and, therefore, there is no need for type decision. Such a command needs only 8 Bit. Whenever a command has just one parameter, the second nibble has the value 0x0, which means no type.

A command can have any operational code between 0x00 and FE. The FE opcode is used as a debugging trap.

During the assembling part, the assembler lexes the Apate Intermediate language. With the help of Yacc an AST gets built from the sourcecode. This AST gets preprocessed by the assembler. Any label and references to labels gets transformed to addresses in a first step. In a second step, the preprocessor checks for wrong (or invalid) addresses, invalid commands or irregular command chains. In a third step, any data that should be stored in a data section gets collected.

Following this step, the assembler will transform the AST to the Apate Intermediate Operating Language, which is in fact some binary code.

In a last step, the assembler generates a binary representation, consisting of a header (inspired by a ELF header), the Apate IL-OC section and a data section.

Out of scope in this research is the ability to store some information about encoding, different instructions sets and other information, which are needed for sophisticated obfuscation and anti disassembling technologies.

E. Hypervisor engine

The hypervisor needs to fulfill different requirements:

- Provide a turing complete language for flexible rules
- Provide a hypervisor to process this language
- Provide a hypervisor that has low resource consumption
- Provide the ability to call system functions, change process memory content
- Embed real x64 or i386 machine code

Another requirements like different instruction sets, Huffman encoding, inbuilt obfuscation and anti-disassembling strategies are not in scope of this paper but part of the real hypervisor prototype. Those (not listed) requirements make it substantially harder to detect and analyze the hypervisor system and their rules.

The Apate Hypervisor has a classical design, based on register, stack and an instruction array. Figure 11 describes the basic architecture for the Apate hypervisor.

The Code Section holds the pure Instruction Code, as provided by the assembler. This Instruction Code gets processed by the Decoder and Execution Unit. The Data Section stores all constants from the source file. Most of the following data storage units are architecture dependent. The underlying Host architecture decides if a value is 32 Bit or 64 Bit.

The Register is able to store 32|64 Bit Values and can be compare with the General Purpose Register from other architectures like x64. The Flag register holds Flags like Zero Flag or Traps for the Debugger. The stack can keep 1024 32|64 Bit values. The Pointer Register is used to store pointer like the instruction pointer, the return pointer and the stack pointer.

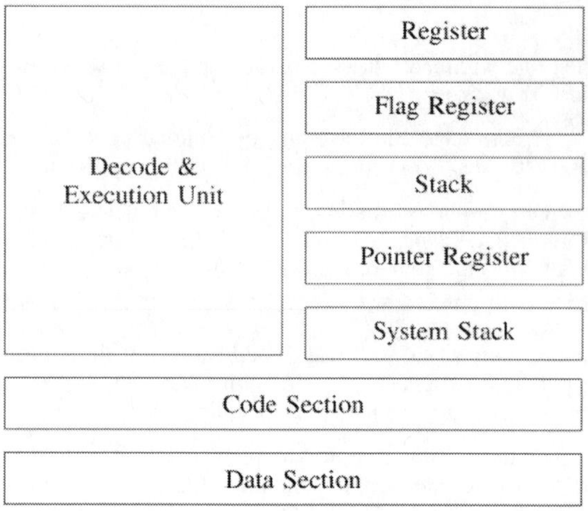

Figure 11: Basic concept of Hypervisor

The System Stack is a special stack to interact with the host system. The hypervisor is able to write values to and read values from this stack, and the internal language is able to do the same. With this communication stack, parameters and other values can be injected into the hypervisor based software.

Table II shows some of the components in Apate Hypervisor.

TABLE II: Register and Stack in Apate

Type	Name	Number	Size (Bit)
Instruction Section	-	n	8
Data Section	-	n	8
General Purpose Register	r0...r9	10	64|32
Stack	-	1024	64|32
Instruction Pointer	eip	1	32
Stack Pointer	stp	1	32
Return Pointer	rtp	1	32
Flag Register	-	1	8
Flag	Zero-Flag	1	1
Flag	Sign-Flag	1	1
Flag	Error-Flag	1	1
Debugger Flag	Next-Flag	1	1
Debugger Flag	Trap-Flag	1	1

The CPU starts with the first address in the code section stored in the instruction pointer. Due performance issues the opcode gets interpreted by index to function pointer translation. In combination with the two nibbles (1 Byte) to identify the correct function it needs two steps and $512 \times 32|64$ Bit to identify an opcode target.

The values stored in the nibbles to identify the param types are used to read the parameter values from the instruction code.

Together with the opcode, the Execution Unit calculates the result of this operation and then sets the next instruction pointer.

VII. Evaluation

The Apate Hypervisor needs to process the custom code inside a hook in an efficient way. Performance tests should assure that Apate is able work under productive usage. The most important factor is the overhead of the hypervisor and the processing of common used code patterns. To evaluate the performance of Apate a common command in *Nix system is hooked.

The experimental setup is shown in Table III.

TABLE III: Experimental setup

Host System	
CPU	2 x XEON
Memory	64 GB Ram
Ethernet	Bridged at 1 GBit Nic
Virtualisation	ESXI
Measurement System	
CPU	2 x VMWare CPU
Memory	8GB Ram
HDD	30 GB Backed by ESXI
HDD Format	ext4

The test scenario is a clone of the cp-command. Aside from command parameter processing, the command uses the commands in Listing 3.

Listing 3: Example code for cp-command

```
for (;;) {
        readed = read(filenosrc, buffer, buffer_size
            );
        if (!readed) {
                //eof
                break;
        }
        written = write(filenodst, buffer,(size_t)
            readed);
}
```

This piece of code reads `buffer_size` bytes from file `filenosrc` and writes `readed` bytes back to file `filenodst`. The variable `buffer_size` is one of the performance variables under *Nix Systems and corresponds to the copybuffer.

The performance test generates a file with 100MB and random data. Then this file gets copied with the cp-command to another file. As reference, a measurement without any hooking has been done. This reference is further called $m1$. Each measurement has been done with different values of `buffer_size`.

Let $l_n \times 1024$ be the value of `buffer_size`. l_n starts with 0. However, a `buffer_size` of 0 is not usable. In this case the `buffer_size` is set to 1.

$$l_n = \begin{cases} l_{n-1} + 4 & \text{if } l_n < 100 \\ l_{n-1} + 100 & \text{if } 100 \leq l_n \\ & \wedge l_n < 1,000 \\ l_{n-1} + 1,000 & \text{if } 1,000 \leq l_n \\ & \wedge l_n \leq 10,000 \end{cases} \tag{2}$$

Each size of l_n has been tested 10 times.

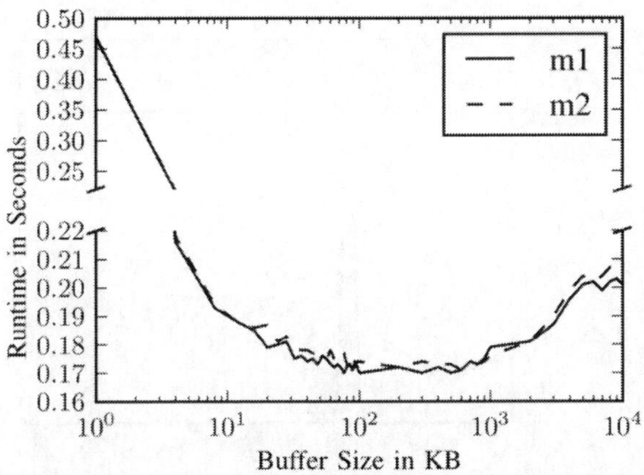

Figure 12: Performance Measurement m1 against m2

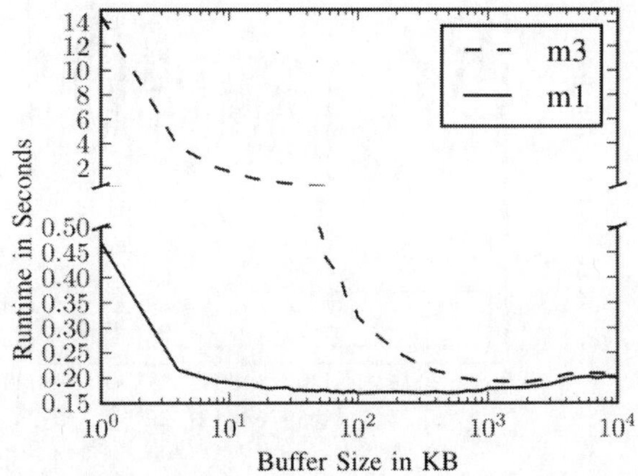

Figure 13: Performance Measurement m1 against m3

To test the overhead the parent function (in this case the function that inherits the code in Listing 3) gets hooked by Apate. The custom code inherits 2500 compare statements. Hence, those statements reflects 50 string compares with 50 chars each. This test is further called $m2$.

Figure 12 compares the reference $m1$ with the overhead of the hypervisor in $m2$.

This measurement shows that the `buffer_size` value has an impact to the overall performance. The outstanding performance for reading and writing (with over 500MB/sec) can be explained with heavy caching due the ESXI Host system. This measurement also shows that the overhead for the hypervisor is not significant.

The next measurement ensures that the hypervisor is able to server even a high amount of custom code calls. For this the `read` function has been hooked with the same custom code than before. Dependent on the `buffer_size` more or less hooks are called by the cp-command. This measurement is further called $m3$. Figure 13 shows the difference between $m1$ and $m3$.

This measurement shows that Apate is able to serve custom code even with a high amount 100.000 custom code calls.

Table IV concludes all 3 measurements.

TABLE IV: Performance Description m1,m2,m3

Measurement	m_1	m_2	m_3
Measurements	4,390	4,390	4,390
min(runtime sec)	0.16	0.17	0.19
max(runtime sec)	0.48	0.48	15.73
mean(runtime sec)	0.186	0.188	0.810
sd(runtime sec)	0.042	0.042	2.017
Throughput(MB/s) mean	536.320	530.566	303.411

In conclusion, the measurement shows that the amount of hooks does not interfere with the performance of one single hook. The Standard deviation is also in an expected range. The throughput row shows that even under high load, and when every system call to —open— is hooked even under worst scenario (`buffer_size==0`), the throughput rate is better than the throughput rate from a standard HDD.

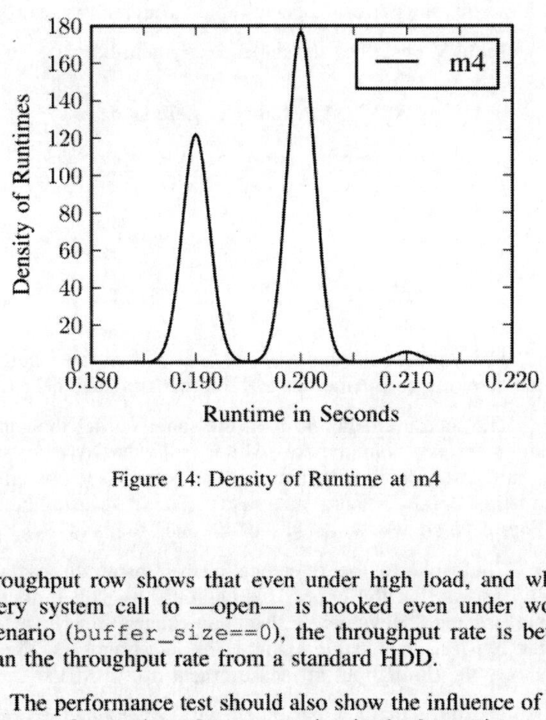

Figure 14: Density of Runtime at m4

The performance test should also show the influence of the amount of operations that are running in the hypervisor.

For this the cp-command has been tested 1000 times with a `buffer_size=8` and a file size of 100MB.

Figure 14 shows the reference measurement. The measurement $m4$ shows the reference measurement without any hypervisor influence. The x-axis shows the runtime in seconds. The y-axis shows the density of each runtime in all measurements. The measurement shows, that the measurement is only in a small range of runtimes, which means a stable runtime for a given buffer and file size to copy. Figure 15 shows the throughput of the reference measurement in MB/s. The throughput is generated with a weighted exponential moving

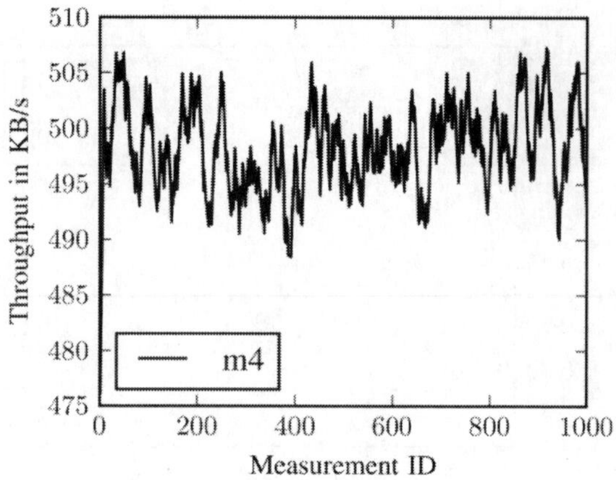

Figure 15: Throughput behavior m4

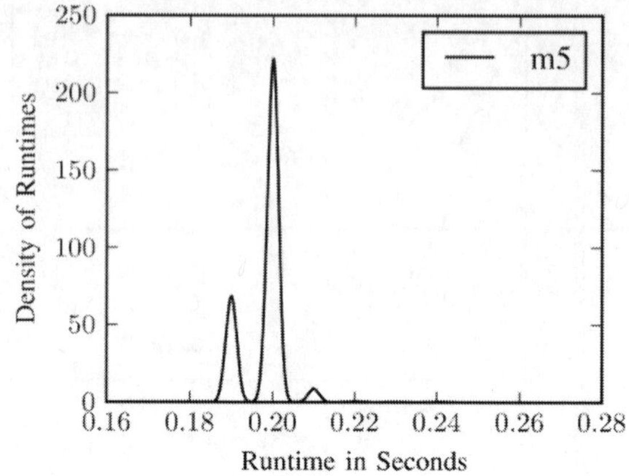

Figure 16: Density of Runtime at m5

average over 20 measurements for more clearance. It also shows that the performance is stable through all measurements.

Table V describes the m4 measurement data.

TABLE V: Performance Description m4

Measurement	*time*	*throughputMB/s*
Measurements	1000	1000
min	0.19 sec	465.029762
max	0.21 sec	513.980263
mean	0.196170	498.168027
standard deviation	0.005221	13.303990

The standard deviation shows that with a given buffer and file size, the command has a stable performance behavior.

The measurement $m5$ uses the same setting than in measurement $m4$, but a hook which calls the hypervisor with a custom code is called once. The hypervisor custom code inherits 2500 compare statements, like in measurement $m2$. Figure 16 shows the density of the measurement $m5$.

Compared to the reference measurement, the data from $m5$ shows that the hypervisor has only a small influence on performance. However, it also shows that the performance of the hypervisor is stable along 1000 measurements. Figure 17 shows the throughput of measurement $m5$ in MB/s.

The throughput is generated with a weighted exponential moving average over 20 measurements. This illustration of data shows that the performance is stable over all measurements. It also shows that it is possible to keep the throughput rate, even with the hypervisor enabled.

Table VI describes measurement $m5$.

The standard deviation shows, that the hypervisor has a stable performance behavior.

In measurement $m6$, the behavior of a productive honeypot scenario is shown. In this case a honeypot, exploitable by timing attacks and with the ability to appear with an HDD with

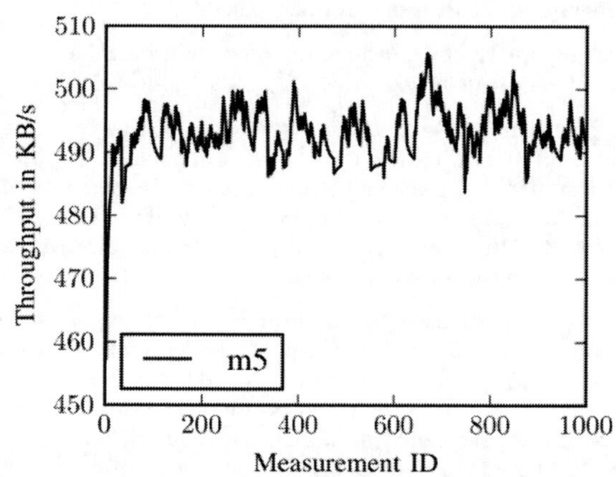

Figure 17: Throughput behavior m5

TABLE VI: Performance Description m5

Measurement	*time*	*throughputMB/s*
Measurements	1000	1000
min	0.19 sec	406.901042
max	0.24 sec	513.980263
mean	0.198180	513.980263
standard deviation	0.005265	12.897778

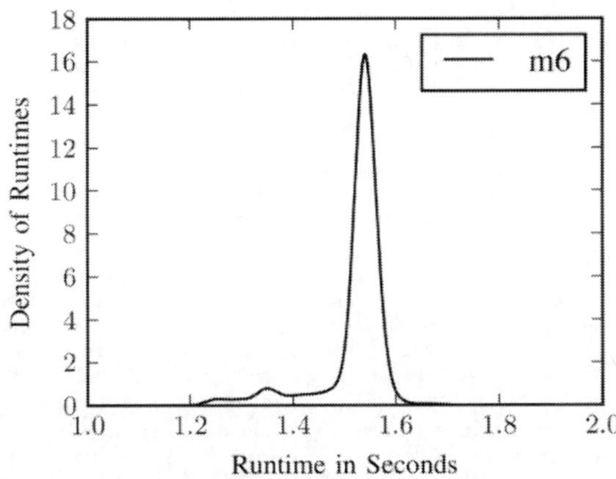

Figure 18: Density of Runtime at m6

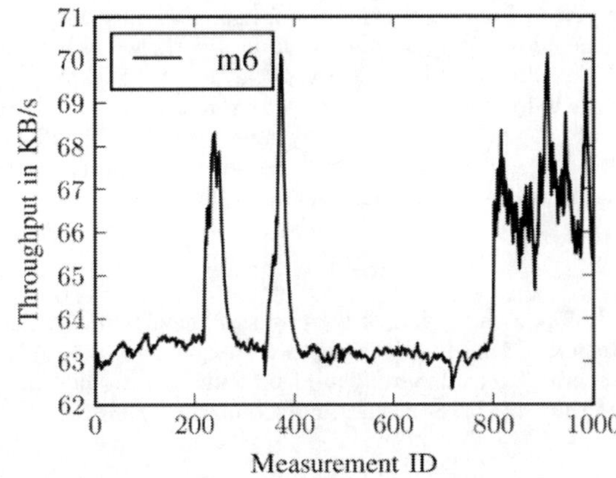

Figure 19: Throughput behavior m6

another throughput rate is built with Apate. The hypervisor should provide a throughput rate of 65 MB/s, instead of the real throughput rate from $m4$. The scenario is the same like in $m4$ and $m5$. A random generated file of 100MB gets copied and the time gets measured. This measurement has been repeated 1000 times.

Let t_{real} be the time to copy one KB on the real system. The real system is the honeypot system. Let t_{honey} be the time to copy one KB on a fictional honeypot system. In the case of this measurement, it is a system with a HDD that provides a throughput rate of 65MB/sec. Let b be the buffer size, used by the cp-command. The hook with the hypervisor is bound to the `read`-function. To decoy the attacker, the hook needs to sleep for a time t_{sleep}, such that:

$$t_{sleep} = b \times (t_{honey} - t_{real}) \quad (3)$$

The calculation $t_{honey} - t_{real}$ is a constant t_{wait} to describe the honeypot system.

The custom code, processed by the hypervisor, reads the variable `buffer_size`. Then, it multiplies this variable with the sleeping rate constant t_{wait}. The result is used to trigger the sleeping function. The full functionality in Apate-IL is shown in Listing 4.

Listing 4: Sleeping function in Apate-IL

```
fpull r1
fpull r2
mul r1 r2
sleep r1
exit
```

The first and second line reads the `buffer_size` and the constant t_{wait} and stores them in register `r1` and `r2`. In the third line, both values stored in the registers gets multiplied. The result gets stored in the most left register `r1`. The sleeping command uses this value to sleep. The exit command quits the hypervisor processing.

Figure 18 describes the density of $m6$.

Compared to $m4$ the measurements show that the sleeping function is able to generate a completely different runtime scenario. It also shows that the performance is stable along all measurements.

Figure 19 shows the throughput of measurement $m6$ in MB/s.

The throughput is generated with a weighted exponential moving average over 20 measurements. This illustration also shows that the throughput is stable over all measurements. It also describes that the target rate of 65 MB/s is stable over all measurements with a small deviation.

Table VII describes the data for measurement $m6$.

TABLE VII: Performance Description m6

Measurement	$time$	$throughput MB/s$
Measurements	1000	1000
min	1.23 sec	58.128720
max	1.68 sec	79.395325
mean	1.521950	64.290778
standard deviation	0.063464	3.020391

This description shows that the mean throughput is very near the expected throughput rate. It also shows that the standard deviation is low, so that the honeypot is able to provide a stable throughput rate.

VIII. Conclusion

This paper presents Apate, a hypervisor for custom code to hook any function in a *Nix Kernel or userland-program. With the possibilities of the proposed solution to detect timing attacks, it is possible to identify the best place to hook a function and to inject the honeypot component. Apate works on a function level, and is able to log, block or manipulate functions. The evaluation shows that Apate has only a low performance overhead and can be used in productive scenarios. The evaluation also shows that Apate is able, with only four commands, to build a honeypot for timing attacks, and to lure an attacker with timings from a completely different hardware system, without any installation, compilation or any other time consuming configuration. As future work, we will implement more commands for usage in honeypot systems. We also plan to include multiprocessing and a more advanced code section. At moment Apate is in a beta status, whenever it is more stable (the assembler does need some tweaking in error detection), Apate will be open source under github.

ACKNOWLEDGMENT

This work is part of the project "Sichere Entwicklung und Sicherer Betrieb von Webanwendungen" of the Munich IT Security Research Group funded by the Bayerisches Staatsministerium für Wissenschaft, Forschung und Kunst.

REFERENCES

[1] C. Pohl and H.-J. Hof, "The all-seeing eye: A massive-multi-sensor zero-configuration intrusion detection system for web applications," in *SECURWARE 2013, The Seventh International Conference on Emerging Security Information, Systems and Technologies*, 2013, pp. 66–72.

[2] C. Pohl, M. Meier, and H.-J. Hof, "Apate-a linux kernel module for high interaction honeypots," in *The Ninth International Conference on Emerging Security Information, Systems and Technologies – SECURWARE 2015*, 2015, pp. 133–138.

[3] C. Pohl, A. Zugenmaier, M. Meier, and H.-J. Hof, "B. hive: A zero configuration forms honeypot for productive web applications," in *ICT Systems Security and Privacy Protection*. Springer, 2015, pp. 267–280.

[4] A. Patcha and J. Park, "An overview of anomaly detection techniques: Existing solutions and latest technological trends," *Computer Networks*, vol. 51, no. 12, pp. 3448–3470, 2007, retrieved 2013-04-11. [Online]. Available: www.scopus.com

[5] C. Kruegel and G. Vigna, "Anomaly detection of web-based attacks," in *Proceedings of the 10th ACM conference on Computer and communications security*, ser. CCS '03. New York, NY, USA: ACM, 2003, p. 251261, retrieved 2013-04-11. [Online]. Available: http://doi.acm.org/10.1145/948109.948144

[6] G. Liepens and H. Vaccaro, "Intrusion detection: Its role and validation," *Computers & Security*, vol. 11, no. 4, pp. 347–355, Jul. 1992, retrieved 2013-04-11. [Online]. Available: http://www.sciencedirect.com/science/article/pii/016740489290175Q

[7] D. Denning, "An intrusion-detection model," *IEEE Transactions on Software Engineering*, vol. SE-13, no. 2, pp. 222–232, 1987, retrieved 2013-04-11.

[8] A. Lakhina, K. Papagiannaki, M. Crovella, C. Diot, E. D. Kolaczyk, and N. Taft, "Structural analysis of network traffic flows," in *Proceedings of the joint international conference on Measurement and modeling of computer systems*, ser. SIGMETRICS '04/Performance '04. New York, NY, USA: ACM, 2004, p. 6172, retrieved 2013-04-11. [Online]. Available: http://doi.acm.org/10.1145/1005686.1005697

[9] P. Barford, J. Kline, D. Plonka, and A. Ron, "A signal analysis of network traffic anomalies," in *Proceedings of the 2nd ACM SIGCOMM Workshop on Internet measurment*, ser. IMW '02. New York, NY, USA: ACM, 2002, p. 7182, retrieved 2013-04-11. [Online]. Available: http://doi.acm.org/10.1145/637201.637210

[10] F. Silveira and C. Diot, "URCA: pulling out anomalies by their root causes," in *2010 Proceedings IEEE INFOCOM*, 2010, pp. 1–9, retrieved 2013-04-11.

[11] H. Javitz and A. Valdes, "The SRI IDES statistical anomaly detector," in *1991 IEEE Computer Society Symposium on Research in Security and Privacy, 1991. Proceedings*, 1991, pp. 316–326, retrieved 2013-04-11.

[12] W. Lee and S. J. Stolfo, "Data mining approaches for intrusion detection," in *Proceedings of the 7th conference on USENIX Security Symposium - Volume 7*, ser. SSYM'98. Berkeley, CA, USA: USENIX Association, 1998, p. 66, retrieved 2013-04-11. [Online]. Available: http://dl.acm.org/citation.cfm?id=1267549.1267555

[13] S. Hofmeyr, S. Forrest, and A. Somayaji, "Intrusion detection using sequences of system calls," *Journal of computer security*, vol. 6, no. 3, pp. 151–180, 1998, retrieved 2013-04-11.

[14] S. Forrest, S. Hofmeyr, A. Somayaji, and T. Longstaff, "A sense of self for unix processes," in *1996 IEEE Symposium on Security and Privacy, 1996. Proceedings*, 1996, pp. 120–128, retrieved 2013-04-11.

[15] A. Frossi, F. Maggi, G. L. Rizzo, and S. Zanero, "Selecting and improving system call models for anomaly detection," in *Detection of Intrusions and Malware, and Vulnerability Assessment*, ser. Lecture Notes in Computer Science, U. Flegel and D. Bruschi, Eds. Springer Berlin Heidelberg, Jan. 2009, no. 5587, pp. 206–223, retrieved 2013-04-11.

[16] W. Masri and A. Podgurski, "Application-based anomaly intrusion detection with dynamic information flow analysis," *Computers & Security*, vol. 27, no. 56, pp. 176–187, Oct. 2008, retrieved 2013-04-11. [Online]. Available: http://www.sciencedirect.com/science/article/pii/S0167404808000369

[17] L. Feng, X. Guan, S. Guo, Y. Gao, and P. Liu, "Predicting the intrusion intentions by observing system call sequences," *Computers & Security*, vol. 23, no. 3, pp. 241–252, May 2004, retrieved 2013-04-11. [Online]. Available: http://www.sciencedirect.com/science/article/pii/S0167404804000732

[18] S. Bhatkar, A. Chaturvedi, and R. Sekar, "Dataflow anomaly detection," in *2006 IEEE Symposium on Security and Privacy*, 2006, pp. 15–62, retrieved 2013-04-11.

[19] F. Qin, C. Wang, Z. Li, H. Kim, Y. Zhou, and Y. Wu, "LIFT: a low-overhead practical information flow tracking system for detecting security attacks," in *39th Annual IEEE/ACM International Symposium on Microarchitecture, 2006. MICRO-39*, 2006, pp. 135–148, retrieved 2013-04-11.

[20] C. Kruegel, G. Vigna, and W. Robertson, "A multi-model approach to the detection of web-based attacks," *Computer Networks*, vol. 48, no. 5, pp. 717–738, Aug. 2005, retrieved 2013-04-11. [Online]. Available: http://www.sciencedirect.com/science/article/pii/S1389128605000083

[21] Honeynet Project, "Know Your Enemy: Sebek," 2003, retrieved: 07, 2015. [Online]. Available: https://www.honeynet.org/papers/sebek

[22] E. Balas, "Sebek: Covert Glass-Box Host Analysis," *login: THE USENIX MAGAZINE*, no. December 2003, Volume 28, Number 6, pp. 21–24, 2003.

[23] T. Holz and F. Raynal, "Detecting honeypots and other suspicious environments," in *Proceedings from the Sixth Annual IEEE Systems, Man and Cybernetics (SMC) Information Assurance Workshop, 2005*. IEEE, 2005, pp. 29–36.

[24] M. Dornseif, T. Holz, and C. Klein, "NoSEBrEaK - Attacking Honeynets," in *Proceedings of the 2004 IEEE Workshop on Information Assurance and Security*, Jun. 2004, pp. 123–129.

[25] C. Song, B. Ha, and J. Zhuge, "Know Your Tools: Qebek – Conceal the Monitoring — The Honeynet Project," retrieved: 07, 2015. [Online]. Available: http://www.honeynet.org/papers/KYT_qebek

[26] T. K. Lengyel, J. Neumann, S. Maresca, B. D. Payne, and A. Kiayias, "Virtual machine introspection in a hybrid honeypot architecture," in *Proceedings of the 5th USENIX Conference on Cyber Security Experimentation and Test*, ser. CSET'12. Berkeley, CA, USA: USENIX Association, 2012, pp. 5–13.

[27] X. Jiang and X. Wang, ""Out-of-the-Box" Monitoring of VM-Based High-Interaction Honeypots," in *Recent Advances in Intrusion Detection*. Springer Berlin Heidelberg, 2007, pp. 198–218.

[28] NSA (Initial developer), "Selinux," 2009, retrieved: 07, 2015. [Online]. Available: https://www.nsa.gov/research/selinux/index.shtml

[29] Open Source Security, "grsecurity," 2015, retrieved: 07, 2015. [Online]. Available: https://grsecurity.net

[30] PAX Team, "Pax," 2015, retrieved: 07, 2015. [Online]. Available: https://pax.grsecurity.net

[31] M. Fox, J. Giordano, L. Stotler, and A. Thomas, "Selinux and grsecurity: A case study comparing linux security kernel enhancements," 2009.

[32] "OpenCms, opencms homepage," http://www.opencms.org, retrieved 2013-04-11. [Online]. Available: http://www.opencms.org

[33] "OpenVZ openvz linux containers," http://openvz.org, retrieved 2013-04-11. [Online]. Available: http://openvz.org

[34] "Apache Tomcat apache tomcat," http://tomcat.apache.org, retrieved 2013-04-11. [Online]. Available: http://tomcat.apache.org

[35] "Owasp Top Ten," https://www.owasp.org/index.php/Category: OWASP_Top_Ten_Project, retrieved 2013-04-11. [Online]. Available: https://www.owasp.org/index.php/Category: OWASP_Top_Ten_Project

[36] S. Marlow, "Haskell 2010 language report," 2010, retrieved: 07, 2015. [Online]. Available: https://www.haskell.org/onlinereport/haskell2010/

[37] OpenBSD, "Pf: The openbsd packet filter," 2015, retrieved: 07, 2015. [Online]. Available: http://www.openbsd.org/faq/pf/

MoNA: Automated Identification of Evidence in Forensic Short Messages

Michael Spranger*, Florian Heinke, Luisa Appelt, Marcus Puder and Dirk Labudde
Department of Applied Computer Sciences & Biosciences
University of Applied Sciences Mittweida
Mittweida, Germany
Email: {*spranger**, *florian.heinke, luisa.appelt, marcus.puder, labudde*}@hs-mittweida.de

***Abstract*—Mobile devices are a popular means for planning, appointing and conducting criminal offences. In particular, short messages (SMS) and chats often contain evidential information. Due to the terms of their use, these types of messages are fundamentally different from other forms of written communication in terms of their grammatical and syntactic structure. Due to the low price of media storage, messages are rarely deleted. On one hand, this fact is quite positive as potentially evidential information is not lost. On the other hand, considering only SMSs, 15,000 and more stored only on one mobile phone is not uncommon. In most cases of organized or gang crime, there is not one but many devices in use. Analysing this large amount of messages manually is time consuming and, therefore, not economically justifiable in the cases of small and medium crimes. In this work, we propose a process chain that enables to decrease the analysis and evaluation time dramatically by reducing the amount of messages, that need to be examined manually. We further present an implemented prototype (MoNA, mobile network analyzer) and demonstrate its performance.**

Keywords–forensic; ontology; German; text processing; expert system; text analysis; short messages

I. Introduction

With our previous work [1] we try to close the gap between backup and recovery of data and its content analysis in the context of mobile forensics. The fast-growing mobile market, constantly emerging or rapidly changing technologies and high hardware diversity require rapid development of new forensic tools. In recent years, many works have dealt with the backup and recovery of data on a variety of platforms [2]. However, there are few works that deal with the analysis of the textual content.

Over the last decade, our understanding of communication and its means have changed drastically. With the introduction of inexpensive messaging technologies and comfortable usability driven by increasingly powerful smart devices, communication has shifted towards conversing via chats and short messages (especially short messaging service, SMS). Besides rising computational power, mobile devices are also provided with significant amounts of memory that allow storing application data, documents, images, and thousands of messages exchanged with a multitude of conversation partners. Although the number of exchanged messages can be in the thousands, they account only for a small fraction of occupied space in general. In consequence, chat and SMS logs are rarely deleted.

In the context of digital forensics, this aspect leads to an ambivalent situation. On the positive side, it has become more likely that confiscated devices yield information relevant for the investigation process and could reveal additional evidential aspects, such as identities of backers or other crime-related intentions of the suspect. On the downside, these information need to be extracted from the raw chat data, which is, considering its scale, barely manageable by manual means. In addition, with the growing amount of available memory and the ongoing popularity growth of text messaging, it can be postulated that manual perusing and annotating will become practically impossible. Hence, there is a necessity in developing computational (semi-) automated technologies that can support the investigator in the process. To achieve this, researches have to cope with a number of issues. Most notably, messages are often enriched with typos and grammar mistakes introduced by lowered language use standards observable in casual text conversations. Such mistakes pose major problems for text mining and computer linguistics.

Based on our previous work [1] a straightforward technique for identifying individual conversations in SMS chat logs is introduced in this paper and evaluated on a manually-annotated SMS dataset. In addition, in Section II we first discuss general background and related work considered in the MoNA development process. In Section III, we define and characterise short message semantic analyses in the context of forensics, providing detailed aspects involved in the motivation of our work. Further, the SMS dataset used to develop and evaluate MoNA is described. We emphasize that the dataset in use has been relevant for a closed drug crime investigation, thus actual information provided in this study are based on a real-life application scenario. In this respect, in Section IV we introduce measures for quantifying the potency of a keyword dictionary provided by investigators that is used by MoNA to classify and score identified conversations. These measures additionally provide statistical figures that can be used to further optimise and refine the dictionary in use. After discussing the evidential conversation detection process utilised by MoNA (Section V), we demonstrate its performance in Section VI and provide future prospects in Section VII.

II. Related Work

Compared with texts from industry, medicine or science, relatively few works deal with the analysis of short messages. Most of these works address the binary classification problem in terms of SPAM detection. For example, in a large-scale study Skudlark [3] examined approaches to detect SPAM activities. However, they rely on the presence of URLs in the text body, which limits the applicability of these methods to forensic short messages on very few cases of fraud, computer sabotage or similar crimes. Ahmed *et al.* [4] presented an SMS classification approach based on Naive Bayes and *a priori* algorithms. A further method has been discussed by Xu *et al.* [5] that relies on content features for classification. Although this method yields reasonable results, an application to most fields of forensics cannot only be based on meta data. But this kind of data can be useful to enlarge the target matching space. In the field of multi class SMS classification Al-Talib *et al.* [6] introduced a technique using an improved TF-IDF weighting, whereas Patel *et al.* exploit artificial neural networks [7]. Another interesting work was presented in 2011 by Ishihara [8]. In this work, the author proposed a likelihood ratio-based approach for SMS authorship classification using n-grams. The model was trained and evaluated using the NUS SMS corpus [9]. Unfortunately, a similar corpus for German forensic SMS is currently not available. The general problem when trying to create such a corpus in the field of forensics is the availability of real-life data. This is the reason why Ishihara considered non-forensic data, while the developed classifier has been trained and evaluated for forensic purposes. Therefore, with respect to forensic short messages and their special characteristics (which are discussed in Section III-B in more detail), the applicability of such a classifier and its performance in the real-life context of forensics remains unsettled. Furthermore, approaches for extracting information from short messages, as discussed in [10], [11], are frequently based on the presence of correct grammatical structures. However, these do not exist in most cases for short messages. Knowledge-based approaches, such as proposed in [12], are more promising since they can include *a priori* knowledge of the investigator to support information retrieval as well as information extraction processes. In the work presented by Nebhi [12] Twitter posts are considered, which, however, are similar to forensic SMS in some degree.

Thus, in general, there is no approach available that can cope with the challenges posed by real-life short message data. In addition, such an approach is required to be both applicable to all the data, and to perform as reliable as required by forensic investigation standards.

III. Background

A. Forensic Short Messages

The analysis of short messages is a particular challenge in the context of forensic text analysis. The reasons for this is the combination of forensic text characteristics and of high information density, which is characterized by limitations in the number of characters. Such limitations arise on the one hand by technical reasons, on the other hand by the kind of use. Thus, short messages are often used in terms of "by the way messages".

Definition 1 (Forensic Short Message): In this study, any textual message having the properties of an incriminated text and is sent or received using a short message service is considered a forensic short message.

Looking at current surveys of the short message traffic in the Federal Republic of Germany (see Fig. 1), a turnaround can be seen in the development starting in 2013. The reason for this is not a decrease in the mobile communications in general, but in a shift to other convenient communication services such as instant messaging services (e. g. Whats App). Nevertheless, every citizen sends one instant message per day on average. The outstanding role of text messages today and in the future, both in general and forensics contexts, was thoroughly discussed in [14]. Since the communication behaviour is mainly influenced by the type of use, the change of the medium has had only a relatively small impact on the writing behaviour of the user. Thus, the results presented in this work can be transferred in principle to other forms of mobile communication in writing. In general, the forensic analysis of incriminated texts is a big challenge for investigators—which is especially the case for short messages. In addition to large message quantities only sent by one individual, such messages have a particular characteristic, which makes the analysis difficult even for experienced investigators. Considering the amount of content that needs to be fully read, this effort is probably justifiable only in cases of severe crime or crime of high public interest. One of the current biggest limitations during the development of an automated solution for forensic purposes is the lack of a gold standard. Yet, an effective and efficient analysis in each relevant case is unthinkable without the usage of computational solutions.

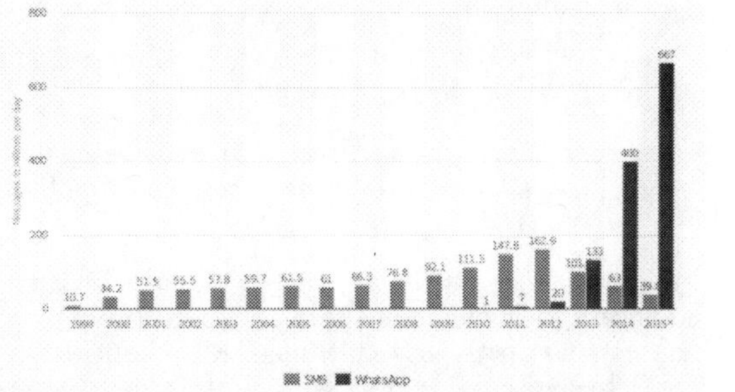

Figure 1: Number of SMS and IM messages (WhatsApp) sent in Germany from 1990 to 2014 in millions per day (2015 estimated) [13].

B. Characteristics of Forensic Short Messages

As already discussed in [1], forensic text's structure and quality regarding grammar, syntax and wording strongly depends on the area of the crime committed by the offenders, their level of education and their social environment. A more detailed description of the general characteristics of forensic texts can be found in [15]. Personalized SMS form the extreme case of these characteristics. They are particularly marked by frequent lack of correct grammatical structures. Therefore, it is difficult to use (lexico)-syntactic pattern as discussed in [16] [17] for extracting information of criminalistic relevance. Further, the usage of non-standardised emoticons, abbreviations, emotionally intended character extensions and especially written effects of language erosion caused by language-economic processes make this task more difficult and lead to a failing of known techniques. The following list shows some example texts to illustrate the problem:

- *"aber was ich mein[e] is[t] wir müss[e]n wenn*

wir weihnacht[e]n gefeiert hab[e]n ***übelst money hab[e]n"***

- *"Beruhig[e] dich* ***ich zieh[e] denn*** *das nächste ma[l] rich[tig]* ***fette ab!*** *:)~~)))))~~"*
- *"Ich schreib jetzt wegen dir hab ich mein 12g nicht bekommen Weil Du* ***ne*** *aus[de]m* ***knick*** *gekommen bist XD"*

Missing characters are included in square brackets, whereas additional characters are shown as strike-through text. Incorrect capitalisations are underlined. Slang-afflicted words and phrases are printed in bold. The most challenging problem in the considered context of SMS with criminalistic relevance is the usage of slang-afflicted language combined with terms of hidden semantics. Hidden semantics refer to one kind of a steganographic code. Such a term is used in its common innocent meaning but its actual semantic background is prearranged by a narrow circle of insiders. For example, the question

"Bringst du ein Wernesgrüner mit?" (Can you bring a Wernesgrüner?)

appears innocent and unsuspicious because the term *Wernesgrüner* (a German beer brand) is used as in asking for a bottle of beer. However, by considering the actual context, the author of this message is actually asking for marijuana. Note that in this example we intentionally do not use slang to avoid misunderstandings. But commonly terms of slang are mixed in regularly. These characteristics make it difficult even for criminalists and linguists with years of experience to read and understand the semantics of forensic SMSs.

Thus, it becomes clear that any information not identified as relevant by an automated system may be crucial in proving the guilt or innocence of a criminal suspect. Eventually, it can be stated that decisions concerning the evidential value of forensic SMSs cannot be made by a machine.

C. Dataset under Consideration

The data used by the authors for the development of MoNA is based on a dataset of a closed case of drug trafficking provided by a cooperating prosecutor for research purposes. Nevertheless, the data is not publicly available. For this purpose the legal framework has to be established, at least in Germany. In the case under consideration a smart phone of the suspect, an HTC Desire A9191, has been seized and a physical image has been generated by using Cellebrite's *UFED Physical Analyzer*. The textual data contained in this image was exported as an Excel Workbook and forms the basis for all further investigations. This dataset includes 14,307 short messages (SMS) and 132,345 chat messages. During the development of MoNA, only SMS messages have been used so far. Through an official of a cooperating police department all short messages were manually read and evidential ones were labelled as relevant. Afterwards, the same work was performed by a member of the research team without criminalistic background.

In summary, only half of the relevant messages were correctly classified as evidential by the research member and, on the contrary, messages considered as insignificant by the investigators were classified as evidential. This shows that subjectivity can introduce significant errors in analyses processes and emphasises the need for expert knowledge. This study thus focuses on the prototypic implementation of MoNA as a strategy for identification and classification of conversations with respect to their relevance to the crime in question.

IV. Word Dictionary Potency

The majority of text mining and computer linguistic algorithms rely on word dictionaries that provide the initial set of words, which are screened against a given text dataset in the process. In computer forensics, the investigator aims at maximizing the number of identified messages containing evidential information, to which we refer to as significant messages in the following text. In general, the basis for the successful identification of significant messages or conversations in large message sets using string matching techniques and phonetic algorithms predominantly requires a potent word dictionary. Word dictionaries are subjected to two major requirements: First, they have a significant impact on classification performances of utilised methods and thus should be optimally composed in this respect. Secondly, word dictionaries are required to be domain-specific, case-independent, and generalized corpora of words—meaning that each should be interchangeable and not be specifically tailored toward the dataset in question. Especially in the field of computer forensics, it needs to be further emphasized that a dictionary is considered to be specific for a certain time period and region as well.

In this study, MoNA has been provided with a dictionary of 90 words specific for the drug scene currently present in the Chemnitz/west Saxony region of Germany. In this section, measures of dictionary potency, which supply simple quantifications of per-word performance, are introduced, demonstrated and discussed on the available data. First, measuring initial classification power of dictionary words is demonstrated. Subsequently, it is shown how word heterogeneity of obtained word matches in the dataset can be measured. Word match heterogeneity provides statistical figures on word diversity in and between matching word sets in significant and insignificant (non-relevant) messages, which in turn can be used to represent per-word specificity. Here, the investigator aims at maximizing diversity between word sets and reduce heterogeneity within the sets, thus reducing ambiguities of obtained matches.

A. Overview on Individual Dictionary Word Potency

Analyses of dictionary potency have been conducted by employing string matching and two phonetic algorithms (Kölner phonetic [18] and Double Metaphone [19]) on the provided SMS dataset. All three algorithms reported a total of 11,665 matches in the dataset, of which 310 had been annotated as significant by the investigators. Interestingly, a large fraction of 42 dictionary words matches exclusively to either significant or insignificant messages (see Table I). The seven words only matching to significant messages account for eighteen of the 310 significant matches. Furthermore, 35 dictionary words yield no significant matches in the dataset, classifying a total of 17% of the matches as insignificant.

In theory, a powerful dictionary yields significant matches only. However, the statistics obtained from actual data show

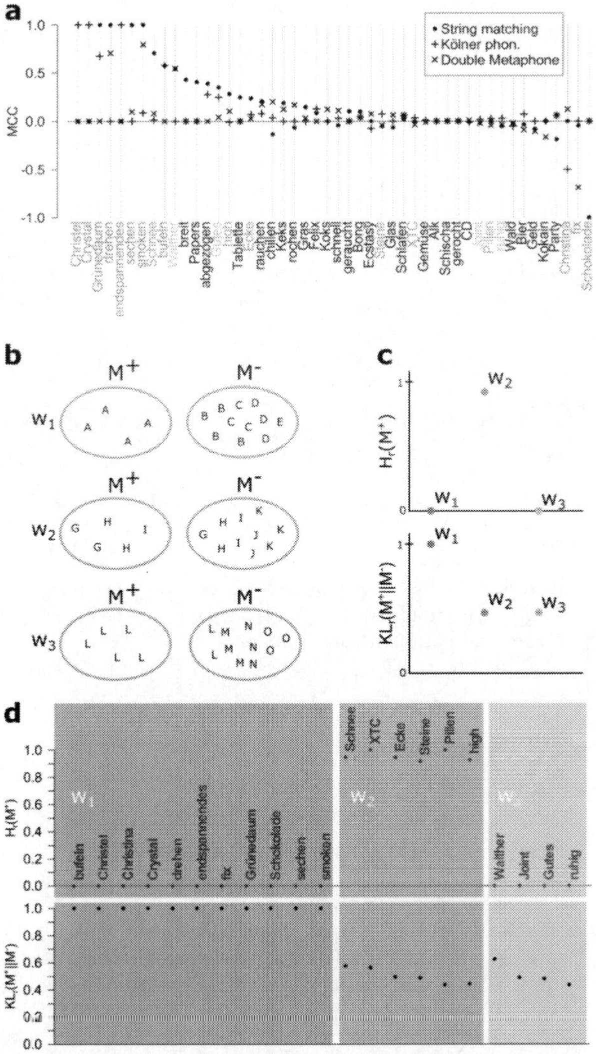

Figure 2: **a:** Predictive performance evaluated by means of Matthews correlation coefficient (MCC) of 90 dictionary words yielding matches in significant and insignificant messages (see Table I). **b** and **c:** Relative entropy (H_r) and relative Kullback-Leibler divergence (KL_r) are measures for assessing word match set homogeneity respectively set divergence. Three illustrative word match homogeneity scenarios for words w_1, w_2, and w_3 are depicted, with schematic plots of H_r and KL_r obtained from these scenarios shown on the right (M^+ and M^-: matching word sets of significant respectively insignificant messages). **d:** Plots of H_r and KL_r of 21 words yielding $KL_r > 0.4$. Colour highlighting is in correspondence to the three word matching scenarios shown in **b** and **c**, indicating varying degrees of ambiguity and, thus, significance to dictionary power.

mixed power of individual dictionary words. The aspect that thirty-five of 90 words are anti-correlated—yielding only insignificant matches—is rather surprising, as one would expect most of the matches to be exclusively significant or at least to be matching to both cases. Although errors should be expected in practice, large fractions of anti-correlated words, as observed in this study, highlight that a given domain-specific dictionary can produce unwanted effects caused by hidden ambiguities in the data. Hence, a dictionary should always be considered as a set of independent words—each of these with its own meaning and power with respect to classification performance.

TABLE I: Results of initial word dictionary testing. 90 domain-specific dictionary words have been matched against the SMS dataset using string matching, Kölner phonetic and Double Metaphone. If a matching message contains evidential information, the match is considered significant.

number of dictionary words	*type of matches*	*% of all matches*
7	only in significant messages	0.2
35	only in insignificant messages	17.0
48	both	82.8

B. Measuring per-word Classification Power

To demonstrate the varying power of words, classification performances of the 48 words matching to significant and insignificant messages have been analysed. Here, the Matthews correlation coefficients (MCC) [20] have been computed for each word and each of the three used algorithms. The MCC is defined as follows:

$$MCC = \frac{TP \times TN - FP \times FN}{\sqrt{(TP+FP)(TP+FN)(TN+FP)(TN+FN)}}. \tag{1}$$

The classification statistics TP (true positives), FP (false positives), TN (true negatives), FN (false positives) correspond in this context to the following numbers:

- TP - number of reported matches corresponding to significant messages
- FP - number of reported matches corresponding to insignificant messages
- TN - number of cases where the algorithm indicates no match in insignificant messages
- FN - number of cases where the algorithm indicates no match in significant messages

The MCC is in the range of -1 and +1, where +1 corresponds to perfect classification, whereas the number of FN and FP cases is 0. In contrast an anti-correlated performance is indicated by an MCC of -1. Furthermore, although the MCC is a more strict measure of classification performance in comparison to the classic F1-measure, it is less prone to errors introduced by class imbalance, which is present for the majority of investigated words. The MCC thus supplies an intuitive representation of dictionary potency, but also provides a measure that is ought to be maximized. The computed individual MCC values are shown in Fig. 2a. As depicted, ten words yield MCC values > 0.5 for any of the three methods. These words include the two phonetically similar words *Christel* (a German nickname) and *Crystal*, as well as *endspannendes* (misspelled German word for 'anything that is relaxing'). In case of these three words, phonetic algorithms reported matches highly correlated to significant messages, however, no string matches have been identified. This is simply due to spelling mistakes made by the conversation partners. Here, phonetic algorithms have been able to successfully identify correspondences missed by string matching that had been proven to be case-relevant. Further, in case of *Schokolade*, a domain-specific synonym for hashish, anti-correlation is observed, yielding string matches only to insignificant messages. Manual inspection of string and phonetic matches revealed spelling differences between significant and insignificant messages, where *Schokolade* is written correctly in the latter, leading to reported anti-correlated string matches. In significant messages, however, a consistent miss-spelling, *Schockolade* instead of *Schokolade*, is present. Although there are only two cases of positive messages, it can be proposed that this typing error is actually made on purpose—where the additional 'c' could abbreviate 'cannabis' and therefore might encode the actual meaning of the message in addition to using the synonym. In summary, for the majority of these 48 words classification performance is insufficiently low. Even though string matching seems to perform superior to the utilised phonetic algorithms in this study, no significant performance difference is observable (one-sided Welch test, $p = 0.24$ for Kölner phonetic, $p = 0.05$ for Double metaphone).

C. Measuring per-word Match Ambiguity

Finally, if a dictionary word results to two sets of matching words in significant and insignificant messages (as in case of forty-eight dictionary words in this study), it is at least desirable to obtain two divergent, homogeneous sets of matches. Divergence indicates that the two sets differ in matching word composition, whereas homogeneity indicates word diversity within the sets. Thus, both measures in combination can provide quantifications of ambiguities present between and within both sets. In order to avoid ambiguity, the researcher aims at increasing divergence and homogeneity. Subfigures 2b and c illustrate resulting hypothetical word match scenarios for three imaginary dictionary words (w_1, w_2, w_3). M^+ and M^- correspond to the sets of matching words in significant respectively insignificant messages. For measuring word set divergence and homogeneity, relative Kullback-Leibler divergence (KL_r) and relative Shannon entropy (H_r) are here proposed. In general, KL_r corresponds to the normalized Kullback-Leibler divergence, which is used to measure the difference between probability distributions P and Q. A probability distribution for a word set M can be simply deduced by considering the relative frequency of each word in the set of unique words U_M derived from M. Thus

$$P(w \in U_M) = \frac{f(w)}{|M|} \tag{2}$$

is obtained. For clarity, $P(M^-)$ is denoted as $Q(M^-)$ in the following. From this, the Kullback-Leibler divergence between sets M^+ and M^- can be readily computed:

$$KL(M^+||M^-) = \sum_{w \in U_M} P(w) \log_2 \frac{P(w)}{Q(w)}, \tag{3}$$

where $M = M^+ \cup M^-$. However, divergence as defined here results to a non-symmetric measure, which also not always strictly considers all unique words in M. In case of a given word w being only present in M^+, $Q(w) = 0$ and the Kullback-Leibler divergence is not defined. Due to these drawbacks, the two-sided divergence is utilised in this study instead:

$$KL(M^+||M^-) = KL(M^+||M) + KL(M^-||M). \tag{4}$$

Finally, KL_r can be computed by normalizing the observed divergence using the theoretical maximal divergence

$$KL_{max}(M^+||M^-) = \log_2\left(\frac{|M|}{|M^+|}\right) + \log_2\left(\frac{|M|}{|M^-|}\right) \tag{5}$$

$$KL_r(M^+||M^-) = \frac{KL(M^+||M^-)}{KL_{max}(M^+||M^-)}. \tag{6}$$

Using the definition of word probability given in equation (2), Shannon entropy can be computed:

$$H(M) = -\sum_{w \in U_M} P(w) \log_2 P(w). \tag{7}$$

In order to obtain normalized comparable quantities $H_r(M)$, $H(M)$ is weighted by taking into account the maximum theoretical entropy, leading to

$$H_r(M) = \frac{H(M)}{\log_2(|U_M|)}. \tag{8}$$

In Fig. 2 KL_r and H_r are illustrated schematically for three word match scenarios w_1, w_2 and w_3 (see subfigures b and c), which are observed for 21 dictionary words. Here, only dictionary words yielding minimal ambiguity ($KL_r > 0.4$) are considered. As illustrated, if all unique words are uniformly distributed over M^+ and M^-, H_r is observed to be 1 (maximal) and KL_r is 0 (minimal). In this case, ambiguity is maximal and, simply by considering matching words, no classification can be achieved. The corresponding dictionary word w is thus of low classification potency. This case is similar to word matching scenario w_3, whereas four dictionary words considered in this study yield similar values (highlighted in green in Fig. 2a and d). Analogously, 11 and 6 dictionary words can be assigned to scenario w_1 (blue) and w_2 (red), respectively. Also, by taking into account MCC values of these words, the dictionary words yielding good classification potency can be identified. In our study, the dictionary words *bufeln, Christel, Crystal, drehen, endspannendes, Grünedaum, sechen, smoken* yield a low degree of ambiguity and good classification performance. Furthermore, dictionary words yielding anti-correlation correspond to word matching scenario w_1 as well.

In summary, these statistics can be used to visualize individual dictionary word potency, but also to provide measures that can aid in identifying unknown correlations and selecting additional potent words from obtained matches, or replacing ambiguous less potent words. In this study, it is apparent that a majority of words provided by the dictionary are of low potency. A large fraction of words are not sensitive to significant messages or provide only low classification potency with respect to message relevance.

V. Identification of Evidential Short Messages

With respect to properties of forensic short messages discussed in Section III-B, the identification of crime-relevant messages within a large message history is a classification problem that is difficult to solve by means of computational approaches as well as manual annotation. However, by taking into account information extracted from related conversations instead of individual messages, automated classification strategies could be developed and applied providing the investigator with a list of conversations, which in turn can be manually perused, put into context, and can thus aid in the investigation process. As a positive side effect the context of the message is maintained in such a preprocessing strategy, which facilitates the understanding when manually perusing obtained classification results. Thus, an automated method for identifying individual conversations in message histories is desirable. In this section, a statistical approach is suggested, which aims at addressing this problem. First, the initial strategy for extracting statistical data from message logs is elucidated and mathematical formalisms are introduced. Furthermore, a statistical measure for quantifying conversation detection performance is introduced and applied to the proposed strategy. In this study, the conversation identification strategy is applied to two drug crime-related message histories both containing manually annotated relevant (evidential) messages, whereas one further contains a conversation index obtained from peruse. The latter message history is eventually used to measure identification performance of the proposed strategy.

A. Conversation Detection

In the context of this study, a conversation is considered as any amount of time- and semantically-coherent messages between at least two people. Formally expressed let M be the set of all messages, where $m \in M$ is corresponding to any message in M. Furthermore, M is in chronological order, creating a temporal connection between the logged messages. Therefore, the chronology of the exchange between the conversational members can be tracked. In addition, the response times (the elapsed time between two sequential messages m_i and m_{i+1}) can be derived. The strategy presented here is based only on derived response times and follows a simple hypothesis: the longer the response time between two messages m_i and m_{i+1}, the lower the likelihood that both messages belong to the same conversation. Based on this hypothesis, the following approaches may gradually lead to the proposed statistical strategy:

1) Response times follow a statistical distribution (frequency distribution). Short response times are thereby more often observed than long response times.
2) Given a sufficiently large dataset and obtained response times, a probability distribution and hence a probability density function can be estimated empirically on the basis of the observed response time frequency distribution.
3) Given any response time t, the relative number of expected response times $\leq t$ in a chat log can be estimated based on the approximated density function.
4) The reversion of the above statement leads to an approach for solving the problem and is as follows: for which response time t is a given fraction p of response times with $\leq t$ to be expected?
5) If p is chosen sufficiently small ($p = 0.05$ is a common statistical threshold), a critical response time t can be determined. Thus, it is expected that for this particular response time $95\%(1-p)$ of all messages are answered within that time period. The remainder of 5% is negligible in accordance to p.
6) If the response time between two messages m_i and m_{i+1} exceeds the critical response time, the probability for both messages belonging to the same conversation is expected to be low. Thus, it can be postulated that both messages do not belong to the same conversation.
7) M can be split into different conversations solely from the sequence of response times with respect the estimated critical response time.

With the general hypothesis elucidated, the underlying formalisms resulting to the identification strategy are now introduced. Let $\delta t = t_{m_{i+1}} - t_{m_i}$ be the response time between two sequential messages of two conversation partners. Then ΔT is the set of all response times which fall within interval $(t_1, t_2]$; thus $\Delta T = \{\delta t \mid t_1 < \delta t \leq t_2\}$. The function of all observed frequencies $h_i = \| \Delta T_i \|$ parallel over time gives a characteristic frequency distribution, which is illustrated in Fig. 3a for a message history containing 1,550 messages. The bin interval is 5 seconds.

In this histogram it can be seen that the frequency distribution follows an exponential decay of form ae^{-bt}. Therefore, short response times are frequently observed. A causal relationship between the observed distribution and response time can be explained by the responsiveness of two callers. However, this responsiveness is not constant, but varies continuously over time. To illustrate this underlying hypothesis, let t be the time that has elapsed since receipt of the last message. The recipient of the last message has not yet responded to this. So the responsiveness is B_t. It should be noted, that B_t is corresponding to a sum of several human factors, for example for this readiness, the duration of the call and already discussed aspects contribute to responsiveness variance. However, a general decrease in responsiveness can be assumed considering a general statement: if the recipient of the last message has seen no reason to answer at time t, readiness to continue the conversation does not increase at a later time $t + dt$. This responsiveness is formally expressed as B_{t+dt}. Although numerous human factors account to variance, the statement $B_t > B_{t+dt}$ is reasonable to assume in the general case. Thus, the responsiveness decreases tendentiously. Here it can be postulated that a constant reduction rate r describes the reduction of B as a function of elapsed time since receipt of the last message. This relationship can be formulated as:

$$\frac{\mathrm{d}B}{\mathrm{d}t} = -rB \tag{9}$$

Hence, the more time has passed since the receipt of a message, the lower is the probability that a response will still be sent. Equation (9) can be readily solved (equation (10)). Thus, from these considerations time-dependent responsiveness B_t results from initial standby responsiveness B_0 and constant reduction rate r. This aspect describes the exponential relation shown in

Fig. 3a.

$$B_t = B_0 e^{-rt} \quad (10)$$

Furthermore, equation (10) can be understood as a probability density function obtainable by fitting parameters B_0 and r to the observed response time distribution. Optimal fitting can be determined by regression errors (see equation (11)).

$$\{r_{opt}, B_{0_{opt}}\} = \underset{r, B_0}{\arg\min} \sum_t |B_t^{calc} - B_t^{obs}| \quad (11)$$

Based on this approximated probability density function, a threshold time t_p is calculated corresponding to a sufficiently low answer probability. If this time t_p is exceeded, the conversation is considered as terminated. This probability can be assumed to be sufficiently small and is hereinafter referred to p. In this study $p = 0.05$ is observed to perform well on both considered message histories. Finally, t_p can be determined by simply integrating the approximated probability density function and corresponding rearranging of the equation:

$$\mathrm{F}(B) = \int_0^{t_p} B_0 e^{-rt} dt = 1 - p \quad (12)$$

The red line in Fig. 3a shows the result of the performed regression on a message history consisting of 1,550 messages. The dashed blue line illustrates the calculated t_p for which the probability of receiving a response to a sent message is lower than $p = 0.05$. For this dataset t_p is 217 seconds. In summary, proposed statistical conversation identification requires to approximate the probability density function from the conversation-characteristic response time distribution, estimate a critical threshold time t_p for a preselected p, and finally split M into disjunct sets of messages, whereas $|t_{m_i} - t_{m_{i+1}}| > t_p$.

To check if conversations containing evidential messages are erroneously split by this approach, their response time distribution has been investigated. As shown in the histogram in Fig. 3b the response time for only one relevant message exceeds the estimated t_p. Hence, all conversations containing evidential information are not falsely split in this case. However, this single message is a solitaire, meaning it is a single unanswered message without contextual references. The algorithm for detecting conversations is only applied to phone numbers at a minimum of 7 digits without any country code or at least 10 digits with country code, because shorter numbers mostly belong to telephone services and, therefore, are of less interest. Furthermore, the cut-off calculation as the first step during the conversation detection is only considered, if the number of messages between two conversation partners is at least 20. To avoid extremely short and, therefore, less meaningful conversations a cut-off value of 2 minutes is set as a minimum. These dialogs also include questions detected via the question mark symbol ("?"), as well as in combination with an exclamation mark ("!"). It was analysed whether and to which extent at these points (between question and answer/reaction) clustering occurs and if, therefore, coherent conversations were cut undesirably. The analysis results on the test dataset can be seen in Table II. Based on a manual review, it could be found out that SMSs, which contain question marks mostly (82.69 to 100%), follow up answers or reactions from the other participant and, therefore, can be treated as a coherent conversation. The cut-off value itself does not change, because the clustering/conversation detection is following the cut-off calculation.

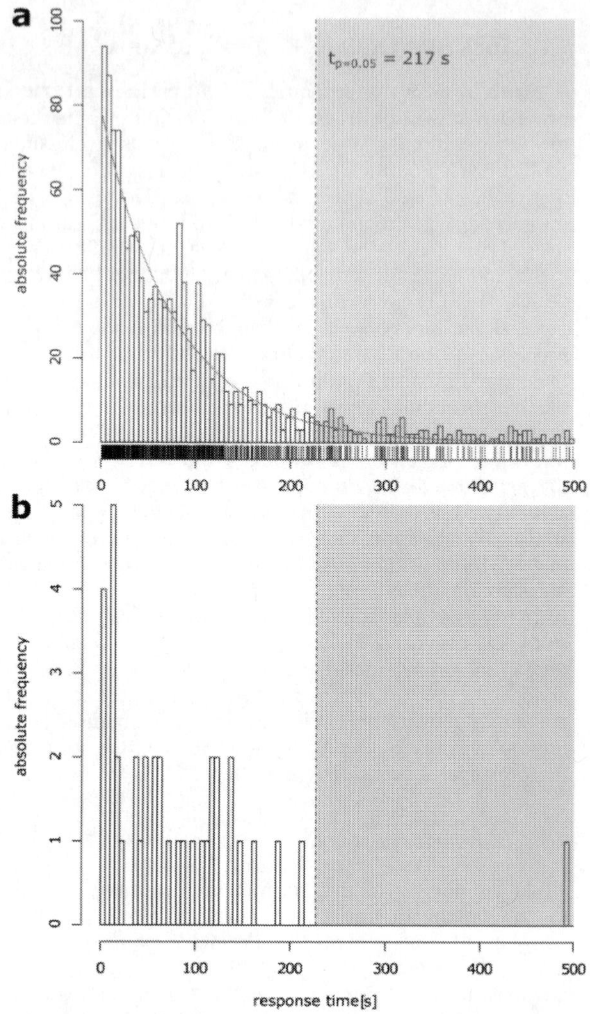

Figure 3: **a:** Response time histogram of a message history containing 1,550 messages, of which 40 were evidential for a recently completed drug crime investigation. Detecting conversations (grouping of chronologically ordered messages into disjunct sets) statistically as proposed in this study utilises a probability density function estimation (shown by red line) based on response time distribution. Employing a probability threshold p gives a critical response time t_p, upon which two consecutive messages are assigned to two separate conversations if the observed response time between said messages exceeds t_p. **b:** Frequency distribution of 40 evidential messages. As shown, utilising a t_p of 217 seconds leads to a set of conversations in which conversations containing evidential messages are not erroneously split by the proposed approach.

By reference to Table II it would appear that special treatment or filtering of question marks has a major impact on the number of clusters in the test dataset. Without question mark treatment 384 clusters arise. If the clustering is extended by the question mark treatment it results in 332 clusters

TABLE II: Comparison of the question mark consideration in the conversation detection of the test dataset.

	without "?" treatment	with "?" treatment
# matches	52	0
# conversations	384	332

(13.54% or alternatively 52 less clusters than before). In view of these results, the question mark treatment is recommended.

B. Evaluation of Conversation Identification

Evaluation of the proposed automated approach is carried out by comparing the similarity of the generated chat log partitioning with the partitioning obtained from manual annotations using an information theoretic approach. More precisely, given the two partitions normalized mutual information is computed, which indicates information coupling between both and reports the degree of uncertainty that the partitioning obtained by the proposed approach is meaningful with respect to manual annotations. A partitioning of a chat log corresponds to a set $C = c_1, \ldots, c_k$ of k identified conversations. Let $t_E(c_i)$ be the time elapsed during conversation c_i. Trivially, the sum of all t_E equals the elapsed time between all messages. According to this the ratio $p(c_i) = t_E(c_i)/\sum(t_E(c_j))$ corresponds to the probability of any randomly chosen message (or any arbitrary point of time between t_1 and t_n) to belong to conversation c_i. In this respect, a pair of conversation sets obtained by manual annotation C^{man} and automated identification C^{auto} can be compared by means of these probabilities. Considering manual conversation identification to be error-free, optimal automated conversation identification is achieved, if $C^{man} = C^{auto}$. By considering underlying probability distributions $P(C^{man})$ and $P(C^{auto})$, the statement holds analogously true if $P(C^{man}) = P(C^{auto})$. In order to evaluate the quality of the proposed approach, both $P(C^{man})$ and $P(C^{auto})$ can be utilised to measure set similarity. However, since both sets are not necessarily of equal size and there is no one-to-one correspondence between conversations in both sets, rather straightforward measures of set similarity, such as the Jaccard index or the previously discussed Kullback-Leibler divergence as well as correlation analyses of conversation indexes, have to be considered as unsuitable. Due to these constraints, normalized mutual information (NMI) is chosen for evaluation instead. In general mutual information quantifies the emitted information (or dependence) between two variables X and Y by means of scaling the joint distribution $P(X, Y)$ of both using the distribution of marginal probabilities $P(X)P(Y)$. This measure is still applicable in case when the sizes of both sets are unequal, and also does not rely on one-to-one relations. Further, mutual information can readily be normalized ($NMI \in [0, 1]$) using the marginal entropies $H(X)$ and $H(Y)$ to obtain comparable quantities. The maximum value of 1 is thus observed if the discrepancy between joint distribution and marginal distribution is maximized— which is only if $P(X) = P(Y)$. With respect to $P(C^{man})$ and $P(C^{auto})$, a maximum value of 1 is only achieved, if both sets are equal and, hence, perfect conversation identification is obtained. If C^{auto} is simply generated by chance and the identified conversation set is thus expected to be of low quality, the discrepancy between both distributions is observed to be relatively small, leading to relatively low NMI. For conversation identification NMI is defined as

$$NMI(C^{auto}, C^{man}) = \frac{2MI(C^{auto}, C^{man})}{H(C^{auto}) + H(C^{man})}, \quad (13)$$

where

$$MI(C_1, C_2) = \sum_{c_i \in C_1} \sum_{c_j \in C_2} p(c_i \cap c_j) \log_2 \left(\frac{p(c_i \cap c_j)}{p(c_i)p(c_j)} \right) \quad (14)$$

and

$$H(C) = - \sum_{c_i \in C} p(c_i) \log_2 (p(c_i)) . \quad (15)$$

$p(c_i \cap c_j)$ corresponds to the time fraction of the overlap between two conversations.

The proposed strategy was applied to a second message history of 2046 messages. The history was manually perused and 116 individual conversations were identified manually. The statistical approach utilised on this dataset yielded a $t_{p=0.05}$ of 2907 seconds. The corresponding NMI was computed and compared to NMI values resulting for critical response times t_c in the range of 30 to 30,000 seconds. This comparison provides a robustness test for the conversation identification obtained from $t_{p=0.05}$. As shown in Fig. 4 NMI_{t_p} is within the response time interval (2000 s - 7000 s) that yields best performance when considering a constant critical response time as proposed here. Note that the NMI for small critical response times ($t_c < 100$ seconds) of about 0.95 corresponds to a message history-characteristic baseline performance, which is the result of marginal correlation between C^{auto} and C^{man} in this t_c range.

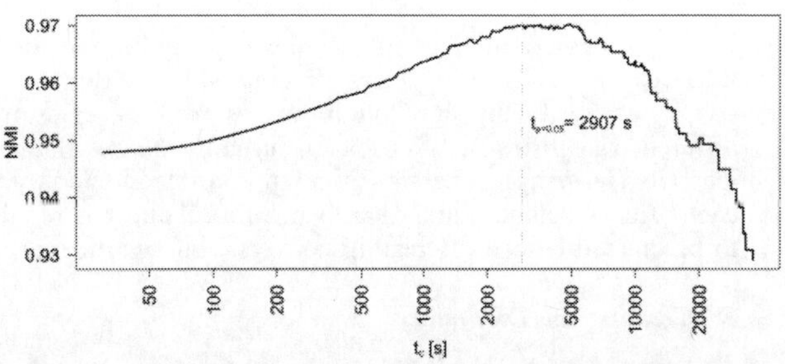

Figure 4: NMI values computed for a message history with available C^{man} determined by peruse. NMI is obtained by deriving C^{auto} for each corresponding critical response time in the range of 30 to 30,000 seconds. The critical response time $t_{p=0.05}$ computed by the proposed statistical approach (2907 seconds) is here highlighted by a green line. Conversation identification obtained by proposed approach is within the critical response time range resulting to best classification.

C. Detecting Evidential Conversations

Given the set of identified conversations $C = \{c_0, ..., c_n\}$, the next step is to determine which of these are significant regarding the object of investigation. With respect to the insights provided in Section III-B, we utilised a bag-of-words model combined with a domain specific dictionary d to assign a significance value to each conversation and hence to each person being part of it. This significance value S can be calculated depending on the frequency of domain-specific terms (see equation (16)).

$$S_i = bag(c_i, d), \forall c \in C \tag{16}$$

These values form the basis of a heat scale we use to colour the contacts in the contact network established using the report data. Fig. 5 shows the overall process. The starting point is a contact network based on the data gathered by *Physical Analyzer* [21]. Exchanged coherent messages are subsequently clustered into conversations as proposed. The significance value is calculated for each of these conversations. Based on these values suspicious contacts and communications are highlighted visually on the contact network using the corresponding heat scale colours via the MoNA user interface.

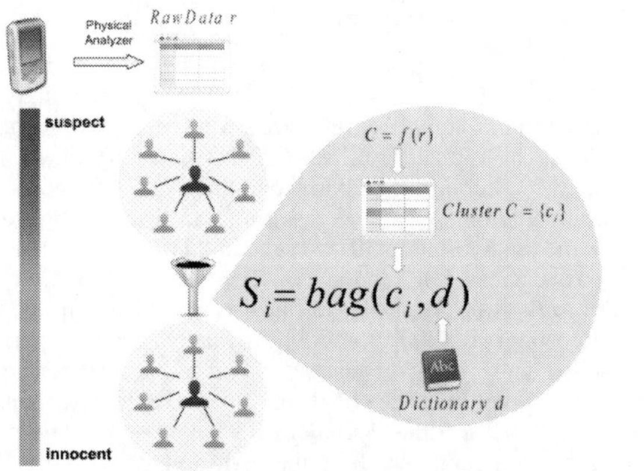

Figure 5: The process of detecting suspicious communication.

As discussed in Section IV, the determining factor for satisfactory results is a potent dictionary. A dictionary that comprises local language conditions, as well as terms from different categories of offences, is currently not available (at least in Germany). Therefore, an appropriate dictionary for each offence category and each local cultural circle is required to be created before calculating conversation significance.

D. Creating the Dictionary

We started dividing the corpus into significant and non-suspicious parts and performing a discriminant analysis involving stop-word elimination and stemming. Considering only the frequency classes 1 and 2 (words exclusively in suspicious texts and words relatively more frequent in such texts) we identified 882 "suspicious" terms. Using these terms in turn for processing the whole dataset for evaluation we achieve 0.98 sensitivity with 1.0 precision. Looking at the distribution of hits, we observed that the most of them are unique. The reason for this is due to the high number of unique spellings, caused by syntactic and typographical errors as well as deliberate word extensions. However, these lists of terms can form a basis for the dictionary, especially if more than one corpus is taken into account and words are removed according to their frequency within all corpora.

In addition, it is useful to integrate the knowledge of local criminalists who deal with similar cases in a similar environment every day. This experiential knowledge is the best source of information for both, slang and hidden semantics. Such manually added terms need to be extended automatically, for example, by twisting letters and transforming in patterns, e. g., regular expressions using an appropriate pattern generator (see Fig. 6). Current work aims at improving dictionary potency by applying a similar bootstrapping algorithm as presented in [15] for the field of categorising forensic texts in general.

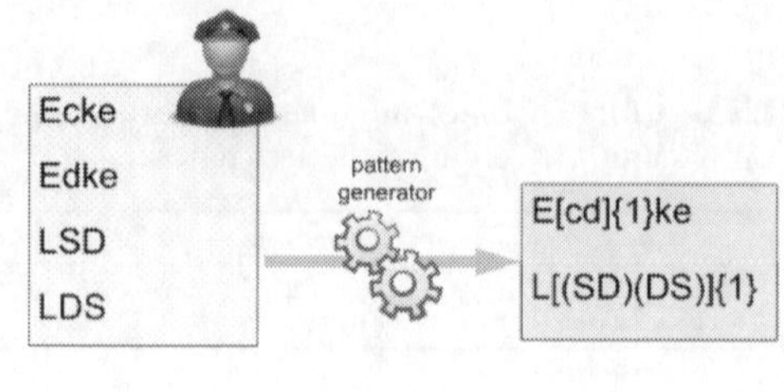

Figure 6: Generating a pattern dictionary by transforming criminalist's knowledge.

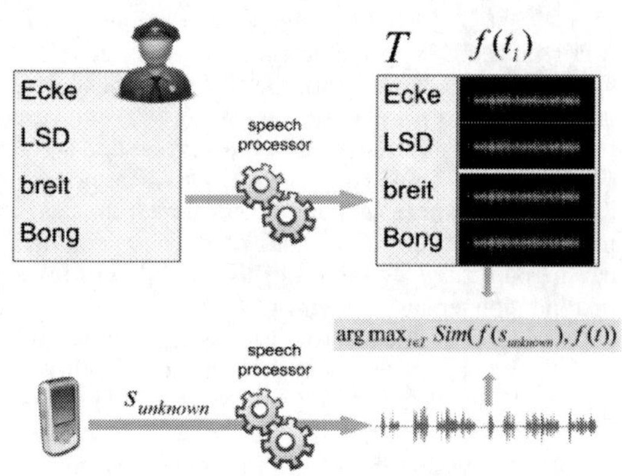

Figure 7: Dictionary containing pronunciation profiles as a basis for matching terms with high failure tolerance.

For testing the universality of the proposed process chain and especially the dictionary additional corpora are required. Fortunately, due to our cooperation with the local prosecutor's office additional data is provided. Finally, initial development of an algorithm, which aims at calculating the conversation significance value with a high failure tolerance as shown in Fig. 7, is currently work in progress. Here, pronunciation profiles are used as a basis for understanding special terms.

VI. Performance of a Prototype

The implemented MoNA prototype show an F_1 score of about 0.80 for both string matching and phonetic matching algorithms in relevance classification of identified conversations. However, both algorithms show opposite performance with respect to sensitivity and recall (string matching: 1.0 sensitivity, 0.67 recall, phonetic algorithms: 0.67 sensitivity, 1.0 recall). In performance testing, a dictionary of keywords commonly used in the local drug scene of the western Saxony area had been provided by investigators with expert knowledge. As demonstrated in the Word Dictionary Potency section, coverage and potency of the provided dictionary is rather low, which is the cause for the discrepancy in recall, respectively, sensitivity and leaves room for improvement. Thus, future research and studies have to focus on keyword selection, dictionary development and refinement. Nevertheless, the workload for manual peruse and annotation has been reduced significantly to 15% by integrating the MoNA prototype into the investigation process chain.

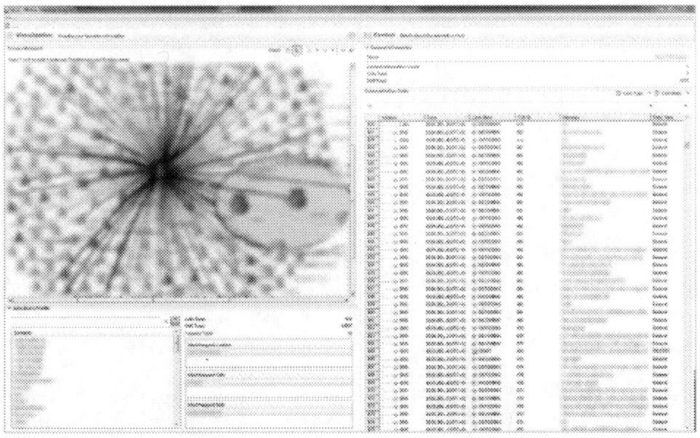

Figure 8: MoNA user interface. The communication network is visualised and highlighted by colour in accordance to scored conversation relevance. Contact information and message histories are further reported and interactively explorable. Sensitive information regarding the closed criminal investigation is disguised.

VII. Conclusion and Future Work

Manual forensic peruse and analyses of SMS and IM messages is a time-demanding and error-prone process. In addition, in case of minor or moderate offences and crimes, such forensic investigations are not justifiable for economical reasons. In recent work it has been shown that automated strategies for information retrieval and mining in message corpora is difficult to realize due to information uncertainty and ambiguity introduced by grammatical and semantic structures usually uncommon in well-written and error-free texts. Existing computational text analyses approaches are predominantly tailored towards a clearly defined semantic domain and are employed to domain-specific corpora of semantically and grammatically correct texts. Successful utilisation of such techniques is thus often limited or even impossible in the context of forensic SMS and IM message analyses.

In this work, a computational approach is proposed that aims at reducing the amount of messages prior to manual peruse by identifying conversations in message histories, which might contain evidential information relevant in investigation. This approach initially identifies conversations in message histories based on statistical analyses of the characteristic behaviour of text communication between participants. Individual identified conversations are subsequently scored with respect to predicted crime-related relevance based on a key word dictionary deduced from practical knowledge of investigators. This evaluation is further used in conversation reporting and visualization within the communication network. As demonstrated, the implemented prototype, MoNA, shows acceptable performance in this respect. Although widely applied software (such as Oxygen Forensics [22], XRY Physical [23] and UFED Touch Ultimate [24]) provide valuable means for data extraction and visualization, the process of data exploration, annotation and peruse is still required to be conducted manually. Here, as a tool for case-based forensic semantic analyses, MoNA could provide a valuable missing link in the process chain. Furthermore, MoNA currently features a data interface to process results and data derived by means of UFED software packages. In the near future, here presented approaches are ought to be refined. Implementations of additional data interfaces compatible with software listed above are currently work in progress.

Acknowledgment

The authors would like to thank the members of the criminal investigation department and the prosecutorial Chemnitz (Germany). We acknowledge funding by the Free State of Saxony and the University of Applied Sciences Mittweida.

References

[1] M. Spranger, E. Zuchantke, and D. Labudde, "Semantic tools for forensics: Towards finding evidence in short messages," in Proc. 4th. International Conference on Advances in Information Management and Mining, IARIA. ThinkMind Library, 2014, pp. 1–4.

[2] K. Barmpatsalou, D. Damopoulos, G. Kambourakis, and V. Katos, "A critical review of 7 years of mobile device forensics," Digital Investigation, vol. 10, no. 4, 2013, pp. 323–349.

[3] A. Skudlark, "Characterizing SMS Spam in a Large Cellular Network via Mining Victim Spam Reports," International Telecommunications Society (ITS) Biennial Conference, Tech. Rep., December 2014.

[4] I. Ahmed, D. Guan, and T. C. Chung, "Sms classification based on naïve bayes classifier and apriori algorithm frequent itemset," International Journal of Machine Learning and Computing, vol. 4, no. 2, April 2014, pp. 183–187.

[5] Q. Xu, E. W. Xiang, Q. Yang, J. Du, and J. Zhong, "Sms spam detection using noncontent features," IEEE Intelligent Systems, November/December 2012, pp. 44–51.

[6] D. G. A. Al-Talib and H. S. Hassan, "A study on analysis of sms classification using tf-idf weighting," International Journal of Computer Networks and Communications Security, vol. 1, no. 5, October 2013, pp. 189–194.

[7] M. B. Deepshikha Patel, "Mobile sms classification: An application of text classification," International Journal of Soft Computing and Engineering, vol. 1, no. 1, March 2011, pp. 47–49.

[8] S. Ishihara, "A forensic authorship classification in sms messages: A likelihood ratio based approach using n-gram," in Proceedings of the Australasian Language Technology Association Workshop 2011, Canberra, Australia, December 2011, pp. 47–56. [Online]. Available: http://www.aclweb.org/anthology/U/U11/U11-1008

[9] T. Chen and M.-Y. Kan, "Creating a live, public short message service corpus: the nus sms corpus," Language Resources and Evaluation, vol. 47, no. 2, 2013, pp. 299–335.

[10] D. H. W. Dannis Muhammad Mangan, "Information extraction from short text message in bahasa indonesia for electronics," Jurnal Sarjana Institut Teknologi Bandung bidang Teknik Elektro dan Informatika, vol. 1, no. 1, April 2012, pp. 29–32.

[11] S. Cooper, R.L.and Manson, "Extracting temporal information from short messages," in British National Conference on Databases, Glasgow, July 2007, LNCS 4587. LNCS, Springer, 2007, pp. 224–234.

[12] K. Nebhi, "Ontology-based information extraction from twitter," in Proceedings of the Workshop on Information Extraction and Entity Analytics on Social Media Data. Mumbai, India: The COLING 2012 Organizing Committee, December 2012, pp. 17–22. [Online]. Available: http://www.aclweb.org/anthology/W12-5502

[13] VATM, "Number of SMS and MMS sent in Germany from 1999 to 2014* (in millions per day)," 2016, URL: http://www.statista.com/statistics/461700/number-of-sms-and-mms-sent-per-day-germany/ [accessed: 2016-01-03].

[14] G. Evans and V. Gosalia, "The coming storm: Companies must be prepared to deal with text messages on employee mobile devices," Digital Discovery & e-Evidence, 2015.

[15] M. Spranger and D. Labudde, "Semantic tools for forensics: Approaches in forensic text analysis," in Proc. 3rd. International Conference on Advances in Information Management and Mining (IMMM), IARIA. ThinkMind Library, 2013, pp. 97–100.

[16] R. Cooper and S. Ali, "Extracting data from short messages," in Natural Language Processing and Information Systems, LNCS 3513. LNCS, Springer, 2005, pp. 388–391.

[17] E. Riloff, "Automatically constructing a dictionary for information extraction tasks," in Proceedings of the Eleventh National Conference on Artificial Intelligence, ser. AAAI'93. AAAI Press, 1993, pp. 811–816.

[18] H.-J. Postel, "Die Kölner Phonetik - Ein Verfahren zur Identifizierung von Personennamen auf der Grundlage der Gestaltanalyse." IBM-Nachrichten, vol. 19, 1969, pp. 925–931.

[19] L. Philips, "The Double Metaphone Search Algorithm." C/C++ Users Journal, vol. 18, no. 6, 2000, pp. 925–931.

[20] B. W. Matthews, "Comparison of the predicted and observed secondary structure of t4 phage lysozyme." Biochim Biophys Acta, vol. 405, no. 2, Oct 1975, pp. 442–451.

[21] Cellebrite Mobile Synchronization LTD. UFED Physical Analyzer - Mobile Daten ermitteln, dekodieren und bereitstellen. [Online]. Available: http://www.cellebrite.com/Mobile-Forensics/Applications/ufed-physical-analyzer [accessed: 2016-03-01]

[22] Oxygen Forensics, Inc. Oxygen Forensics. [Online]. Available: http://www.oxygen-forensic.com/de/ [accessed: 2016-03-01]

[23] MSAB. XRY Physical. [Online]. Available: https://www.msab.com/products/xry/#physical [accessed: 2016-03-01]

[24] Cellebrite Mobile Synchronization LTD. UFED Touch - Eine hochleistungsfähige Lösung für hochleistungsfähige Geräte. [Online]. Available: http://www.cellebrite.com/de/Mobile-Forensics/Products/ufed-touch [accessed: 2016-03-01]

Secure Scrum and OpenSAMM for Secure Software Development

Christoph Pohl
and Hans-Joachim Hof

MuSe - Munich IT Security Research Group
Munich University of Applied Sciences
Email: christoph.pohl0@hm.edu, hof@hm.edu

***Abstract*—Recent years saw serious attacks on software, e.g., the Heartbleed attack. Improving software security should be a main concern in all software development projects. Currently, Scrum is a popular agile software development method, used all around companies and universities. However, addressing IT security in Scrum projects is different to traditional security planning, which usually requires detailed planning in an initial planning phase. After this planning phase, only minor adjustments are expected. In contrast, Scrum is known for very little initial planning and for constant changes. This paper presents Secure Scrum, an extension to Scrum, that deals with the characteristics of security planning in Scrum. Secure Scrum is a variation of the Scrum framework that puts an emphasis on implementation of security related issues without the need of changing the underlying Scrum process or influencing team dynamics. To implement Secure Scrum in an organization, it helps to utilize a framework for strategic security planning. This paper uses the example of the OpenSAMM (Open Software Assurance Maturity Model) to show how Secure Scrum could be implemented in the field. A field test of Secure Scrum shows that the security level of software developed using Secure Scrum is higher then the security level of software developed using standard Scrum and that Secure Scrum is even suitable for use by non-security experts.**

Keywords*–*Scrum; Secure Scrum; Secure Software Development; SDL; OpenSAMM.

I. Introduction

This paper presents Secure Scrum and how Secure Scrum can be used in conjunction with OpenSAMM for the development of secure software. Secure Scrum was first presented in [1].

In times of the Internet of Things, even refrigerators now have network support and run a whole bunch of software. As software is so ubiquitous today, software bugs that lead to successful attacks on software systems are becoming a major hassle, see, e.g., [2]. To deal with the constant presence of attacks on systems, modern software development should focus on developing SECURE software, meaning software with little or no vulnerabilities.

Scrum [3][4] is a very popular software develpoment framework at the moment [5]. Unfortunately, Scrum comes without security support. This paper presents Secure Scrum, an extension of the Scrum framework that supports developers in implementing secure software. Secure Scrum is even suitable for non-security experts.

Scrum groups developer in small developer team, which have a certain autonomy to develop software. It is assumed in Scrum that all developers can implement all tasks at hand. Software development projects are split into so-called sprints. A sprint is a fixed period of time (between 2 and 4 weeks). During a sprint, the team develops an increment of the current software version, typically including a defined number of new features or functionality, which are described as user stories. User stories are used in Scrum to document requirements for a software project. All user stories are stored in the Product Backlog. During the planning of a sprint, user stories from the Product Backlog are divided into tasks. These tasks are stored in the Sprint Backlog. A so-called Product Owner is the single point of communication between customer and developer team. Regular feedback of customers on the state of the current increment of the software introduces agility to software development. Changes of user stories reflects this agility. The Product Owner also prioritizes the features to implement. Traditional Scrum does not include any security-specific parts.

One major driver of software security in Secure Scrum is the identification of security relevant parts of a software project. The identification of security critical system parts is very important in any software project, because only in this case, developers can implement appropriate security controls. Traditional software development processes typically use methods of security requirements engineering to identify security critical components of a system. However, the planning moments of Scrum (Product Backlog Refinement, Sprint Planning, and Sprint Review) have very tight time constraints, hence it is very hard to apply time-consuming traditional security requirements engineering methods. In Secure Scrum, security relevance of parts of the emerging software is visible to all team members at all times. This approach is considered to increase the security level, because developers place their focus on things that they had evaluated themselves, which they fully understand, and when their prioritization of requirements does not differ from prioritization of others [6][7].

Secure Scrum aims on achieving an appropriate security level for a given software project. The term "appropriate" was chosen to avoid costly over engineering of IT security in software projects. The definition of an appropriate security level is the crucial point in resource efficient software development (e.g., time and money are important resources during software development). For the definition of an appropriate security level, Secure Scrum relies on the definition in [8]: Software needs to be secured until it is no longer profitable for an intruder to find and exploit a vulnerability. This means that an appropriate security level is reached once the cost of an attack is higher then the expected gain of the attack. So, Secure Scrum offers a way to not only identify security relevant parts of the project but to also judge on the attractiveness of attack vectors in the sense of ease of exploitation.

The identification of security issues is not the only important part of achieving software security, the developers also need to implement effective controls to avoid potential security risks. In Scrum, each team member is responsible for the completeness of his solution (Definition of Done). However, there is a huge number of choices of methodologies to verify completeness. Thus, Secure Scrum must be able to integrate different verification methods. This leads to the issue that Secure Scrum needs to support team members with verification, but without the use of predefined verification methods. This means that a team member can use any method for verification (same as with normal tests, Scrum does not tell the developer how to test). Secure Scrum helps developers to identify appropriate security testing means for security relevant parts of a software project.

One last challenge solved by Secure Scrum is the availability of security knowledge when needed. In standard Scrum, each team member is responsible for his own work, this also means that the team member needs the knowledge to solve the requested task. Nowadays, the availability of security knowledge and experience among software developers does not reflect the importance of this issue. To keep many benefits of standard Scrum, Secure Scrum assumes that the vast majority of requirements should and could be handled by the team itself. However, for some security related issues, it could be necessary or more cost effective to include external resources like security consultants or in-house security experts in the project. Secure Scrum offers a way to include these external resources into the project without breaking the characteristics of Scrum and with little overhead in administration.

The rest of this paper is structured as follows: The following section summarizes related work on software security relevant for Secure Scrum. Section III shows the design of Secure Scrum in detail. Section IV shows how Secure Scrum can be implemented in an arbitrary organization using the framework OpenSAMM. Secure Scrum is evaluated in a field test in Section V. Section VI summarizes the findings of this paper.

II. Related Work

There are several methods for achieving software security, e.g., Clean Room [9], Correctness by Construction [10], CMMI-DEV [11][12], etc. However, these methods cannot be used in Scrum as they do not blend well with the characteristics of agile software development and specifically Scrum. Correctness by Construction [10], for example, advocates formal development in planning, verification and testing. This is completely different to agility and flexible approaches like agile methodologies. Especially Scrum has a strong focus on fast changes to running code, the overhead of Correctness by Construction would be significant. Other models like CMMI-DEV [11][12] can deal with agile methods. The main difference is that CMMI focuses on processes and Scrum on the developers [12]. This means that Scrum and other agile methodologies are developer centric, while CMMI is more process oriented. Restricting developers by rigid processes would break the idea of self-organization of Scrum, hence would introduce significant overhead. Concepts like Microsoft SDL [13] are designed to integrate agile methodologies, but is also self-contained. It can not be plugged into Scrum or any other agile methodology. Scrum focuses on rich communication, self-organisation, and collaboration between the involved project members. This conflicts with formalistic and rigid concepts.

To sum it up, the major challenge of addressing software security in Scrum is not to conflict with the agility aspect of Scrum.

S-Scrum [14] is a "security enhanced version of Scrum". It modifies the Scrum process by inserting so-called spikes. A spike contains analysis, design and verification related to security concerns. Further, requirements engineering (RE) in story gathering takes effect on this process. For this, the authors describe to use tools like Misuse Stories [15]. This approach is very formalistic and needs lot of changes to standard Scrum, hence hinders deployment in environments already using Scrum. Secure Scrum in contrast is compatible with standard Scrum, hence can be used in environments where Scrum is already used.

Another approach is described in [16]. It introduces a Security Backlog beside the Product Backlog and Sprint Backlog. Together with this artifact, they introduce a new role. The security master should be responsible for this new Backlog. This approach introduces an expert, describes the security aware parts in the backlog, and is adapted to the Scrum process. However, it lacks flexibility (as described in the introduction) and does not fit naturally in a grown Scrum team. Also, the introduction of a new role changes the management of projects. With this approach, it is not possible to interconnect standard Scrum user stories with the introduced security related stories. Secure Scrum in contrast keeps the connect between security issues and user stories of the Product Backlog respectively tasks of the Sprint Backlog.

In [17] an informal game (Protection Poker) is used to estimate security risks to explain security requirements to the developer team. The related case study shows that this is a possible way to integrate security awareness into Scrum. It solves the problem of requirements engineering with focus on software security. However, it does not provide a solution for the implementation and verification phase of software development, hence it is incomplete. Especially, Protection Poker does not ensure that security considerations actually affect the code itself, which is of crucial importance [18]. Secure Scrum in contrast provides a solution for all phases of software development, especially for the important implementation phase.

Another approach is discussed in [19]. An XP Team is accompanied by a security engineer. This should help to identify critical parts in the development process. Results are documented using abuse stories. This is similar to the definition in [20]. This approach is suitable for XP-Teams but not for Scrum.

To sum it up, none of the related work mentioned above integrates well into Scrum, comes with little overhead for Scrum, allows for easy adaption for teams already using standard Scrum, and focuses on all phases of software development. Secure Scrum in contrast solves all of these problems. The design of Secure Scrum is described in detail in the following.

III. Design of Secure Scrum

Secure Scrum consists of four components. These four components are put on top of the standard Scrum framework. Secure Scrum influences six stages of standard Scrum as can be seen in Figure 1.

The components of Secure Scrum are:

- *Identification component*: The identification component is used to identify security issues during software development. To make security issues visible to the team, security issues are marked in the Product Backlog of Scrum. The identification component is used during the initial creation of the Product Backlog as well as during Product Backlog Refinement, Sprint Planning, and Sprint Review.
- *Implementation component*: The implementation component raises the awareness of the Scrum team for security issues during each sprint. The implementation component is used in Sprint Planning, as well as during the Daily Scrum meetings. Hence, all software developers are aware of software security issues all the time.
- *Verification component*: The verification component ensures that team members are able to test the software with focus on the non-functional requirement software security. The verification component gets managed within the Daily Scrum meeting.
- *Definition of Done component*: The Definition of Done component enables the developers to define the Definition of Done for security related parts of the software in a way compatible with standard Scrum. The verification component especially addresses the problem of long-running security tests, e.g., penetration tests, that could not be performed at the end of a Scrum sprint.

In the following, each component of Secure Scrum is described in detail.

A. Identification Component

The identification component is used to identify and mark security relevant user stories. It is used during the initial creation of the Product Backlog as well as during Product Backlog Refinement, Sprint Planning, and Sprint Review. As Product Backlog Refinement, Sprint Planning, and Sprint Review have a very tight time constraint, the identification component does not use traditional methods of security requirements engineering.

Secure Scrum takes a value-oriented approach to security: Software needs to be secured until it is no longer profitable for an intruder to find and exploit a vulnerability. This means that an appropriate security level is reached once the cost of an attack is higher then the expected gain of the attack. Secure Scrum focuses security implementation effort on parts of the emerging software that are of high value for the stakeholders. Hence, in a first step, stakeholders (may be represented by

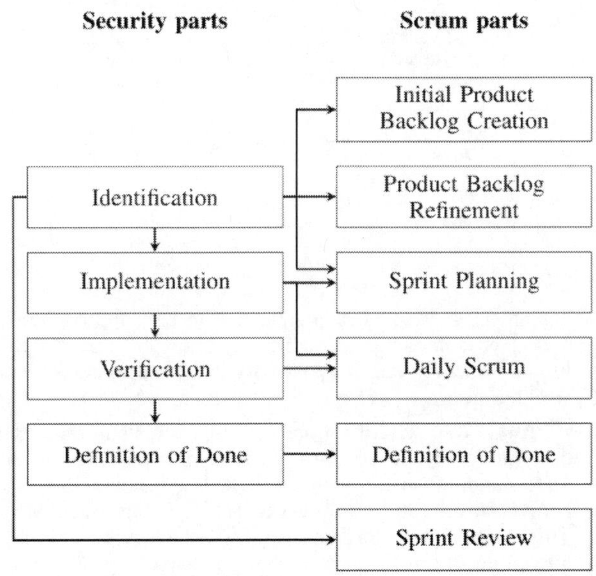

Figure 1. Integration of Secure Scrum components into standard Scrum

the Product Owner) and team members rank the different user stories according to their loss value. The loss value of a user story is not the cost of development neither the benefit of the functionality that implements the user story. The loss value of a user story is the loss that may occur whenever the functionality that implements the user story gets attacked or data processed by this functionality gets stolen or manipulated. For example, one can formulate "Whenever someone will get access to these data, our company will have high damage". Even better the cost gets listed with a numerable value like USD or Euro. However, such money estimates tend to be imprecise.

In a next step, stakeholders and team members evaluate misuse cases and rank them by their risk. At this point, it can be useful to incorporate external security expertise to moderate by asking the right questions and proposing security aware user stories.

If an organization often develops software for the same domain (e.g., financial service sector, medical sector), it is advisable to compile a list of misuse cases from prior projects in the same domain that could be used for future projects. Also, checklists may be used. Other useful sources for risk estimation are other risk rating methodologies, e.g., the OWASP Risk Rating [21].

After using the identification component, team members and stakeholders have a common understanding of security risks in the Product Backlog. To keep awareness for security risks at a high level, the initial understanding about security risks is documented in the Product Backlog. To do this, Scrum uses so-called *S-Tags*. Figure 2 shows the basic principle of an *S-Tag*. An *S-Tag* consists of one or more *S-Marks*, a Backlog artifact, and a connection between the Backlog artifact and one or more *S-Tags*. An *S-Tag* identifies Product Backlog items that have security relevance with a marker called *S-Mark*. This ensures that the security relevance of certain items in the Product Backlog is visible at all times. The technology

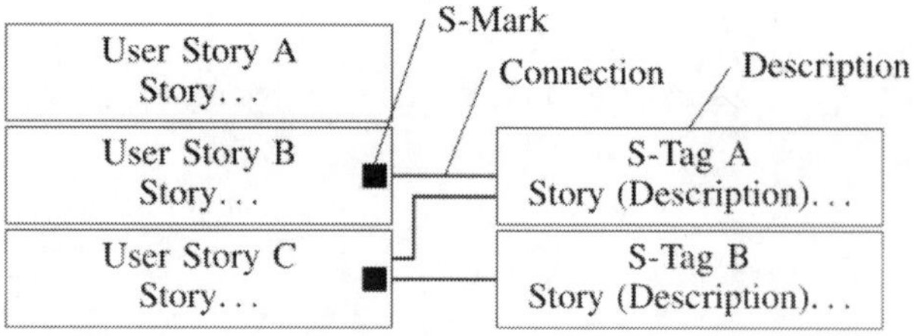

Figure 2. Usage of S-Tags to mark user stories in the Product Backlog and to connect user stories to descriptions of security related issues.

behind the *S-Mark* is negligible (it can be a red background, a dot, or something else), it only must be ensured that a Product Backlog item with security relevance contrasts to other Backlog items.

An *S-Tag* describes one security concern. A detailed description of the security issue helps the Scrum team to understand the security concern. The description of the security concern itself can be formulated in a separate Backlog item. This can be a user story, misuse story, abuse story, or whatever a team decides to use as description technology. The description may include elements from a knowledge base that gives advice on how to deal with this specific security concern. If such a knowledge base is maintained over the course of several projects, it is very likely a valuable source of information for the Scrum team. A knowledge base could also increase the time-efficiency of the identification component.

An *S-Tag* links one security concern to one or more Backlog items. A security concern is any security related problem, attack vector, task, or security principle that should be considered during implementation. One-to-many-connections between security concern and affected Product Backlog items allow for grouping of items that share the same security concern (and hopefully may use the same security mechanisms) as well as expressing security on a high level. Connections between *S-Tags* could be realized by using unique identifiers for *S-Tags* that are part of the *S-Mark* (e.g., written on a red dot that is used as *S-Mark*). Using meaningful identifiers helps in understanding security concerns at one glance.

B. Implementation Component

Original Scrum has a strong focus on implementation and running code. Hence, it is obvious that security efforts must affect the code itself [18]. Thus, Secure Scrum makes security concerns visible for the developers at all time. To ensure that security concerns are visible in daily work of the developers, they must be present in the Sprint Backlog. Subsection III-A describes how security concerns are included in the Product Backlog. The Product Backlog lists the required functionalities of the product. This includes the *S-Tags*. Usually, a sprint implements a subset of these functionalities (for example user stories). During a sprint, some user stories are broke down to tasks (or similar conceptual parts). Whenever a user story is marked with an *S-Mark*, the corresponding *S-Tag* must also be present in the corresponding Sprint Backlog and the *S-Tag* must be handled by the developer during the sprint. An *S-Tag* can be handled like any other Backlog item. But whenever an *S-Tag* gets split into tasks, these tasks must also be marked with an *S-Mark* and connected to the original *S-Tag*. This ensures that developers are always aware of the original security concern and the security concern can be linked back to the origin description. Using the implementation component of Secure Scrum ensures that developers are aware of the relevant security concerns of the product in each sprint and that security concerns do not get lost during implementation.

C. Verification Component and Definition of Done Component

Increased awareness for security related concerns is not the only advantage of the use of *S-Tags*. *S-Tags* are also very useful when identifying requirements for verification of the emerging software. In the first place, *S-Tags* clearly identify parts of the emerging software that need security verification. In the second place, *S-Tags* are useful to estimate the effort needed for verification. Some security verifications may need a long time (e.g., penetration testing), hence could not be performed at the end of a sprint.

For further simplification, the term "task" is used for some work that is performed by one developer in one sprint and that needs one Definition of Done.

Secure Scrum proposes two different approaches for verification to deal with the problem of long running tests and, therefore, two variants of the Definition of Done exist:

- *Same-Sprint-Verification:* Whenever the verification process (whatever the developer or team chooses to use) for one task can be performed during the same sprint and by the same developer, the verification must be part of the task itself. This ensures that the verification is also part of the Definition of Done.
- *Spin-off Verification Task:* This variant is used if a developer does not have the required knowledge for verification, or the verification needs external resources, extra time for testing, or anything else that hinders an immediate verification. In this case, the verification cannot be part of the Definition of Done. In such cases, a new task must be created that inherits only the verification part of the original task. This new task ("spin-off verification task") must be marked with an *S-Mark* and should be connected to the original *S-Tag*, together with the original task. In this case, the developer can define the Definition of Done without the verification, hence a Definition of Done compatible to standard Scrum is available. It is of crucial importance that spin-off verification tasks are subject of sprints in the near future. However, if external experts are used for certain verification tasks (see Subsection III-D), it is beneficial if spin-off verification tasks can be pooled. In any case, it must be ensured that there are no unhandled spin-off verification tasks at the end of software development.

The proposed approach for the definition of the Definition of Done ensures that the connection between an *S-Mark* and its corresponding *S-Tag* keep existing throughout the project, hence no security concern can get lost.

D. Integration of External Ressources

IT security knowledge may be rare in a Scrum team or special knowledge not present in the Scrum team may be necessary for certain parts of the emerging software (e.g.,

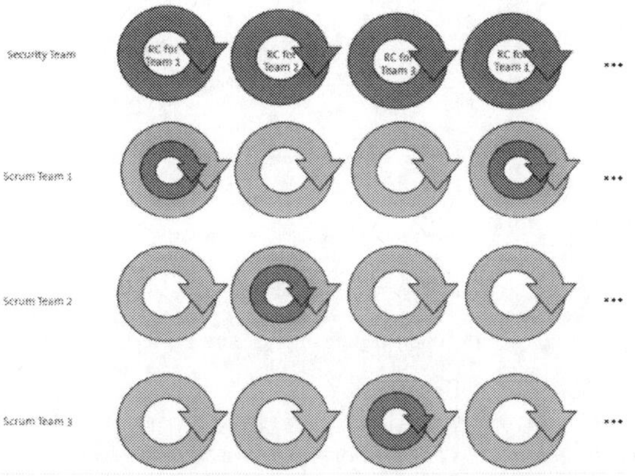

Figure 3. Running Coach approach: one security team provides security services to multiple scrum teams

implementation and testing of cryptographic algorithms, penetration testing of software increments). Or a company prefers to pool security experts in a special team that supports multiple other scrum teams. Such a security team allows for a running coach approach: the security team supports exactly one team at each scrum sprint. If sprints are synchronized in a company, this helps to have a good use of the security experts. Figure 3 shows this so-called running coach approach with one security team that supports three Secure Scrum teams.

Secure Scrum offers ways to include external resources (e.g., external security consultants or internal running coaches) in all components of Secure Scrum. External resources could have one or more of the following three functions:

- Enhance knowledge and provide guidance
- Solve challenges
- Provide external view

These three functions are described in the following.

Enhance knowledge and provide guidance: This function includes security-related training for the Scrum team to help them to gain a better understanding of a specific security-related area. Doing so on the job during a project offers a chance to teach IT security with a specific example at hand (e.g., a certain *S-Tag* that is linked to many user stories) and may be more efficient than security training between two projects. Training may be necessary for aspects that are not part of everyday work, e.g., the usability of security mechanisms [22], [23].

Solving Challenges: Some *S-Tag*s represent hard security challenges that require special expertise or special experience, such that it is more cost efficient to let external resources solve this challenge. To avoid breaches in Scrum, it is necessary that these external solutions can be handled like a tool, a well defined part of development, a framework, or a "black box", which is ready to use. This means that this external solution should be encapsulated and therefore does not influence Scrum or the Scrum team. For example, this can be a functional part of software (with special IT Security concerns) or parts of the project, which can be used with an API by the Scrum team. Another challenge is the integration of external services like penetration testing into the development process. One way to do so is that external resources provide test cases (e.g., for Metasploit [24]) that can be used for every increment of the emerging software at any time. Results of tests can be documented as artifacts in the Backlog. Then they can be handled like any other change request.

Providing external view: One major part in IT Security is to recognize ways to exploit the own system. In other words, one must think like an attacker to recognize potential attack vectors. Usually, it is easier for an outsider to spot potential weaknesses of a system than it is for the developer of a system. Hence, external resources may introduce a valuable external viewpoint on a project. When using the identification component of Secure Scrum, an external consultant can be helpful to point the team to security concerns. When using the implementation component, external resources can be helpful in the sprint planning or could perform code reviews. When using the verification component, an external consultant can help to create tests for security concerns. These interventions by external resources should not be part of the normal Scrum processes, the external resource should only help to ask questions (in the meaning of: he should show relevant concerns in scope of IT Security). In conclusion, the external resource should help to set focus on problems the team is not aware of.

IV. Implementation of Secure Scrum Using OpenSAMM

This section gives some hints on how to successfully implement Secure Scrum in an organization. Implementation of a new security approach is a non-trivial task for many organizations. Secure Scrum is compatible with many frameworks for implementation of security strategies, and if there is already a framework in use in an organization, it is a good idea to use this framework to implement Secure Scrum. Existing frameworks may be for example Microsoft SDL [25] or CLASP (Comprehensive Lightweight Application Security Process) [26]. This section uses OpenSAMM (Open Software Assurance Maturity Model) [27] as an example to show possible implementation activities. OpenSAMM was chosen because it can be used with arbitrary security strategies, has a small overhead, is open and flexible enough to be a good fit for security in agile software development. One big advantage of OpenSAMM compared to Micrsoft SDL, CLASP, and many other frameworks is, that it it is not necessary to introduce Secure Scrum in one big project at one time, but many small steps are possible, using so-called maturity levels. Especially this feature of OpenSAMM makes it a good fit for small and medium size companies with small security budgets.

OpenSAMM consists of four business functions that are typical for organizations developing software. Each business function has three security practices (see Figures 5, 6, 7, and 8). Each security practices has levels between 0 (no security yet) and 3 (mature security). The meaning of these maturity levels is described in the following:

- Maturity level 0: No activities for this security practice are implemented. In most organizations, this is the starting point.
- Maturity level 1: There is a basic understanding of the security practice and first implementations of the security practice exist.

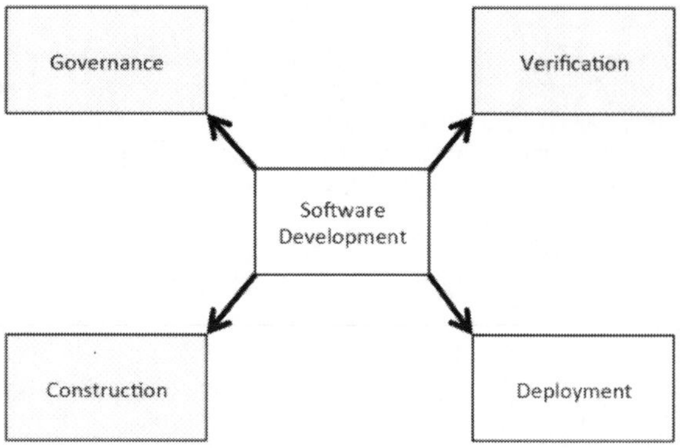

Figure 4. Overview OpenSAMM (parts relevant for the implementation of Secure Scrum in yellow)

- Maturity level 2: Efficiency and/or effectiveness of implementations of this security practice get enhanced at this level.
- Maturity level 3: The security practice is at a high level of competence.

This section describes security activities for Secure Scrum security practices on levels 1 through 3. The level approach helps to introduce Secure Scrum in multiple steps. OpenSAMM includes methodologies to verify the successful implementation of activities on a certain level of a security practice before proceeding further. Also, OpenSAMM offers roadmap templates for typical domains. Figure 4 gives an overview of the four business functions of OpenSAMM. The four business functions of the software development process in OpenSAMM are:

- *Governance*: The focus of the business function Governance lies on the overall processes and activities for software development in an organization.
- *Construction*: The focus of the business function Construction lies on how to create software in a software project. This business function is the most important business function for the implementation of Secure Scrum.
- *Verification*: The focus of the business function Verification lies on how to test software produced during software development. Typical activities include penetration testing, general software quality assurance actions as well as manual review of source code or even design documents.
- *Deployment*: The focus of the business function Deployment lies on how to manage releases of software. This includes shipping of products to the end user, installation of products as well as operational aspects of software. There is no need to adapt this business function for Secure Scrum as operation of software is out of scope of Secure Scrum.

Secure Scrum needs to be included in the business functions Governance, Verification, and Construction. The business function Deployment is out of scope of Secure Scrum, but nevertheless, it is very important for achieving software security in general.

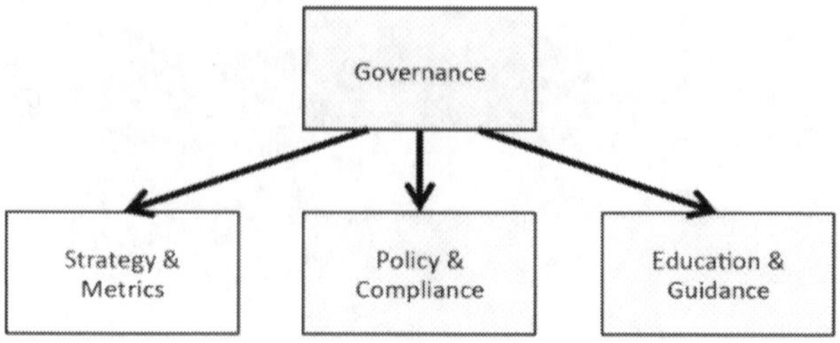

Figure 5. Security practices of business function Governance (parts relevant for the implementation of Secure Scrum in yellow)

Figure 5 shows the security practices for the business function Governance. They are:

- *Strategy & Metrics*: This security practice includes the overall strategy for development of secure software as well as metrics to measure progress in enhancing the security level of software.
- *Policy & Compliance*: This security practice includes setting up control mechanisms to check that all processes for development of secure software are followed.
- *Education & Guidance*: This security practice includes all activities that enhance knowledge of software developers.

Security practice Strategy & Metrics does not need changes for Secure Scrum. Secure Scrum can be used in many different security strategies and all kind of metrics can be used. See [28] for an overview of common metrics.

Security practice Policy & Compliance includes Secure Scrum activities at the following maturity levels:

- Maturity Level 1: Establish compliance guidelines for Secure Scrum usage. Guidelines should include mandatory use of Secure Scrum as well as responsibilities of the Scrum roles (process owner, Scrum Master, team members) in Secure Scrum, e.g., who is responsible for risk rating.
- Maturity Level 2: Establish compliance guidelines for risk rating in software projects. Establish regular audits of projects.
- Maturity Level 3: Establish a solution for audit data collection. Establish compliance gates, e.g., check compliance with Secure Scrum guidelines every 6th sprint.

Security practice Education & Guidance includes Secure Scrum activities at the following maturity levels:

- Maturity Level 1: Establish a technical guideline for Secure Scrum. This should include a description of the Secure Scrum components Identification, Implementation, Verification, and Definition of Done components (see Section III), a comprehensive description of S-Marks and S-Tags as well as a description of the integration of Secure Scrum in Scrum. Establish a knowledge base of security concerns as described in Section III-A.

- Maturity Level 2: Each scrum role (product owner, scrum master, scrum team member) gets role-specific security training, an introduction to Secure Scrum as a methodology as well as an introduction to the supporting systems. Project teams are supported by Secure Scrum running coaches to support the transition to Secure Scrum.
- Maturity Level 3: Establish mandatory Secure Scrum training for all roles. Establish a role-based Secure Scrum exam or a role-based Secure Scrum certification.

Figure 6 shows the security practices for the business function Construction. They are:

- *Threat Assessment*: Identification of threats and risk assessment.
- *Security Requirements*: Specification of security requirements.
- *Secure Architecture*: Activities to achieve a secure software design.

All three security practices need to include Secure Scrum related activities.

Security practice Threat Assessment includes Secure Scrum activities at the following maturity levels:

- Maturity Level 1: Establish a knowledge base of application-specific typical attacks for use in the identification component of Secure Scrum.
- Maturity Level 2: Adopt a system for rating relevant attacks per application. Such a system could for example be based on the OWASP Risk Rating [21]. Establish a knowledge base of misuse-cases that are typical for the developed applications.
- Maturity Level 3: Include external experts in risk assessment, see Section III-D for details.

Security practice Security Requirements includes Secure Scrum activities at the following maturity levels:

- Maturity Level 1: Establish mandatory use of the identification component of Secure Scrum. Use knowledge base in identification of relevant attacks. Connect affected user stories with knowledge base articles.
- Maturity Level 2: Establish a risk-based approach for the identification component.
- Maturity Level 3: Audit S-Mark usage explicitly during software development. Audit use of spin-off verification tasks. Ensure no spin-off verification tasks exist at the end of software development.

Security practice Secure Architecture includes Secure Scrum activities at the following maturity levels:

- Maturity Level 1: Maintain a list of security design principles in a knowledge base and make sure that S-Marks for each product are connected to them.
- Maturity Level 2: Maintain a list of security design patterns [29] and make sure that S-Marks are connected to them.
- Maturity Level 3: Maintain a list of reference architectures and make sure that S-Marks connect to them. Use audits to ensure that secure frameworks, patterns, and platforms are used. Establish regular audits by external security experts.

Figure 7 shows the security practices for the business function Verification. They are:

- *Design Review*: Inspection of the design regarding the use of adequate security mechanisms
- *Code Review*: Inspection of code to find potential vulnerabilities.
- *Security Testing*: Testing of software increments produced during software development for vulnerabilities.

All three security practices need to include Secure Scrum related activities.

Security practice Design Review includes Secure Scrum activities at the following maturity levels:

- Maturity Level 1: Establish mandatory use of S-Marks at the start of a project to tag security relevant user stories.
- Maturity Level 2: Establish audit of all S-Marks by external security experts.
- Maturity Level 3: Establish periodic audits (e.g., every 6th Scrum sprint) by all roles of Scrum as well as by external security experts to review the user stories and assign S-Marks.

Security practice Code Review includes Secure Scrum activities at the following maturity levels:

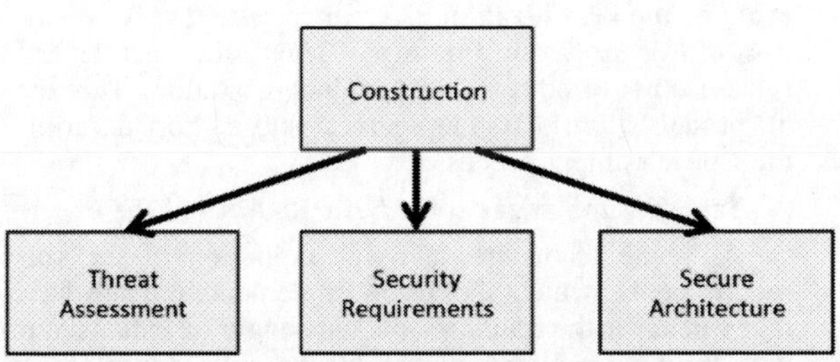

Figure 6. Security practices of business function Construction (parts relevant for the implementation of Secure Scrum in yellow)

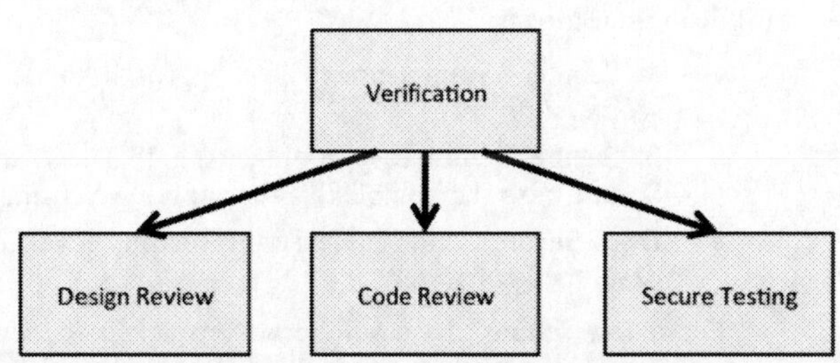

Figure 7. Security practices of business function Verification (parts relevant for the implementation of Secure Scrum in yellow)

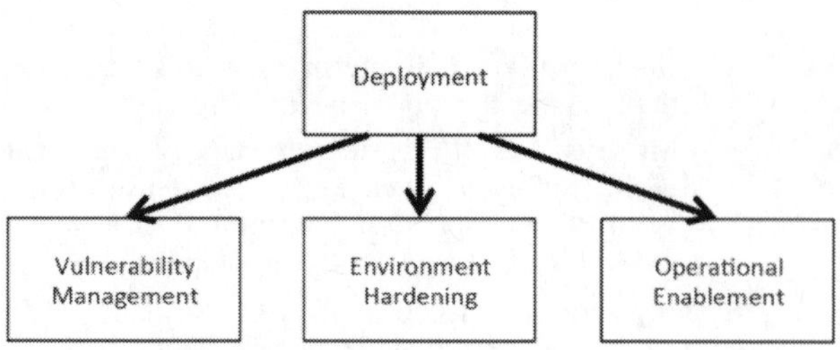

Figure 8. Security practices of business function Deployment (parts relevant for the implementation of Secure Scrum in yellow)

- Maturity Level 1: Establish spin-off verification gates: At certain points during the software development make sure, that spin-off verification task in backlogs are cared for.
- Maturity Level 2: Offer support of security experts to verify verification artifacts.
- Maturity Level 3: Use experts to verify all verification artifacts (e.g., running coaches, see Section III-D, or external penetration testers).

Figure 8 shows the security practices for the business function Deployment. They are:

- *Vulnerability Management*: Establish processes to handle vulnerability reports.
- *Environment Hardening*: Increase security level of systems that run software provided by the organization
- *Operational Enablement*: Provide security information to administrators that use the organizations software. This information includes secure configuration, secure deployment, and security operation.

None of these security practices is relevant to Secure Scrum. However, the three security practices of the business function Deployment are very important for software security in general, hence should hold activities appropriate for the implementing organization.

The OpenSAMM Guide [27] offers several roadmap templates, giving a schedule for security practice level changes. In most cases, the roadmap template "Independent Software Vendor" is a good fit.

V. Evaluation

The evaluation presented in this paper focuses on the following questions:

- Is Secure scrum a practicable approach to develop secure software?
- Is Secure Scrum easy to understand? Does Secure Scrum raise the complexity for applying Scrum?
- Does Secure Scrum increase the security level of the developed software?

For a test setting, 16 developers were asked to develop a small piece of software. The developers were third year students in a computer sciences and business informatics (BSc) study program. They were not aware that they are part of this evaluation. The students showed programming skills that were on the usual level of a third year bachelor student. No participant attended a specialized course in IT Security before beside the compulsory lecture in IT Security (basic level) in the second year of the bachelor. When asked about their practical experience in IT security, all students said that they have no practical experience. Hence, it is expected that none of the students has IT security as a hobby and all students are on the same level concerning IT security knowledge and experience. All developers had average theoretical knowledge about Scrum. Only two students had practical experiences (less than 2 months) with Scrum.

The developers were divided into three groups:

1) Team 1 (T1): The Anarchist group: They could manage themselves as they like, except using Scrum.
2) Team 2 (T2): The Scrum group: They should use standard Scrum.
3) Team 3 (T3): The Secure Scrum group: They should use Secure Scrum.

To avoid influences on the evaluation, teams 1 and 2 thought that team 3 also uses standard Scrum. All groups got a list of six basic requirements for a new software product. They were asked to develop a prototype for a social network with the following features:

- registration,
- login and logout,
- personal messages,
- wall messages,
- bans, and
- friend lists.

Each group had only one week to develop a prototype of this application using Java and a preconfigured spring framework template (based on BREW (Breakable Web Application) [30]). Each group was asked to implement as many requirements as possible. However, it was known that it is impossible to implement all requirements for the final version of the application considering the harsh time constraints. This setting of the evaluation assures a high time pressure (as in real projects), hence allows to observe the prioritization of security-related tasks. Developers were also told that they need to "sell" their prototype on the last day of the experiment in front of a jury. In fact they should learn how to present their prototype and act like a team that wants to have a contract for further development. This should ensure that every team needs to define for itself the selling points of their prototype, putting a high pressure on feature richness. Again, this setting helps to evaluate the prioritization of security-related task. Team 3 has a short Secure Scrum briefing of about one hour. Every team is advised to produce a proper documentation. This includes all produced artifacts, the sources, and a short description of their development process.

Table I summarizes some basic findings of the experiment.

All three teams had a rough definition of the six basic requirements, which should be implemented. They were told that whenever the requirements list should be enhanced to deal with the 6 requirements given by the customer, they are free to define new requirements. Team 1 did not define any new requirements. Team 2 defined one new requirement to enhance

TABLE I. Results of the evaluation of the efficiency and effectiveness of Secure Scrum

#	Metric	T1	T2	T3
1	Lines of code	1149	758	458
2	Number of basic requirements	6	6	6
3	Number of additional requirements defined	0	1	8
4	Number of basic requirements documented	0	6	6
5	Number of basic requirements implemented	6	5	4
6	Number of requirements documented	0	7	14
7	Number of requirements implemented	6	6	9
8	Number of vulnerabilities sp	18	12	3
9	Group size	6	5	5

performance. Team 3 defined 8 new requirements that had a focus on IT Security. These requirements are an excerpt of the descriptions for the *S-Tag*. Overall, they defined 29 new stories focused on IT Security. This shows that even with beginner skills in computer sciences and only basic skills in IT Security, it is possible to define a high amount (compared to the original requirements) of security related requirements. It also shows that it is possible to describe the most problematic vulnerabilities or problems with the help of risk identification.

Metrics 4 – 7 of Table I are used to evaluate if the teams documented all requirements and how many of the requirements were implemented. The evaluation shows that the teams did not take care of any further requirements when not specified by the customer. This sounds trivial, but it also shows that the developer did not take care of IT Security when not specified. The Secure Scrum team (team 3) is the only team that did not implement all given basic requirements. Instead, they obviously prioritized some of the security requirements over the basic requirements as some of the additional requirements that were added by the team were implemented. This finding shows that Secure Scrum succeeds in putting focus on software security.

Metric 8 shows the number of security problems that were created by the developers. The number of security problem is calculated as follows:

Let sl be a vulnerability listed in the OWASP Top 10 list OTT ($sl \in OTT$). The OWASP Top 10 project [31] lists the most common security vulnerabilities for web applications:

- Injection,
- Broken Authentication and Session Management,
- Cross-Site Scripting (XSS),
- Insecure Direct Object References,
- Security Misconfiguration,
- Sensitive Data Exposure,
- Missing Function Level Access Control,
- Cross-Site Request Forgery,
- Using Components with Known Vulnerabilities, and
- Unvalidated Redirects and Forwards.

Let OS be the complete source code of the developed software and SC the part of the software written by the students ($SC \subset OS$). Let cf be a Java function. Let $cpf(sl)$ be a function that counts the amount of sl for one cf. By definition, $cpf(sl)$ increments a vulnerability counter by one whenever the current function is the source ms function for a vulnerability. A function cf is considered as a source ms whenever $cf \in SC$ and when the function is the reason for the vulnerability or it calls a function cf_1 where $cf_1 \notin SC$ and cf_1 is the reason for the vulnerability. The amount of vulnerabilities sp is the sum of all $cpf(cf)$. Such a definition of the number of security problems only counts code that is responsible for vulnerabilities of a software system. It also takes into consideration the use of vulnerable code. For example, when a developer creates an SQL statement with a potential SQL Injection vulnerability, the function holding the database call with this statement is regarded as the reason of the vulnerability.

TABLE II. Results of the evaluation of the practicality of Secure Scrum

#	Metric	Team 2	Team 3
1	Number of requirements	7	14
2	Number of user stories	7 (13)	14 (62)
3	Number of tasks	18	35
4	Number of user stories with *S-Mark*	-	14
5	Number of tasks with *S-Mark*	-	8(35)

The results of the evaluation shows that team 1 and team 2 had a high amount of vulnerabilities in their software (team 1: 18, team 2: 12). Both teams built software exploitable by SQL Injection, XSS, CSRF, and had a vulnerable session management. Team 3 had significantly less vulnerabilities. It should be noted that every team has the same level of security knowledge. The benefit of team 3 is, that their usage of Secure Scrum raised the awareness for security issues. Hence, the evaluation shows that the use of Secure Scrum increase the security level of the developed software.

The first metric (Lines of Code (LOC)) of Table I shows the amount of code, which was generated during the week. There are significant differences between the three teams. The teams that identified additional requirements (performance (team 2) and security (team 3)) were not as productive as the other teams. The difference between team 2 and team 3 shows that Secure Scrum raises the complexity of applying Scrum. This shows the overhead that comes with a broadened focus on software quality, especially on non-functional requirements. However, it should be noted that it is expected that the overhead of Secure Scrum decreases over time as team members get used to it and as a knowhow transfer over project takes place, e.g., in the form of knowledge base entries on security issues (see Section III-A) or security checklists from previous projects (see Section III-A).

Secure Scrum is considered to be easy to use and practicable, if even students with a weak background in IT security are able to identify security relevant parts of the software. To evaluate ease of use and practicality of Secure Scrum, the documentation of the Scrum teams was evaluated. The documentation consists of the Backlogs and a timetable. There, it can be seen if the Secure Scrum team did identify security relevant parts of the software.

Table II summarizes the results of this evaluation for team 2 (Scrum) and team 3 (Secure Scrum) to compare standard Scrum to Secure Scrum.

Numbers in braces give the total amount of user stories. The numbers not in braces (aggregated number) show the amount of user stories when grouped together. This means a group of user story is a "bigger" user story, which reflects a requirement. Team 2 broke down every user story to a different task. Team 3 broke down tasks for only the stories that they also implemented. This is why they defined more user stories than tasks. Team 3 found for every user story some security concerns, this is why they tagged all user stories. Metric 5 shows that all tasks also had *S-Marks*, overall they had 8 different groups in the tasks. Team 3 decided to create the links by grouping, they simply used red cards for the descriptions to show security problems (*S-Mark*). This also shows that the proposed tools are simple enough to adapt them very fast in a Scrum process.

In conclusion, the evaluation shows that Secure Scrum is able to improve the security level of the developed software. Secure Scrum is easy to understand, can be used in practice, and is even suitable for teams that have no deepened security knowledge. The evaluation also shows that it is possible to have a proper documentation through all stages of the experiment. The tools of Secure Scrum harmoniously blend into the standard Scrum toolset without the need of much overhead for training.

VI. Conclusion

This paper presents Secure Scrum, an extension of the software development framework Scrum. Secure Scrum enriches Scrum with features focusing on building secure software. One of the main contributions of Secure Scrum are *S-Tags*, a way to annotate Backlog items with security related information. Such annotations help software developers to keep security in mind during software development. The paper also presents how OpenSAMM can be used to implement Secure Scrum in an organization. The maturity level approach of OpenSAMM helps to implement Secure Scrum step by step, hence does not overburden organizations. Secure Scrum was evaluated in a small software development project. The evaluation shows that Secure Scrum can be used in practice, is easy to use and understand, and improves the level of software security.

References

[1] C. Pohl and H.-J. Hof, "Secure Scrum: Develpoment of Secure Software with Scrum," in SECURWARE 2015: The Ninth International Conference on Emerging Security Information, Systems and Technologies. Venice, Italy: IARIA XPS Press, 2015, pp. 15–20.

[2] Symantec, "2015 internet security threat report.", retrieved: 05, 2016 [Online]. Available: https://www4.symantec.com/mktginfo/whitepaper/ISTR/21347932_GA-internet-security-threat-report-volume-20-2015-social_v2.pdf

[3] K. Beck, M. Beedle, K. Schwaber, and M. Fowler, "Manifesto for agile software development,", retrieved: 05, 2016 [Online]. Available: http://www.agilemanifesto.org/

[4] K. Schwaber, "SCRUM development process," in Business Object Design and Implementation, D. J. Sutherland, C. Casanave, J. Miller, D. P. Patel, and G. Hollowell, Eds. Springer London, pp. 117–134.

[5] VersionOne, "9th Annual State of Agile Survey.", retrieved: 05, 2016 [Online]. Available: http://info.versionone.com/state-of-agile-development-survey-ninth.html

[6] C. Riemenschneider, B. Hardgrave, and F. Davis, "Explaining software developer acceptance of methodologies: a comparison of five theoretical models," IEEE Transactions on Software Engineering, vol. 28, no. 12, Dec. 2002, pp. 1135–1145.

[7] L. Vijayasarathy and D. Turk, "Drivers of agile software development use: Dialectic interplay between benefits and hindrances," Information and Software Technology, vol. 54, no. 2, Feb. 2012, pp. 137–148.

[8] C. Herley, "Security, cybercrime, and scale," Communications of the ACM, vol. 57, no. 9, Sep. 2014, pp. 64–71.

[9] H. D. Mills and R. C. Linger, "Cleanroom Software Engineering: Developing Software Under Statistical Quality Control - Encyclopedia of Software Engineering - Mills - Wiley Online Library," 1991.

[10] A. Hall and R. Chapman, "Correctness by construction: developing a commercial secure system," IEEE Software, vol. 19, no. 1, 2002, pp. 18–25.

[11] M. B. Chrissis, M. Konrad, and S. Shrum, CMMI for Development, ser. Guidelines for Process Integration and Product Improvement. Pearson Education, Mar. 2011.

[12] H. Glazer, J. Dalton, D. Anderson, M. D. Konrad, and S. Shrum, "CMMI or Agile: Why Not Embrace Both!" 2008, pp. 1–48.

[13] M. Howard and S. Lipner, The security development lifecycle. O'Reilly Media, Incorporated, 2009.

[14] D. Mougouei, N. F. Mohd Sani, and M. Moein Almasi, "S-scrum: a secure methodology for agile development of web services." World of Computer Science & Information Technology Journal, vol. 3, no. 1, 2013, pp. 15–19.

[15] G. Sindre and A. L. Opdahl, "Eliciting security requirements with misuse cases," Requirements Engineering, vol. 10, no. 1, Jan. 2005, pp. 34–44.

[16] Z. Azham, I. Ghani, and N. Ithnin, "Security backlog in scrum security practices," in Software Engineering (MySEC), 2011 5th Malaysian Conference in. IEEE, 2011, pp. 414–417.

[17] L. Williams, A. Meneely, and G. Shipley, "Protection poker: The new software security," IEEE Security & Privacy, no. 3, 2010, pp. 14–20.

[18] S. B. Lipner, "Security Assurance - How can customers tell they are getting it?" Communications of the ACM, vol. 58, no. 11, 2053, pp. 24–26.

[19] G. Boström, J. Wyrynen, M. Bodn, K. Beznosov, and P. Kruchten, "Extending XP practices to support security requirements engineering," in Proceedings of the 2006 international workshop on Software engineering for secure systems. ACM, 2006, pp. 11–18.

[20] J. Peeters, "Agile security requirements engineering," in Symposium on Requirements Engineering for Information Security, 2005.

[21] Open Web Application Security Project (OWASP), "OWASP Risk Rating Methodology." , retrieved: 05, 2016 [Online]. Available: https://www.owasp.org/index.php/OWASP_Risk_Rating_Methodology

[22] H.-J. Hof, "Towards Enhanced Usability of IT Security Mechanisms - How to Design Usable IT Security Mechanisms Using the Example of Email Encryption," International Journal On Advances in Security, vol. 6, no. 1&2, 2013, pp. 78–87.

[23] H. J. Hof, "User-Centric IT Security - How to Design Usable Security Mechanisms," in The Fifth International Conference on Advances in Human-oriented and Personalized Mechanisms, Technologies, and Services (CENTRIC 2012), 2012, pp. 7–12.

[24] Rapid7, "Metasploit," 2015, retrieved: 05, 2016. [Online]. Available: http://www.metasploit.com/

[25] M. Howard and S. Lipner, The Security Development Lifecycle: SDL: A Process for Developing Demonstrably More Secure Software (Developer Best Practices), ser. Secure Software. Microsoft Press, Jun. 2006.

[26] Open Web Application Security Project (OWASP), "CLASP (Comprehensive, Lightweight Application Security Process).", retrieved: 05, 2016 [Online]. Available: https://www.owasp.org/index.php/Category:OWASP_CLASP_Project

[27] P. Chandra, "Software assurance maturity model.", retrieved: 05, 2016 [Online]. Available: http://www.opensamm.org/downloads/SAMM-0.8.1-en_US.pdf

[28] N. Fenton and J. Bieman, Software Metrics - A Rigourous and Practical Approach. CRC Press, 2015.

[29] E. Fernandez-Buglioni, Security Patterns in Practice: Designing Secure Architectures Using Software Patterns(Wiley Series in Software Design Patterns). John Wiley & Sons, 2013.

[30] C. Pohl, K. Schlierkamp, and H.-J. Hof, "BREW: A Breakable Web Application for IT-Security Classroom Use," in Proceedings: European Conference on Software Engineering Education 2014. ECSEE, 2014, pp. 191–205.

[31] Open Web Application Security Project (OWASP), "OWASP Top Ten Project.", retrieved: 05,2016 [Online]. Available: https://www.owasp.org/index.php/Top10#OWASP_Top_10_for_2013

Securing Card data on the Cloud

Application of the Cloud Card Compliance Checklist

Hassan El Alloussi, Laila Fetjah, Abdelhak Chaichaa
Department of Mathematics and Computer Science
Faculty of Sciences Aïn Chock
Hassan II University of Casablanca, P.O Box 5366
Casablanca, Morocco
e-mail: halloussi@gmail.com, l.fetjah@fsac.ac.ma, chaichaa@fsac.ac.ma

Abstract—**Cloud Computing did come up with so many attractive advantages such as scalability, flexibility, accessibility, rapid application deployment, user self-service and mainly cost effectiveness. However, security issues and lack of governance let users hesitating before deciding. In the other side, with the advent of many means of payment, other than coins and banknotes, the security is also the big issue. Many tools has been developed to help Card Industry stakeholder to develop their products with minimal concern, like Payment Card Industry Data Security Standard. In fact, the Payment Card Industry Data Security Standard is a standard that aims to harmonize and strengthen the protection of Card Data in the whole lifecycle. Since its introduction, it has always been an efficient tool for controlling Card data on a platform deployed internally. In addition, it has been proved that this standard is among the best one for gauging data security, because it dictates a series of scrupulous controls and how they could be implemented. However, with the coming of the Cloud, the strategies have changed and the issues in protecting Card data become more complex. In this paper, we work on developing a checklist that will be a reference for the Cloud tenant to control the security of Card data and information on the Cloud Computing. Also, we will evaluate our result by applying our checklist on a real Cloud environment. In next steps, we will focus on evaluating Risk Management of deployed Card Transaction Platform on a Public Cloud and all the strategies to reduce impacts of all potential risks.**

Keywords- Cloud Computing; PCI-DSS; Card Industry; PCI-SSC; Cloud Computing Alliance (CSA); Cloud Controls Matrix (CCM), Checklist.

I. Introduction

As the competition puts pressure on companies to increase productivity and decrease capital investments, solutions like distributed computing, that offer scalable systems with low fees, are attractive options for management to take in consideration. However, when you are responsible for the security of the access and the network, the idea of migrating everything to an environment that is not controlled and even owned, probably makes the decision more difficult.

Therefore, many banks and card transactions companies, which are attracted to outsourcing card solution outside their premises, encounter several obstacles, mainly related to security and data governance. The client has the responsibility to know where its data are and where it is going. This concept is the basis to data security, developed in [1], and plays a significant role in achieving and maintaining compliance with security norms, mainly the PCI-DSS [2].

Unfortunately, most of the requirements focus on the merchant's ability to implement network access controls, data control, and insuring that the applications installed respect the security norms by periodically test their effectiveness. In addition, it may be difficult to do it and insufficient in a Cloud platform, where the infrastructure is outsourced [3].

In this paper, we will expose our complete work by developing our methodology to get an exhaustive tool for auditing that will be an efficient tool for banks and Card companies to control if the Cloud platform is ready to receive Card solutions or not. Also, we illustrate our work by a real use case. We based our contribution on two mains frameworks: Cloud Controls Matrix (CCM) [4] developed by Cloud Computing Alliance (CSA) and PCI-DSS.

In the next section, we illustrate some basic aspects of the Cloud Computing and the Card Payment Industry. In Section III, we explain the main advantages of the CCM [4] and its domains. Section IV explains the choices of domains on what we focus on. Section V details the matrix developed and the correspondent checklist for client that allow them to verify the effectiveness of the platform outsourced (we give an extract of the checklist in Table IV). Section V brings a critical view to PCI-DSS standard insufficiency in Cloud computing. A use case is illustrated in Section VII. And finally, we draw a conclusion in Section VIII.

II. Background

As mentioned before, in this section we explain the basics aspects; Cloud Computing, The Payment Industry, the CSA and the PCI-DSS.

A. *Cloud Computing: the new opportunity*

Cloud Computing means outsourcing your data and its processing on remote servers, which eliminates the need to store these on premises. The interest is to access that data from any Internet-connected computer and synchronization across multiple devices.

The benefits are many; including a gain of space, resources, time and money. The user can freely access documents without worrying about the machine he uses. Cloud computing is, essentially, an economic commercial offer subscription to external services.

However, to adopt the Cloud, the customer should manage security issues, including legal and contractual aspects. Indeed, the advent of cloud computing brings new solutions to significant improvement in security. The data are stored in the cloud and should be always accessible no matter what happens to all access devices (laptop, Tablet, Smartphone, etc.).

B. *Payment Card Industry: The evolution*

Electronic payment means all electronic flows of information and treatment needed to manage credit cards and associated transactions. Electronic money transfers have been conducted by banks since the 1960's and bank customers have been able to draw cash from ATM's since the 1970's (NCR, Diebold, Wincor, etc.).

Historically, the first credit Cards, were existed before 1970, and were equipped with only "Embossing" (i.e., customer data printed in relief on the physical media). Information is the number of the card (backed by a bank account), the name and surname of the owner, date of expiry, etc.

In the mid-90s, electronic banking has evolved to include a new fully electronic channel and e-Commerce, which is buying and selling of products or services via the web, Internet or other computer networks while M-commerce (or mobile commerce) is the buying of products or services via a device like Smartphone, PDA, etc.

1) *The stakeholders involved with payment card transactions:*

- **Card holder**: a person holding a payment card (the consumer in B2C).
- **Merchant**: the business organization selling the goods and services (The merchant sets up a contract known as a merchant account with an acquirer).
- **Service provider**: this could be the merchant itself (Merchant service provider (MSP)) or an independent sales organization providing some or all of the payment services for the merchant.
- **Acquirer or acquiring bank**: this connects to a card brand network for payment processing and also has a contract for payment services with a merchant.
- **Issuing bank**: this entity issues the payment cards to the payment card holders.
- **Card brand**: this is a payment system (called association network) with its own processors and acquirers (such as Visa, MasterCard or CMI card in Morocco).

In Figure 1, we illustrate the relation between the stakeholders in Card Payment.

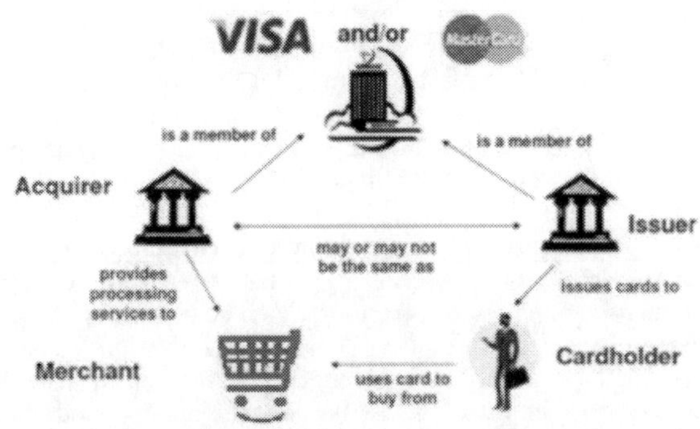

Figure 1. Payment card stakeholders

2) *Payment cards flowchart:*

Basically payment cards work using two components (Figure 2). The first one, the 'transaction authorization', is where a message containing the transaction details is sent to the card issuer requesting authorization for the payment. The card issuer then authorizes the payment. This guarantees payment to the merchant.

The second component known as 'clearing' is where the merchant submits the authorized transaction for payment (automatically or manually; daily or periodically) to Service Provider. The transaction then appears in the card holder's statement.

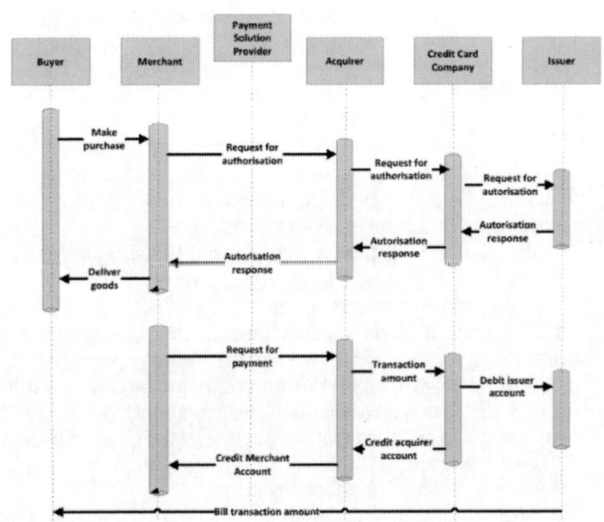

Figure 2. Payment Card Flowchart

However, in e-commerce/m-commerce, the payment methods are slightly different.

3) *The e-commerce/m-commerce system model*

Generally, most e-commerce/m-commerce systems can be designed as a three tier model. The three component parts are the client side, the service system and the back end system. These two last components are commonly known as 'Server Side'.

The client side connects users to the Server Side, which deals the users' requests. From a business perspective the client side provides the customer interface, the service system provides the business logic and the back-end provides the required data to complete a transaction to its fate.

E-commerce/m-commerce system vulnerabilities

The transaction process highlights the requirement for communication between the users, merchant, card issuer and may be the service provider. These communications must be protected to ensure confidentiality and integrity of the transaction details. This will prevent spying and data manipulation of the transaction details.

By understanding the e-commerce/m-commerce system architecture it becomes apparent that the payment card data will be vulnerable if someone having obtained the payment card information details or can access the component parts of the server side system. Additionally, the communications between the component parts of the server side must be protected to ensure confidentiality and integrity of the transaction details.

C. *The CSA: Cloud Security Alliance*

The Cloud Security Alliance is a not-for-profit organization with a mission to promote the use of best practices for providing security assurance within Cloud Computing, and to provide education on the uses of Cloud Computing to help secure all other forms of computing. It is led by a broad coalition of industry practitioners, corporations, associations and other key stakeholders.

The Cloud Security Alliance has designed many tools to manage control and governance on Cloud. Its main tool is Cloud Controls Matrix (CCM), which aims to provide fundamental security principles to guide cloud vendors and to assist prospective cloud customers in assessing the overall security risk of a cloud provider.

Cloud Control Matrix: a reliable tool to assess security risk of Cloud environment

The Cloud Security Alliance's Cloud Controls Matrix is a rich source of cloud security best practices designed as a framework to provide fundamental security principles to cloud vendors and cloud customers. It provides a controls framework that gives detailed understanding of security concepts and principles that are aligned to the Cloud Security Alliance guidance in 16 domains (latest version 3.0.1):

1. Application & Interface Security
2. Audit Assurance & Compliance
3. Business Continuity Management & Operational Resilience
4. Change Control & Configuration Management
5. Data Security & Information Lifecycle Management
6. Datacenter Security
7. Encryption & Key Management
8. Governance and Risk Management
9. Human Resources
10. Identity & Access Management
11. Infrastructure & Virtualization Security
12. Interoperability & Portability
13. Mobile Security
14. Security Incident Management, E-Discovery & Cloud Forensics
15. Supply Chain Management, Transparency and Accountability
16. Threat and Vulnerability Management

The CCM serves as the basis for new industry standards and certifications. It is the first ever baseline control framework specifically designed for managing risk in the Cloud Supply Chain:

- Addressing the inter- and intra-organizational challenges of persistent information security by clearly delineating control ownership.
- Providing an anchor point and common language for balanced measurement of security and compliance postures.
- Providing the holistic adherence to the vast and ever evolving landscape of global data privacy regulations and security standards.

The foundations of the Cloud Security Alliance Controls Matrix rest on its customized relationship to other industry-accepted security standards, regulations, and controls frameworks such as the ISO 27001/27002, ISACA COBIT, PCI, NIST, Jericho Forum and NERC CIP and will provide internal control direction for service organization control reports attestations provided by cloud providers. As a framework, the CSA CCM provides organizations with the needed structure, detail and clarity relating to information security tailored to the cloud industry. The CSA CCM strengthens existing information security control environments by emphasizing business information security control requirements, reduces and identifies consistent security threats and vulnerabilities in the cloud, provides standardized security and operational risk management, and seeks to normalize security expectations, cloud taxonomy and terminology, and security measures implemented in the cloud.

PCI DSS [6]: is an industry wide set of requirements that affects any company or organization that accepts, processes, transmits or stores card details or any sensitive data linked to the payment card. It aims to encourage merchants and service providers to protect payment card data. This ultimately leads to the reduction of fraud losses for banks, merchants and card brands.

ISO 27001/27002 [7]: are the best practice recommendations on information security management, risks and controls within the context of an overall information security management system (ISMS), published jointly by the International Organization for Standardization (ISO) and the International Electro-technical Commission (IEC). While ISO27017 and ISO27018 are respectively for Information security management for cloud systems and Data protection for cloud systems are as draft now, the main framework still now ISO 27001/27002.

ISO 27001 is an internationally accepted standard framework for an information security management system that includes control requirements in 11 domains. Those that do implement ISO 27001 may further choose to have their compliance independently audited to obtain ISO 27001 certification.

ISACA COBIT [8]: is a framework created by ISACA for information technology (IT) management and IT governance. It is a supporting toolset that allows managers to bridge the gap between control requirements, technical issues and business risks. It aims to research, develop, publish and promote an authoritative, up-to-date, international set of generally accepted information technology control objectives for day-to-day use by business managers, IT professionals and assurance professionals. The benefits that frameworks such as COBIT offer is that they produce a summary assessment of the business risks and achieved business value of an application, and they can help practitioners evaluate (often to a highly granular degree) many security or value issues.

NIST [9]: The National Institute of Standards and Technology (NIST) has been designated by the Federal Chief Information Officer (CIO) to accelerate the federal government's secure adoption of cloud computing by leading efforts to identify existing standards and guidelines.

BITS [10]: stands for "Banking Industry Technology Secretariat, however a BITS Shared Assessment provides an assessment of an organization's implementation of its controls using a standardized questionnaire, which is based on the ISO 27002 standard, with additional input from Shared Assessments Program members. The approach is more rigidly defined (e.g., answers are Yes, No, or N/A, making the completed SIG easy to read by machine. The original idea was that service providers could complete the SIG just once, and then provide the completed SIG to multiple clients.

In short, the BITS Shared Assessment cost is a little more and is a little less flexible – but it provides a higher level of interim attestation in return.

GAPP (Generally Accepted Privacy Principles) [11]: are privacy principles and criteria developed and updated by the AICPA and Canadian Institute of Chartered Accountants to assist organizations in the design and implementation of sound privacy practices and policies.

HIPAA/HITECH (Health Insurance Portability and Accountability Act) [12]: The HIPAA Privacy Rule provides federal protections for individually identifiable health information held by covered entities and their business associates and gives patients an array of rights with respect to that information. At the same time, the Privacy Rule is balanced so that it permits the disclosure of health information needed for patient care and other important purposes.

The Security Rule specifies a series of administrative, physical, and technical safeguards for covered entities and their business associates to use to assure the confidentiality, integrity, and availability of electronic protected health information. The Health Information Technology for Economic and Clinical Health (HITECH) Act, enacted as part of the American Recovery and Reinvestment Act of 2009, was signed into law on February 17, 2009, to promote the adoption and meaningful use of health information technology. Subtitle D of the HITECH Act addresses the privacy and security concerns associated with the electronic transmission of health information, in part, through several provisions that strengthen the civil and criminal enforcement of the HIPAA rules.

Jericho Forum [13]: is an international group of organizations working together to define and promote the solutions surrounding the issue of de-perimeterisation. It was officially founded at the offices of the Open Group in Reading, UK, on Friday 16 January 2004. It had existed as a loose affiliation of interested corporate CISOs (Chief Information Security Officers) discussing the topic since the summer of 2003.

NERC CIP (North American Electric Reliability Corporation- Critical infrastructure protection) [14]: is a concept that relates to the preparedness and response to serious incidents that involve the critical infrastructure of a region or nation.

In our work, we focus firstly on PCI DSS framework to provide a questionnaire to control card data on the cloud and give a critical review to improve the framework and add more requirements for Cloud Computing. Afterward, we extend the work to the other frameworks in order to have a complete checklist a standard for Cloud Computing adopters

D. The PCI DSS

The PCI DSS was created jointly in 2004 by four major credit-card companies: Visa, MasterCard, Discover and American Express.

The PCI Security Standards Council is an open global forum, launched in 2006, that is responsible for the development, management, education, and awareness of the PCI Security Standards, including the Data Security Standard (PCI DSS), Payment Application Data Security Standard (PA-DSS), and PIN Transaction Security (PTS) requirements.

The Council's five founding global payment brands - American Express, Discover Financial Services, JCB International, MasterCard Worldwide, and Visa Inc - have agreed to incorporate the PCI DSS as the technical requirements of each of their data security compliance programs. Each founding member also recognizes the QSAs (Qualified Security Assessors) PA-QSAs (Payment application Qualified Security Assessors) and ASVs (Approved Scanning Vendor) certified by the PCI Security Standards Council.

1) What are the PCI DSS requirements?

PCI DSS is a set of requirements for protecting cardholder data and may be enhanced by additional controls and practices to further mitigate risks.

The PCI DSS specifies and elaborates on six major objectives and twelve requirements (Table I).

These requirements are intended to reduce the risk of transactions and promote a holistic approach to the security of the Card Data Environment (CDE). It is important for companies to understand the scope of PCI DSS and how to implement the controls to meet the requirements.

TABLE I. THE PCI-DSS REQUIREMENTS

Activities	Describing the Requirements
Build and Maintain a Secure Network and Systems	1. Install and maintain a firewall configuration to protect cardholder data
	2. Do not use vendor supplied defaults for system passwords and other security parameters.
Protect cardholder data.	3. Protect stored cardholder data
	4. Encrypt transmission of cardholder data across open, public networks
Maintain a vulnerability management program.	5. Protect all systems against malware and regularly update anti-virus software or programs
	6. Develop and maintain secure systems and applications
Implement strong access control measures.	7. Restrict access to cardholder data by business need to know
	8. Identify and authenticate access to system components
	9. Restrict physical access to cardholder data
Regularly monitor and test networks.	10. Track and monitor all access to network resources and cardholder data
	11. Regularly test security systems and processes
Maintain an Information security policy.	12. Maintain a policy that addresses information security for all personnel

2) PCI DSS compliance in Cloud environments:

PCI DSS, as stated earlier in this section, applies to any company or organization that accepts, processes, transmits or stores payment card details or any sensitive data associated with a payment card. Merchants and service providers must comply with the all the requirements regardless of their size and how many transactions they process.

On February 2013 PCI DSS Cloud Computing Guidelines state, The responsibilities delineated between the client and the Cloud Service Provider (CSP) for managing PCI DSS controls are influenced by a number of variables, including but not limited to:

- The purpose for which the client is using the cloud service
- The scope of PCI DSS requirements that the client is outsourcing to the CSP
- The services and system components that the CSP has validated within its own operations
- The service option that the client has selected to engage the CSP (IaaS, PaaS or SaaS)
- The scope of any additional services the CSP is providing to proactively manage the client's compliance (for example, additional managed security services)

Hereafter, we show, in Table II, an example of how the responsibilities are sharing following the Cloud Layers.

TABLE II. RESPONSIBILITIES SHARING ON CLOUD LAYERS

(light shading)	*Client*
(dark shading)	*CSP*

Cloud Layer	Service Models		
	IaaS	PaaS	SaaS
Data			
Interface (APIs, GUIs)			
Application			
Solution Stack (Programming languages)			
Operating Systems (OS)			
Virtual Machines			
Virtual network infrastructure			
Hypervisors			
Processing and memory			
Data Storage (hard drives, removable disks, backups, etc)			
Network (Interfaces and devices, communications			
Physical facilities / data centers			

Also, we show, in Table III, how the responsibilities are sharing following PCI DSS Requirements.

TABLE III. RESPONSIBILITIES SHARING ON PCI DSS REQUIREMENT

	Client
	CSP
	Both Client and CSP

PCI DSS Requirement	Service Models		
	IaaS	PaaS	SaaS
1. Install and maintain a firewall configuration to protect cardholder data	Both	Both	CSP
2. Do not use vendor supplied defaults for system passwords and other security parameters.	Both	Both	CSP
3. Protect stored cardholder data	Both	Both	CSP
4. Encrypt transmission of cardholder data across open, public networks	Client	Both	CSP
5. Protect all systems against malware and regularly update anti-virus software or programs	Client	Both	CSP
6. Develop and maintain secure systems and applications	Both	Both	Both
7. Restrict access to cardholder data by business need to know	Both	Both	Both
8. Identify and authenticate access to system components	Both	Both	Both

9. Restrict physical access to cardholder data	CSP	CSP	CSP
10. Track and monitor all access to network resources and cardholder data	Both	Both	CSP
11. Regularly test security systems and processes	Both	Both	CSP
12. Maintain a policy that addresses information security for all personnel	Both	Both	Both
PCI DSS Appendix A: Additional PCI DSS Requirements for Shared Hosting Providers	CSP	CSP	CSP

3) Considerations in managing PCI DSS on the Cloud computing:

a) Segmentation of the Cloud:

a. Segmentation on a cloud-computing infrastructure must provide an equivalent level of isolation as that achievable through physical network separation
b. Other client environments running on the same infrastructure are to be considered untrusted networks
c. The CSP needs to take ownership of the segmentation between clients
d. The client is responsible for the proper configuration of any segmentation controls implemented within their own environment

b) Recommendations for Reducing Scope:

a. Do not store, process or transmit payment card data in the cloud
b. Implement a dedicated physical infrastructure that is used only for the in-scope cloud environment
c. Minimize reliance on third-party CSPs for protecting payment card data
d. It can be challenging to verify who has access to cardholder data processed, transmitted, or stored in the cloud environment
e. It can be challenging to collect, correlate, and/or archive all of the logs necessary to meet applicable PCI DSS requirements
f. Organizations using data-discovery tools to identify cardholder data in their environments, and to ensure that such data is not stored in unexpected places, may find that running such tools in a cloud environment can be difficult and result in incomplete results.

Many large providers might not support right-to-audit for their clients. Clients should discuss their needs with the provider to determine how the CSP can provide assurance that required controls are in place

III. The CCM and the PCI-DSS: The State of the Art

The Cloud Security Alliance's CCM is a rich source of cloud security best practices designed as a framework to provide fundamental security principles to cloud vendors and cloud customers. It provides a controls framework that gives detailed understanding of security concepts and principles that are aligned to the Cloud Security Alliance guidance in 16 domains (latest version 3.0.1) [6]. This tool provides the holistic adherence to the vast and ever evolving landscape of global data privacy regulations and security standards.

The CCM serves as the basis for new industry standards and certifications. It is the first ever baseline control framework specifically designed for managing risk in the Cloud Supply Chain:

- Addressing the inter- and intra-organizational challenges of persistent information security by clearly delineating control ownership.
- Providing an anchor point and common language for balanced measurement of security and compliance postures.

The PCI-DSS is a broadly accepted set of policies and procedures intended to optimize the security of credit, debit and cash card transactions and protect cardholders against misuse of their personal information. Therefore, it is not possible for a client to leverage the benefits of cloud systems without jeopardizing security, and mainly Card Data.

In our work, we focus on creating for each topic on CCM list a matching PCI-DSS requirement in order to get a series of checklists on what the client could depend on to verify the trustworthiness of the Cloud before deciding to outsource.

IV. The Domains of Application

In our work, we focused on 4 main areas (domains) because they represent a basis for any tenant to check and control Cloud before deciding to outsource or not. Figure 3 shows the four domains, which are Network and Transport security, Data Security, Application and interface security, and Business Continuity management.

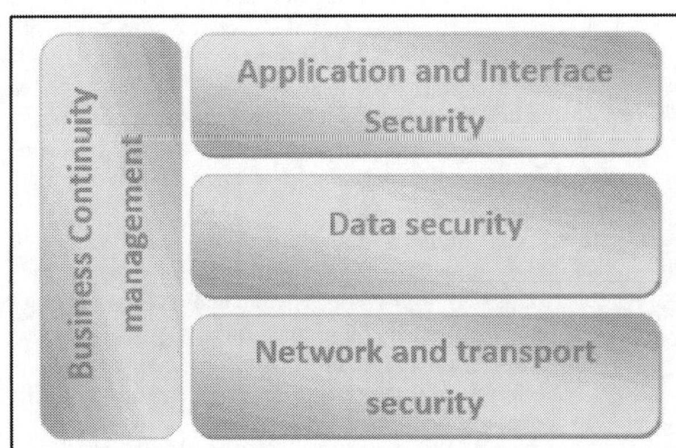

Figure 3. The domains developed in the checklist

- **<u>Network and Transport security</u>**: These controls allow verifying the security of the Card Data on network while it is transmitted. It is essential for the tenant to check this aspect scrupulously before deploying on the Cloud.

- **Data Security**: These controls allow verifying the security of the Card data and preventing it from any leakage.
- **Application and interface security**: These controls aim to ensure that any Application and Programming Interface (APIs) is designed, developed, deployed and tested respecting the PCI-DSS norms in order to avoid any leakage.
- **Business Continuity management**: These controls aim at insuring the business continuity of the activities in any issue or disaster. The client should be sure that the activity could continue without any deterioration.

In the next section, we describe the checklist developed with an exhaustive questionnaire as a tool for any Cloud specialist to verify the compliance of a cloud and its readiness to outsource or not.

V. The Checklist Matrix

Our work, as described above, is developing a checklist based on 4 domains and 32 controls. Each control addresses a part of securing Transaction payment on the Cloud. In the first part, we describe each control and in the second one, we present a small extract of the Cloud Checklist. For the full and exhaustive Checklist, as the document size is limited, we suggest to refer to the authors.

A. *Network security*

1) Network Security (Infrastructure & Virtualization Security)

In this control, the auditor must ensure that:

- The Network environments and virtual instances are designed and are configured to restrict and monitor traffic between trusted and untrusted connections.
- The configurations of the Network are reviewed at least annually, and are supported by a documented justification for use for all allowed services, protocols, and ports, and compensating controls.

2) Network Architecture (Infrastructure & Virtualization Security)

In this control, the auditor must ensure that:

- The network architecture diagrams have clearly identified high-risk environments and data flows that may have legal compliance impacts.
- The technical measures are implemented and apply defense-in-depth techniques for detection and timely response to network-based attacks associated with anomalous ingress or egress traffic patterns (e.g., MAC spoofing and ARP poisoning attacks) and/or distributed denial-of-service (DDoS) attacks.

3) VM Security - vMotion Data Protection (Infrastructure & Virtualization Security)

In this control, the auditor must ensure that:

- The secured and encrypted communication channels are used when migrating physical servers, applications, or data to virtualized servers
- There is a network segregation from production-level networks for such migrations.

4) Wireless Security (Infrastructure & Virtualization Security)

In this control, the auditor must ensure, in order to protect wireless network environments, that:

- There are policies and procedures that restrict the use of the this technology,
- The supporting business processes and technical measures are implemented.

5) Standardized Network Protocols (Interoperability & Portability)

In this control, the auditor must ensure that:

- The provider uses secure standardized network protocols for the import and export of data and to manage the service,
- The provider makes available a document to consumers (tenants) detailing the relevant interoperability and portability standards that are involved.

6) Audit Logging / Intrusion Detection (Infrastructure & Virtualization Security)

In this control, the auditor must ensure that:

- The provider is adhering to applicable legal, statutory or regulatory compliance obligations
- The provider is providing unique user access accountability to detect potentially suspicious network behaviors and/or file integrity anomalies, and to support forensic investigative capabilities in the event of a security breach.

7) Encryption (Encryption & Key Management)

In this control, the auditor must ensure, for the use of encryption protocols for protection of sensitive data in storage and data in transmission, that:

- The Policies and procedures are established,
- The supporting business processes and technical measures are implemented, as per applicable legal, statutory, and regulatory compliance obligations.

8) Antivirus / Malicious Software (Threat and Vulnerability Management)

In this control, the auditor must ensure, in order to prevent the execution of malware on organizationally-owned or managed user end-point devices and IT infrastructure network and systems components, that:

- The policies and procedures are established.
- The supporting business processes and technical measures are implemented.

9) Configuration Ports Access (Identity & Access Management)

In this control, the auditor must ensure that the user access to diagnostic and configuration ports is restricted to authorized individuals and applications.

10) Independent Audits (Audit Assurance & Compliance)

In this control, the auditor must ensure that independent reviews and assessments are performed at least annually to ensure that the organization addresses nonconformities of established policies, standards, procedures and compliance obligations.

11) User Access Policy (Identity & Access Management)

In this control, the auditor must ensure, in order for ensuring appropriate identity, entitlement, and access management for internal corporate and customer (tenant) users with access to data and organizationally-owned or managed (physical and virtual) application interfaces and infrastructure network and systems components, that:

- The user access policies and procedures are established,
- The supporting business processes and technical measures are implemented.

12) Segmentation (Infrastructure & Virtualization Security)

In this control, the auditor must ensure that the Multi-tenant organizationally-owned or managed (physical and virtual) applications, and infrastructure system and network components, are designed, developed, deployed and configured such that provider and customer (tenant) user access is appropriately segmented from other tenant users.

B. Data Security & Information Lifecycle Management

1) Data Inventory / Flows

In this control, the auditor must ensure that the policies and procedures are established to inventory, document, and maintain data flows for data that is resident (permanently or temporarily) within the service's applications and infrastructure network and systems (in particular, providers shall ensure that data that is subject to geographic residency requirements not be migrated beyond its defined bounds)

2) Classification

In this control, the auditor must ensure that data and objects containing data are assigned a classification by the data owner based on data type, value, sensitivity, and criticality to the organization.

3) eCommerce Transactions

In this control, the auditor must ensure that the data related to electronic commerce (e-commerce) that crosses public networks is appropriately classified, and protected from fraudulent activity, unauthorized disclosure, or modification in such a manner to prevent contract dispute and compromise of data.

4) Handling / Labeling / Security Policy

In this control, the auditor must ensure that:

- The policies and procedures are established for labeling, handling, and the security of data and objects that contain data.
- The mechanisms for label inheritance are implemented for objects that act as aggregate containers for data.

5) Nonproduction Data

In this control, the auditor must ensure that the production data are not replicated or used in non-production environments.

6) Ownership / Stewardship

In this control, the auditor must ensure that all data is designated with stewardship, with assigned responsibilities defined, documented, and communicated.

7) Secure Disposal

In this control, the auditor must ensure that any use of customer data in non-production environments requires explicit, documented approval from all customers whose data is affected, and must comply with all legal and regulatory requirements for scrubbing of sensitive data elements.

C. Application & Interface Security

1) Application Security

In this control, the auditor must ensure that the APIs are designed, developed, deployed and tested in accordance with leading industry standards (e.g., OWASP [19] for web applications) and are adhered to applicable legal, statutory, or regulatory compliance obligations.

2) Customer Access Requirements

In this control, the auditor must ensure that prior to granting customer's access to data, assets, and information systems, all identified security, contractual, and regulatory requirements for customer access are addressed and are remediated.

3) Data Integrity

In this control, the auditor must ensure that the data input and output integrity routines (i.e., reconciliation and edit checks) are implemented for application interfaces and databases to prevent manual or systematic processing errors, corruption of data, or misuse.

4) Data Security / Integrity

In this control, the auditor must ensure, in order to guarantee protection of confidentiality, integrity, and availability of data exchanged between one or more system interfaces, jurisdictions, or external business relationships to prevent improper disclosure, alteration, or destruction, that:

- The policies and procedures are established,
- The supporting business processes and technical measures are implemented.

D. Business Continuity Management & Operational Resilience

1) Business Continuity Planning

In this control, the auditor must ensure if all business continuity plans are consistent in addressing priorities for testing, maintenance, and information security requirements, that a consistent unified framework for business continuity planning and plan development is established, documented and adopted.

2) Business Continuity Testing

In this control, the auditor must ensure that:

- The business continuity and security incident response plans are subject to testing at planned intervals or upon significant organizational or environmental changes.
- The incident response plans involve impacted customers (tenant) and other business relationships that represent critical intra-supply chain business process dependencies.

3) Datacenter Utilities / Environmental Conditions (Power / Telecommunications)

In this control, the auditor must ensure that datacenter utilities services and environmental conditions (e.g., water, power, temperature and humidity controls, telecommunications, and internet connectivity) are secured, monitored, maintained, and tested for continual effectiveness at planned intervals.

4) Documentation

In this control, the auditor must ensure that information system documentation (e.g., administrator and user guides, and architecture diagrams) is made available to authorized personnel, in order to:

- Configure, install, and operate the information system,
- Effectively use the system's security features.

5) Environmental Risks

In this control, the auditor must ensure that the physical protection, against damage from natural causes and disasters, is anticipated, designed, and have countermeasures applied.

6) Equipment Location

In this control, the auditor must ensure, in order to reduce the risks from environmental threats, hazards, and opportunities for unauthorized access, that the equipment are kept away from locations subject to high probability environmental risks and are supplemented by redundant equipment located at a reasonable distance.

7) Equipment Maintenance

In this control, the auditor must ensure, for equipment maintenance ensuring continuity and availability of operations and support personnel, that:

- The policies and procedures are established,
- The supporting business processes and technical measures are implemented.

8) Policy

In this control, the auditor must ensure, for appropriate IT governance and service management to ensure appropriate planning, delivery and support of the organization's IT capabilities supporting business functions, workforce, and/or customers based on industry acceptable standards (i.e., ITIL v4 and COBIT 5), that:

- The policies and procedures are established,
- The supporting business processes and technical measures are implemented.

9) Retention Policy

In this control, the auditor must ensure, for defining and adhering to the retention period of any critical asset as per established policies and procedures, as well as applicable legal, statutory, or regulatory compliance obligations, that:

- The policies and procedures are established,
- The supporting business processes and technical measures are implemented.

In Table IV, we illustrate an extract of the developed checklist. For each domain (from the main four described above), and for each sub-domain, we developed the questions that the auditors should verify and also how to verify the condition.

TABLE IV. EXAMPLE OF CONTROL MATRIX (EXTRACT)

PCI-DSS Requirements Correspondent	Question	Expected Testing	In place	Not In Place	Reserves
A.1. Network Security					
PCI-DSS v3.0 1.1.2 Current network diagram that identifies all connections between the cardholder data environment and other networks, including any wireless networks	Does a current network diagram exists and that it documents all connections to cardholder data, including any wireless networks?	• Examine diagram(s) • Observe network configurations	☐	☐	☐
	Is the network diagram kept updated?	• Interview responsible personnel	☐	☐	☐
PCI-DSS v3.0 1.1.3 Current diagram that shows all cardholder data flows across systems and networks	Does the diagram show all cardholder data flows across systems and networks?	• Examine data-flow diagram • Interview personnel	☐	☐	☐
	Is the diagram kept current and updated as needed upon changes to the environment?	• Examine data-flow diagram • Interview personnel	☐	☐	☐
....	...	• .	☐	☐	☐

PCI-DSS Requirements Correspondent	Question	Expected Testing	In place	Not In Place	Reserves
B.3. eCommerce Transactions					
PCI-DSS v3.0 4.2 Never send unprotected PANs by end-user messaging technologies (for example, e-mail, instant messaging, chat, etc.)	Are end-user messaging technologies used to send cardholder data? (verify that PAN is rendered unreadable or secured with strong cryptography whenever it is sent via end-user messaging technologies)	• Observe processes for sending PAN • Examine a sample of outbound transmissions as they occur	☐	☐	☐
	Is there a policy stating that unprotected PANs are not to be sent via end-user messaging technologies?	• Review written policies	☐	☐	☐
....	…	•.	☐	☐	☐
C.1. Application Security					
PCI-DSS v3.0 6.5 : Address common coding vulnerabilities in software-development processes as follows: • Train developers in secure coding techniques, including how to avoid common coding vulnerabilities, and understanding how sensitive data is handled in memory. • Develop applications based on secure coding guidelines.	Are developers required training in secure coding techniques based on industry best practices and guidance?	• Review policies and procedures for training • Interview personnel	☐	☐	☐
	Are developers knowledgeable in secure coding techniques, including how to avoid common coding vulnerabilities, and understanding how sensitive data is handled in memory?	• Interview personnel • Examine records of training	☐	☐	☐
	Are processes to protect applications from the following vulnerabilities, in place?		☐	☐	☐
D.7. Equipment Maintenance					
PCI DSS v3.0 10.8 Ensure that security policies and operational procedures for monitoring all access to net-work resources and cardholder data are documented, in use, and known to all affected par-ties.	Are security policies and operational pro-cedures for monitoring all access to net-work resources and cardholder data docu-mented, In use, and Known to all affected parties?	• Examine documentation • Interview personnel	☐	√	☐

VI. Critical view to the standard PCI-DSS on the Cloud

Many controls specifications in the 4 domains treated above are not specified in any requirement in the recent version 3.0 of the PCI-DSS norm. These control specifications are:

- Network and Infrastructure Services: this control specification aims verifying that the Business-critical or customer (tenant) impacting (physical and virtual) application and system-system interface (API) designs and configurations, and infrastructure network and systems components, is designed, developed, and deployed in accordance with mutually agreed-upon service and capacity-level expectations, as well as IT governance and service management policies and procedures.
- Equipment Power Failure: this control specification aims verifying Information security measures and redundancies are implemented to protect equipment from utility service outages (e.g., power failures and network disruptions).
- Impact Analysis: this control specification aims verifying that there is a defined and documented method for determining the impact of any disruption to the organization that must incorporate the following:
  - Identify critical products and services
  - Identify all dependencies, including processes, applications, business partners, and third party service providers
  - Understand threats to critical products and services
  - Determine impacts resulting from planned or unplanned disruptions and how these vary over time
  - Establish the maximum tolerable period for disruption
  - Establish priorities for recovery
  - Establish recovery time objectives for resumption of critical products and services within their maximum tolerable period of disruption
  - Estimate the resources required for resumption.

In the next step, we will evaluate, as a use case, this new framework by applying it on a real Card platform outsourced on the Cloud and we check its vulnerability and resilience. Afterward, we continue our work by focusing on developing recommended requirement for PCI-DSS for these control specification that could be added in the next update version of the norm.

VII. Use Case

In this section, we describe how we applied the framework on a Card Transaction Platform developed as part of this project. Firstly, we will describe the solution HibaPay, its functionalities and its architecture. Afterward, we will apply the framework checklist and we will describe the result on the platform.

However, the solution HibaPay is deployed in a public Cloud and it is ready for processing.

A. *Card Data Processins Solution on Cloud*

HibaPay is an electronic Card Transaction Platform that allows banks to convert the opportunities offered by the development of smartphones and increase in revenue by setting up financial services that are simple and powerful.

The design of the platform HibaPay considers integrated manner the interests and constraints of the various stakeholders: the Client, the Merchant and the Bank. It also includes a prospective view of the state of the art either in the world of Mobile Phones or that of Electronic Card payment.

The platform HibaPay allows banks and operators to explore all business development opportunities offered by the financial Solutions in meeting with the specific needs of each market. HibaPay includes modules able to realize synergies between market players of mobile financial services.

In Figure 4, we illustrate the architecture of the solution HibaPay.

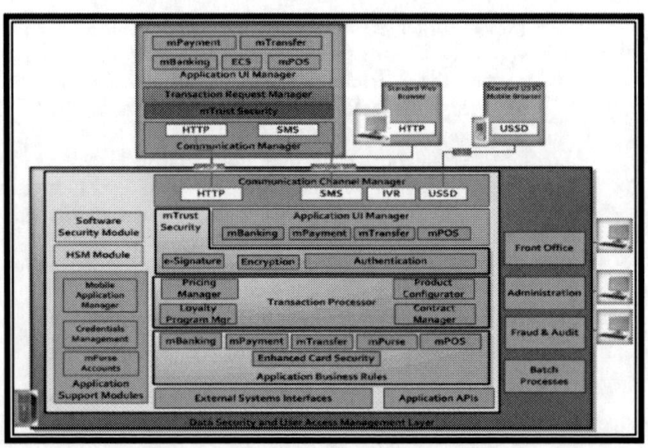

Figure 4. The Card Processing Solution Architecture

The HibaPay main modules are:

The server Modules:

- mTrust Security
- Software Security Module
- Transaction Manager
- Credentials Manager
- Applications UI Manager
- Communication Channels Manager
- Mobile Application Manager
- mPurse Accounts Manager

The application Modules:

- mBanking
- mPayment
- mTransfer
- mPurse
- mPoS
- Enhanced Card Security

B. *Appraisal*

Once we deployed the solution, we audit the solution and we illustrate in Table V an extract of the result.

TABLE V. Sample of the Audit Result

PCI-DSS Requirements Correspondent	Question	Expected Testing	In place	Not In Place	Reserves
A.1. Network Security					
PCI-DSS v3.0 1.1.2 Current network diagram that identifies all connections between the cardholder data environment and other networks, including any wireless networks	Does a current network diagram exists and that it documents all connections to cardholder data, including any wireless networks?	• Examine diagram(s) • Observe network configurations	✓	☐	☐
	Is the network diagram kept updated?	• Interview responsible personnel	✓	☐	☐
PCI-DSS v3.0 1.1.3 Current diagram that shows all cardholder data flows across systems and networks	Does the diagram show all cardholder data flows across systems and networks?	• Examine data-flow diagram • Interview personnel	✓	☐	☐
	Is the diagram kept current and updated as needed upon changes to the environment?	• Examine data-flow diagram • Interview personnel	☐	☐	✓
….	…	• …	☐	☐	☐
B.3. eCommerce Transactions					
PCI-DSS v3.0 4.2 Never send	Are end-user messaging	• Observe	✓	☐	☐

PCI-DSS Requirements Correspondent	Question	Expected Testing	In place	Not In Place	Reserves
unprotected PANs by end-user messaging technologies (for example, e-mail, instant messaging, chat, etc.)	technologies used to send cardholder data? (verify that PAN is rendered unreadable or secured with strong cryptography whenever it is sent via end-user messaging technologies)	processes for sending PAN • Examine a sample of outbound transmissions as they occur			
	Is there a policy stating that unprotected PANs are not to be sent via end-user messaging technologies?	• Review written policies	☐	☐	√
....	...	• ...	☐	☐	☐
C.1. Application Security					
PCI-DSS v3.0 6.5 : Address common coding vulnerabilities in software-development processes as follows: • Train developers in secure coding techniques, including how to avoid common coding vulnerabilities, and understanding how sensitive data is handled in memory. • Develop applications based on secure coding guidelines.	Are developers required training in secure coding techniques based on industry best practices and guidance?	• Review policies and procedures for training • Interview personnel	☐	☐	√
	Are developers knowledgeable in secure coding techniques, including how to avoid common coding vulnerabilities, and understanding how sensitive data is handled in memory?	• Interview personnel • Examine records of training	☐	☐	√
	Are processes to protect applications from the following vulnerabilities, in place?		☐	☐	☐
D.7. Equipment Maintenance					
PCI DSS v3.0 10.8 Ensure that security policies and operational procedures for monitoring all access to net-work resources and cardholder data are documented, in use, and known to all affected par-ties.	Are security policies and operational pro-cedures for monitoring all access to net-work resources and cardholder data docu-mented, In use, and Known to all affected parties?	• Examine documentation • Interview personnel	☐	√	☐
PCI DSS v3.0 11.6 Ensure that security policies and operational procedures for security monitoring and testing are documented, in use, and known to all affected parties.	Are security policies and operational pro-cedures for security monitoring and testing documented, in use, and known to all affected parties?	• Examine documentation • Interview personnel	√	☐	☐

C. *Analysis*

In our audit of the platform, we stated that many requirements are not in place or there are reserves. So, many actions must be in place to remove these differences.

For example, in the "Network Security", we noted a reserve on "Cloud Provider" (see Table VI).

TABLE VI. SAMPLE OF AUDIT RESULT WITH "RESERVES"

PCI-DSS Requirements Correspondent	Question	Expected Testing	In place	Not In Place	Reserves
A.1. Network Security					
PCI-DSS v3.0 1.1.3 Current diagram that shows all cardholder data flows across systems and networks	Is the diagram kept current and updated as needed upon changes to the environment?	• Examine data-flow diagram • Interview personnel	☐	☐	√

Indeed, after auditing, we found that the cloud provider does not update the network diagram after a change on environment. For this, we asked to add a firewall to improve access security. However, we found that the chart was not updated in time.

Another example, Table VII, we found during the audit that security policies and operational procedures for monitoring all access to network resources and cardholder data documented are not known by the provider staff Cloud. For this, training must be established to prepare the personnel of Cloud Provider for the types of data they will handle.

TABLE VII. SAMPLE OF AUDIT RESULT WITH REQUIREMENT "NOT IN PLACE"

PCI-DSS Requirements Correspondent	Question	Expected Testing	In place	Not In Place	Reserves
D.7. Equipment Maintenance					
PCI DSS v3.0 10.8 Ensure that security policies and operational procedures for monitoring all access to net-work resources and cardholder data are documented, in use, and known to all affected par-ties.	Are security policies and operational pro-cedures for monitoring all access to net-work resources and cardholder data docu-mented, In use, and Known to all affected parties?	• Examine documentation • Interview personnel	☐	√	☐

In the next steps, in order to prepare a successful deployment, we monitor the implementation of all necessaries actions to eliminate all reserves and implementing all the requirement, which are not "In place".

VIII. CONCLUSION AND FUTURE WORK

The goal of the PCI-DSS is to protect cardholder data that is processed, stored or transmitted by providers, issuers or merchants. The security controls and processes required by PCI-DSS are vital for protecting cardholder account data. With all the advantages that give Cloud, Issuers, and Merchants and any other service providers involved with payment card processing must insure that the platform virtually and physically is sufficiently protected.

In this paper, we have developed an exhaustive checklist as a tool for any card stakeholder who wants to outsource a part or the whole card processing in a Cloud. In the next steps of the work, we will focus evaluating Risk Management of deployed Card Transaction Platform on a Public Cloud and all the strategies to reduce impacts of all potential risks.

REFERENCES

[1] H. El Alloussi, L. Fetjah, and A. Chaichaa, "Cloud Card Compliance Checklist : An Efficient Tool for Securing Deployment Card Solutions on the Cloud," IARIA SECURWARE 2015 : The Ninth International Conference on Emerging Security, ISBN: 978-1-61208-427-5 98, August 2015, pp. 98-104.

[2] PCI Security Standards Council, "Requirements and Security Assessment Procedures," Version 3.1, May 2015, https://www.pcisecuritystandards.org [retrieved: May, 2016].

[3] G. Ataya, "PCI-DSS audit and compliance," In information security technical report 15 (2010) 138 -144.

[4] Cloud Security Alliance (CSA), "CCM 3.0.1," https://cloudsecurityalliance.org/research/ccm/ [retrieved: May, 2016].

[5] H. El Alloussi, L. Fetjah, and A. Chaichaa, "Securing the Payment Card Data on Cloud environment: Issues & perspectives," International Journal Of Computer Science and Network Security, Vol. 14, no. 11, Nov. 2014, pp. 14-20, http://paper.ijcsns.org/07_book/html/201411/201411003.html.

[6] PCI Security Standards Council, Summary of Changes from PCI DSS Version 3.0 to 3.1," April 2015, https://www.pcisecuritystandards.org [retrieved: May, 2016].

[7] The ISO 27000 Directory, http://www.27000.org/, [retrieved: May, 2016].

[8] ISACA Global Organization/ COBIT, http://isaca.org/cobit, [retrieved: May, 2016].

[9] The National Institute of Standards and Technology, http://www.nist.gov/, [retrieved: May, 2016].

[10] The Technology Policy Division of the Financial Services Roundtable, http://www.bits.org, [retrieved: May, 2016].

[11] Generally Accepted Privacy Principles, https://www.cippguide.org/2010/07/01/generally-accepted-privacy-principles-gapp/, [retrieved: May, 2016].

[12] Health Insurance Portability and Accountability Act (HIPAA), http://www.ohii.ca.gov/calohi/PrivacySecurity/HIPAA.aspx, [retrieved: May, 2016].

[13] Jericho Forum, http://www.jerichoforum.org, [retrieved: May, 2016].

[14] North American Electric Reliability Corporation- Critical infrastructure protection, http://www.nerc.com/, [retrieved: May, 2016].

[15] Cloud Special Interest Group (PCI Security Standards Council), "PCI-DSS Cloud Computing Guidelines," February 2013, https://www.pcisecuritystandards.org [retrieved: May, 2016].

[16] PCI Security Standards Council, "Payment Card Industry (PCI), Data Security Standard (DSS) and Payment Application Data Security Standard (PA-DSS), Glossary of Terms, Abbreviations, and Acronyms," Version 3.0, January 2014, https://www.pcisecuritystandards.org [retrieved: May, 2016].

[17] H. Rasheed, "Data and infrastructure security auditing in cloud computing," In International Journal of Information Management 34 (2014) 364–368.

[18] W. Spangenberg, "PCI Compliance in the Cloud: What are the Risks?," http://www.ioactive.com/pdfs/PCIComplianceInTheCloud.pdf.

[19] The Open Web Application Security Project (OWASP) Vulnerable Web Applications Directory Project, https://www.owasp.org/index.php/OWASP_Vulnerable_Web_Applications_Directory_Project [retrieved: May, 2016].

[20] G. Parann-Nissany, "Introduction to PCI-DSS and the Cloud," Sep 2013, http://www.infoq.com/articles/cloud-pci-compliance.

[21] J. P. de Albuquerque and P. L. de Geus. "A Framework for Network Security System Design," WSEAS Transactions on Systems, Piraeus,Greece, vol. 2, no. 1, 2003, pp. 139-144.

[22] N. Carr, "The Big Switch: h: Rewiring the World, from Edison to Google," W.W. Norton & Co., NY, 2008.

[23] A. Toffler, "The Third Wave," Bantam (1980).

New Applications of Physical Unclonable Functions

Rainer Falk and Steffen Fries
Corporate Technology
Siemens AG
Munich, Germany
e-mail: {rainer.falk|steffen.fries}@siemens.com

***Abstract*—Physical Unclonable Functions (PUF) realize the functionality of a "fingerprint" of a digital circuit. They can be used to authenticate devices without requiring a cryptographic authentication algorithm, or to determine a unique cryptographic key based on hardware-intrinsic, device-specific properties. It is also known to design PUF-based cryptographic protocols. This paper presents several new applications of PUFs. They can be used to check the integrity, or authenticity of presented data. A PUF can be used to build a digital tamper sensor or a digital degradation sensor. An identifying information in a communication protocol can be determined using a PUF, or a licensing mechanism can be realized. The bootstrapping of cryptographic credentials can be protected by a PUF.**

Keywords–physical unclonable function; key extraction; embedded security; licensing; configuration integrity

I. INTRODUCTION

The need for technical information technology (IT) security measures increases rapidly to protect products and solutions from manipulation and reverse engineering. Cryptographic IT security mechanisms have been known for many years, and are applied in smart devices (internet of things, industrial and energy automation, operation technology). Such mechanisms target authentication, system and communication integrity and confidentiality of data in transit or at rest.

Critical Infrastructures (CI) and especially cyber security in critical infrastructures has gained more momentum over the last years. The term "critical infrastructure" in the context of this paper is used to describe technical installations, which are essential for the functioning of the society and economy of a country, but also globally. Typical critical infrastructures in this context are the smart energy grid (including central or distributed energy generation, transmission, and distribution), water supply, healthcare, transportation, telecommunication services, just to state a few. The increased threat level becomes visible, e.g., through reported attacks on critical infrastructure, but also through legislation, which meanwhile explicitly requires the protection of critical infrastructures and reporting about serious attacks.

Information Technology (IT) security in the past was addressed mostly in common enterprise IT environments, but there is a clear trend to provide more connectivity to operational sites, which are quite often part of the critical infrastructure. Examples for operational sites are industrial automation or energy automation. This increased connectivity leads to a tighter integration of IT and Operational Technology (OT). IT security in this context evolves to cyber security to underline the mutual relation between the security and physical effects.

One essential basis for the operation of security mechanisms is typically a cryptographic key that has to be stored securely on devices. A significant effort is often required in practical realizations to protect the storage of cryptographic keys, e.g., by securely integrating external or internal hardware integrated circuits (IC). In current security research on PUFs, methods are investigated that directly use a unique physical property of an object as a physical fingerprint. The problem addressed in this paper is the practical application of physical unclonable functions (PUF) in new, innovative ways, being an extended version of [1]. Upcoming industrial security standards for industrial automation and control systems as IEC 62443 [2] require explicitly a hardware-bound storage for cryptographic keys. A hardware-bound key store or hardware trust anchor can be realized by using a separate security integrated circuit (IC), or by using in integrated hardware trust anchor of a microcontroller. In both cases, a dedicated hardware security functionality has to be realized.

Small random differences of physical properties are used by a PUF to identify an object directly, or to derive a cryptographic key for conventional cryptographic IT security mechanisms [3]. A digital circuit, i.e., a semiconductor integrated circuit, can contain a digital circuit element called a PUF to determine the physical device fingerprint. Minimal differences in the semiconductor structure, like for instance the doping of a semiconductor, the layer thickness, or the width of lines arise at the production randomly. This is similar to the random surface structure of paper sheets. These chip individual properties are "simply there" without being designed-in explicitly, or being programmed by a manufacturer during production. Such a device fingerprint shall be unique, and not be reproducible easily (unclonability). In addition, the fingerprint can be modified, or even destroyed when the IC is manipulated physically. A PUF can be used as simple low-cost alternative to a dedicated hardware key store security circuit, or as additional protection mechanism to conventional cryptographic security mechanisms. It may be useful for simple devices in the Internet of Things to bootstrap cryptographic security credentials using an intrinsic device-specific fingerprint to protect the bootstrapping process. Much research has been spent on constructions for realizing a PUF, and for extracting a cryptographic key from a PUF [4][5][6][7].

After giving an overview of some major realization possibilities for a digital PUF in Section II, basic usages of a PUF are summarized in Section III. The main contribution of the paper is in Section IV, describing several new applications of PUF technology. Section VI concludes with a summary, and an outlook.

II. Physical Unclonable Functions as Digital Device Fingerprint

A PUF can be realized on a semiconductor circuit to determine a device-specific piece of information depending on variations in the target physics due to the manufacturing process. The information provided by the PUF can be used directly for low-cost authentication, to determine a serial number as an identifier, or as cryptographic key. The semiconductor circuit can be an application-specific integrated circuit (ASIC), or a field-programmable gate array (FPGA). This section gives a short overview about PUFs. More detailed information is available in tutorials on PUFs [4][5][6][7].

PUFs have been a major topic of academic research. However, PUF technology is already applied commercially. Examples are Intrinsic ID [8], Verayo [9][10], Microsemi Smartfusion2 FPGAs [11], and NXP smart card ICs [12].

Common digital circuits are designed to provide identical behavior on different ICs. However, a PUF circuit is designed to provide different results on different ICs, but identical or at least similar results on the same IC when the function is executed repeatedly.

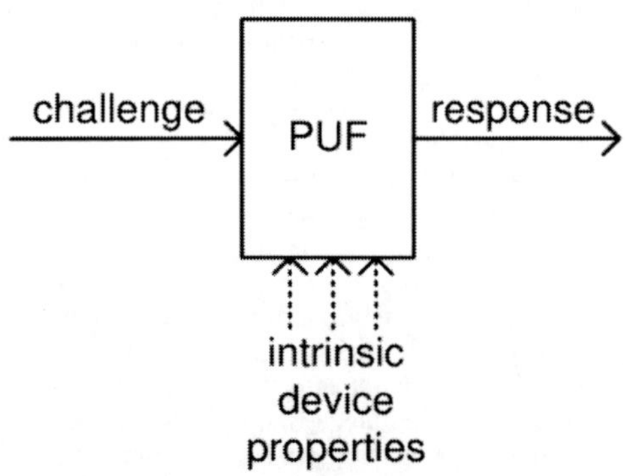

Figure 1. Challenge-Response-PUF

Figure 1 shows a challenge-response PUF, in which the PUF circuit determines a response value depending on a provided challenge value. Weak PUFs and strong PUFs are distinguished: while a strong PUF has a wide range of challenge input values, a weak PUF has no, or only a very limited set of challenge values. A strong digital PUF can be realized by reconfiguring a digital PUF circuit depending on the challenge value.

A PUF performs a computation to determine a response value depending on a given challenge value. Intrinsic device properties influence the PUF calculation so that the calculation of the response is different on different devices, but reproducible – with some bit errors – on the same device.

The objective of a PUF circuit is that on the same IC, the response value for a given challenge value is stable (reproducibility), while on different ICs, the response values are different (uniqueness). As binary values are used for challenge and response values, the similarity can be measured by the Hamming weight, i.e., the number of different bits. The measure for reproducibility is the intra-device Hamming distance, i.e., the mean value of the number of different bits when the PUF is executed multiple times for a given challenge value. The measure for the uniqueness is the inter-device Hamming distance, i.e., the mean value of the number of different bits when executed in different ICs.

Figure 2 shows three examples of well-known constructions of PUFs and their mechanical analogon:

- SRAM-PUF: power-up value of static random-access memory (SRAM) cells
- RO-PUF (Ring oscillator PUF): oscillator frequency
- Arbiter PUF: time delay

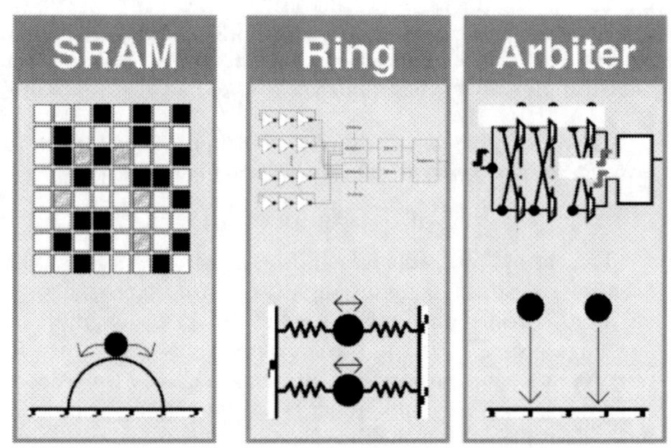

Figure 2. Example PUF Realizations and Their Mechanical Analogon

Many more constructions for a digital PUF have been proposed, e.g., bi-stable Ring PUF, Flip-Flop-PUF, Glitch PUF, Cellular Non-linear Network PUF, or Butterfly-PUF.

A. *SRAM-PUF*

A digital memory can store binary values 0 and 1. After power-up, some memories show a device-specific initialization pattern. The power-up value of a memory cell can be either 0 or 1, or being instable (sometimes 0, sometimes 1). The pattern of power-up values of its memory cells is characteristic of a memory IC, depending on small variations of the semiconductor physics of each memory cell.

A mechanical analogon for the power-up is a ball placed on the top of a hill [13]. When the whole geometry is exactly symmetric, the ball will roll-down to the left side and to the right side with the same probability. If the hill, or the ball, would have some asymmetries from manufacturing, the ball will tend to roll-down either to the left side or to the right side.

B. Ring Oscillator PUF (RO-PUF)

A digital circuit can realize an oscillator using a delay circuit with a feedback loop (ring oscillator). The oscillation frequency depends on manufacturing variations. The frequency of two identically designed oscillators can be compared using a counter, and comparator. Depending on the IC, one or the other will oscillate with a higher frequency. Realizing multiple oscillators, a "fingerprint" of the digital circuit can be obtained.

A mechanical analogon is an oscillating mass, and spring. Two identical physical realizations will in practice have a slightly different oscillation frequency, depending on small physical variations.

C. Arbiter PUF

A further effect that can be used to build a PUF is time delay. Two identically designed signal paths will show minimal differences in the respective delay. After giving in input signal to both signal paths at the same time, an arbiter circuit determines the faster signal path, i.e., the signal path on which the signal appears first,

A mechanical analogon is a drop test for two identically manufactured masses. Depending on variations in the height, or the surface of the masses, one will tend to impact first on the floor.

III. Basic PUF Applications

A PUF can be used for security purposes in different ways. It can be used as low-cost object authentication, or to determine a cryptographic key. This section describes these two basic applications, and gives examples for some specific usages of PUFs.

A. Object Authentication

Authentication is an elementary security service proving that an entity in fact possesses a claimed identity. Often natural persons are authenticated. The basic approaches a person can use to prove a claimed identity are by something the person knows (e.g., a password), by showing something the person has (e.g., passport, authentication token, smart card), or by exposing a physical property the person has (biometric property, e.g., a fingerprint, voice, iris, or behavior).

Advanced authentication techniques make use of multiple authentication factors, and performing authentication continuously during a session. With multi-factor authentication, several independent authentication factors are verified, e.g., a password and an authentication token. With continuous authentication, also called active authentication, the behavior of a user during an authenticated session is monitored to determine if still the authenticated user is using the session.

With ubiquitous machine-oriented communication, e.g., coming with the Internet of Things and interconnected cyber physical systems, also devices have to authenticate in a secure way. Considering the threat of counterfeited products (e.g., consumables, replacement parts) and the increasing importance of ubiquitous machine-based communication, also physical objects need to be authenticated in a secure way. Various different technologies are used to verify the authenticity of products, e.g., applying visible and hidden markers, using security labels (using, e.g., security ink or holograms), and by integrating cryptographic authentication functionality in wired product authentication tokens, or Radio Frequency Identification (RFID) authentication tags.

An object or digital circuit can be identified by a serial number. For authentication, a cryptographic authentication protocol can be used, requiring a secret/private key to be available on the object to be authenticated.

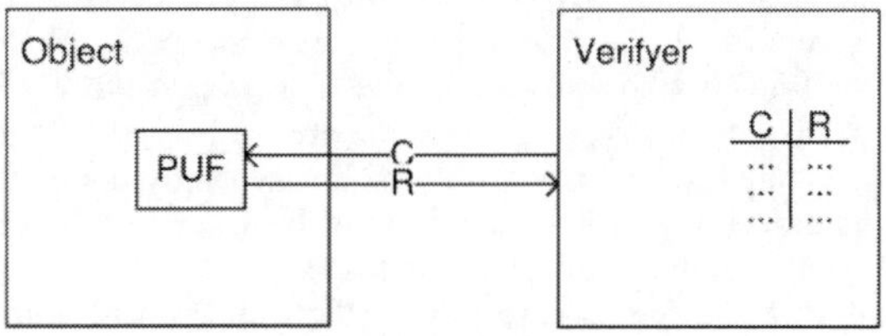

Figure 3. Challenge-Response-Authentication

For authentication, a challenge value is sent to the object to be authenticated. A corresponding response value is sent back and verified. The response is determined by the PUF. As only an original product can determine the correct response value corresponding to a challenge, the product entity or a dedicated part of the product is thereby authenticated.

Figure 3 shows how an object becomes authenticated by a verifier. The verifier maintains a database of reference challenge response pairs. For example, the database was filled during production of the object by recording arbitrary challenge-response-pairs. During the authentication the verifier selects a challenge value of the database and sends it to the object to be authenticated. The response value R is determined by means of the PUF, and transferred back to the verifier. The verifier compares the received response value with the reference value stored in the database. If these are similar, i.e., the number of different bits does not exceed a threshold, the object is authenticated successfully.

B. Cryptographic Key Extraction

A cryptographic key can be determined based on inexact, noisy data. A "fuzzy key extractor" is a functionality that determines a stable cryptographic key using a PUF, and helper data [14][15]. The helper data allows to correct bit errors of responses (noisy data), and to map the PUF output to a given cryptographic key. A main advantage is that no secure non-volatile memory is needed on the device to store a cryptographic key.

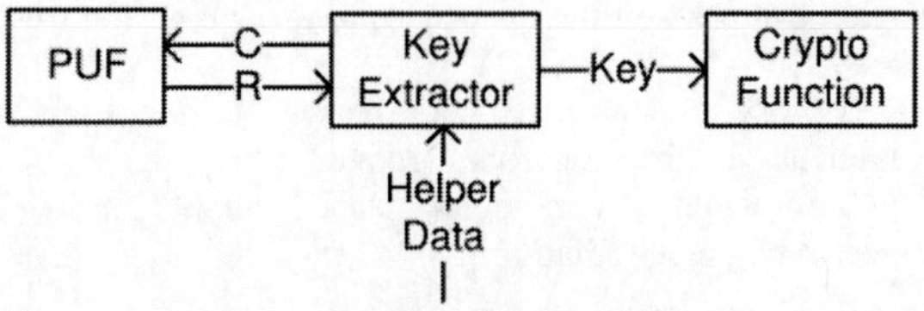

Figure 4. PUF Key Extraction

The PUF is used internally within a digital circuit to determine response values, see Figure 4. The helper data does not have to be stored securely. It can be used only by a single IC to determine the cryptographic key on the device.

C. Further PUF Applications

Several further applications, besides the two basic PUF usages outlined above, have been proposed and designed. The following list section gives an overview on related work.

- A PUF can be used to prevent utilizing specific features of semiconductor ICs. Without chip-specific aiding information, the performance of an IC is reduced or access to certain memory partitions is prevented. Also, a PUF can be used to bind software intellectual property to a FPGA device by encrypting the software code using a PUF-generated device key [16], which is typically done during manufacturing. This solution can be used to protect for instance remote software updates [17].
- A PUF can be used to protect the execution of software code: the Control Flow Graph of an executed program depends on the output of a PUF [18].
- It is known to include a measurement value determined by a sensor as part of the challenge of a PUF to authenticate the sensor measurement [19][20]. This allows authenticating sensor measurements.
- A PUF can be used also in data communication to determine a message integrity checksum (message integrity code, message authentication code) [21]. While a real, physical PUF is used to determine the message authentication code by the sender, a simulated, algorithmic model of the PUF is used to verify the checksum by the receiver.
- Furthermore, the cryptographic key derived by a PUF of a semiconductor can be used to decrypt configuration data [22].
- A PUF can, as security primitive, be integrated in a cryptographic protocol directly [23][24].

D. Limitations of PUF

Building security solutions using PUFs, it is important to understand their limitations. Important issues to be considered are:

- Attacks on the PUF itself, and attacks to PUF support functions as a fuzzy key extractor need to be taken into account. This relates for instance to the PUF model building, to physical attacks on PUFs, and to side channel and fault injection attacks [24][25].
- Robustness of a PUF implementations with respect to tampering, e.g., how vulnerable is a solution in fact against attacks on the opened chip, using e.g., focused ion beams.
- Reliability of the PUF with respect to the long term application in devices related to ageing, and environmental conditions as temperature and electromagnetic radiation.
- Required processes for enrollment of helper data and security management data, which relates on one hand to data on the PUF device, and to data maintained within backend security systems. On the other hand, depending on the PUF application the handling of the recorded challenge response pairs needs to be defined, as this information is sensitive and can be system critical. The latter may be compared to the handling of symmetric device keys, which require a similar level of sensitivity. Besides the initial enrollment, also requirements during the whole lifecycle have to be covered, e.g., the update of keys or helper data, ownership transfer of a device, and taking a device out of service securely.

Based on these points, it becomes even more obvious that a security solution exposing the PUF functionality to other elements needs to designed PUF aware, especially considering reliability and resilience requirements for deployments intended for long usage periods (long term security).

IV. New Applications of Phyiscal Unclonable Functions

The main applications of PUFs fall basically in two categories: A PUF is used directly for object authentication using challenge-response authentication, e.g., for low cost RFID Tags. Here, the PUF is used by the authenticated object to determine the response. Another way of using a PUF is to reconstruct a symmetric cryptographic key that is determined by a fuzzy key extractor using the device's PUF and stored helper data. The reconstructed cryptographic key can be used independently from the specific PUF properties. That means, any cryptographic security mechanism can be used based on the reconstructed key material.

In this section, we describe potential new applications of PUFs in the context of security services.

A. Authentication Verification

It is known to use a PUF to authenticate an integrated circuit or a device respectively. Here, a PUF is used to authenticate the device on which the PUF is realized. However, the reverse usage of a PUF is possible as well: The PUF can be used to *verify* access of an external party. This approach has the clear advantage that no cryptographic algorithm has to be implemented to perform authentication checks. Furthermore, no cryptographic key has been established and stored on the verifier device. An entity that authenticates towards the device has to store a certain number of PUF challenge-response pairs as authentication credentials. The verifying device uses the PUF to check the validity of challenge-response pairs provided by the authenticating entity.

One application for this authentication verification can be, e.g., in the context access verification to a diagnosis or debug interface of an integrated circuit, or to protect the wake-up functionality of a battery-power Internet of Things device or a wireless sensor node.

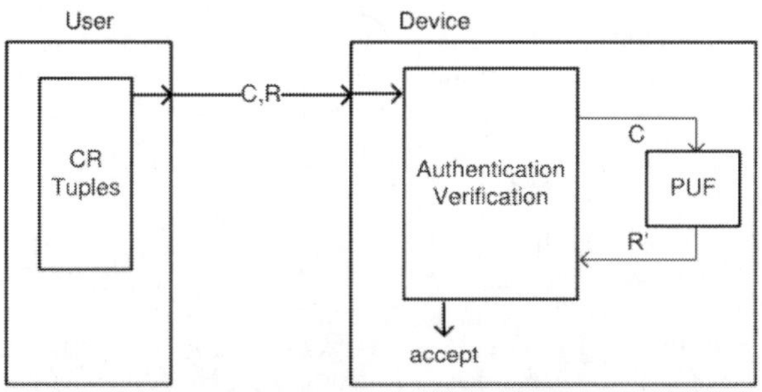

Figure 5. PUF Authentication Verification

Figure 5 illustrates how a PUF can be used to check authenticated access to a device or device functionality by a user as authenticating entity: A user presents a C/R pair of challenge C and response R. The PUF determines the response R' for the given challenge C. If the presented response R, and the determined response R' are identical or differ only in a limited number of bits, access is granted (accept). To increase attack robustness, it may be required to provide multiple valid C/R pairs. The set of challenges of the C/R pairs may be checked for validity. This means that no arbitrary set of CR pairs may be presented, but that the set of challenges of the presented CR pairs is verified to be a valid set of challenge values (e.g., consecutive values). Furthermore, different authorization levels may be associated with different sets of challenge values. So, depending on the presented set of C/R pairs, access to different functionality is granted (e.g., read diagnostic information, or modify configuration parameters).

The C/R pair, respectively the set of C/R pairs, can be determined in different ways:

- During an initialization phase, C/R pairs can be read out from the device, and stored in a secure data base of the authenticating entity. Before the IC is put in operation, the interface allowing to read out C/R pairs is blocked, e.g., by burning a security fuse.
- During an initialization phase, a first set of C/R pairs is read out from the device, and stored in a secure data base. Before the IC is put in operation, the interface allowing to read out C/R pairs without having authenticated is blocked, e.g., by burning a security fuse. Only after having authenticated successfully, the device would allow to read-out additional C/R pairs.
- Should the PUF be a PUF for which an algorithmic model can be determined (as described in [21], the algorithmic model of the PUF can be used to compute C/R pairs. During an initialization phase, C/R pairs are read out to determine the parameters of the PUF model for this device. Before the IC is put in operation, the interface allowing the reading out of C/R pairs can be blocked, e.g., by burning a security fuse.

This inverse usage of a challenge-response PUF for verifying an authentication has the advantage that the verifying device uses the PUF only internally during the operation phase. After the initialization phase, it does not offer an external interface to unauthenticated users that allows to access the PUF directly, i.e., to get responses for given challenges. So, PUF modeling attacks [26] requiring access to PUF responses are avoided.

B. Configuration Integrity Check

In a similar way, the integrity of externally stored configuration data can be verified by a device using its PUF. The configuration data, as the model and serial number, and the configuration and calibration data of a sensor element, can be stored, e.g., in an electrically erasable programmable read only memory (EEPROM).

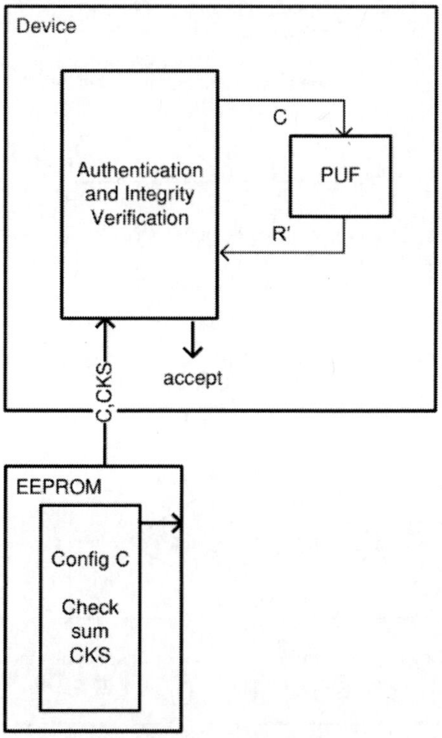

Figure 6. PUF-based Protection of Configuration Data

Figure 6 shows a system where a device uses a PUF to check the integrity of configuration data loaded from an EEPROM memory using its internal PUF. A specific case of configuration data is PUF helper data. The helper data used to reconstruct a cryptographic key could be checked for integrity and authenticity before it is applied with a PUF fuzzy key extractor.

Figure 7 shows the performed steps of a realization option: Configuration data is read from an external, unprotected configuration memory, e.g., a serial EEPROM. Besides the actual configuration data (CD), a PUF checksum (PCS) is also stored on the EEPROM. Once the configuration CD and its PUF checksum PCS have been read, the device verifies the integrity of the read data using its PUF. A PUF challenge value is determined depending on the read configuration data, e.g., a cryptographic hash value computed over the configuration data. The corresponding PUF response value R' is determined using the device PUF.

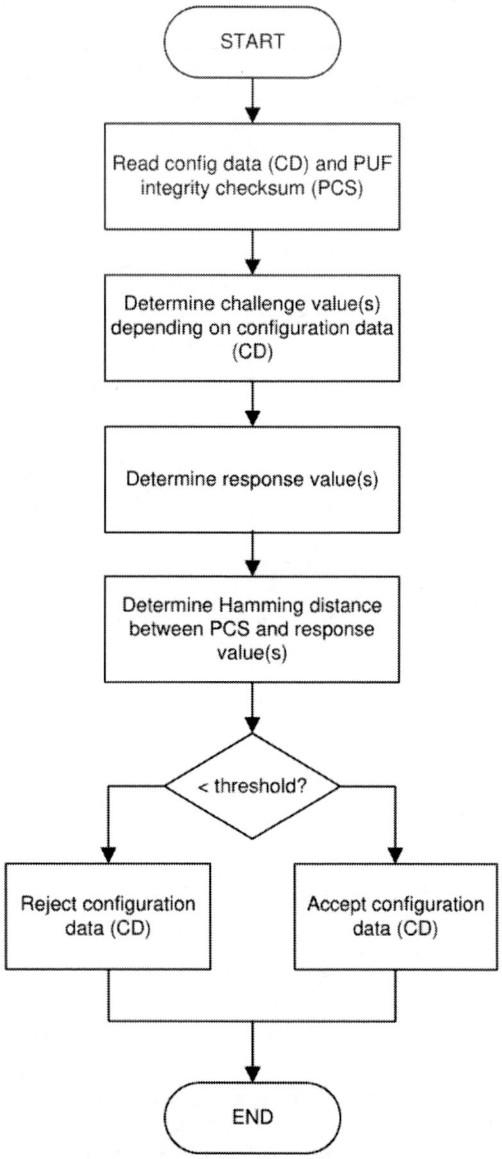

Figure 7. PUF-based Integrity Check of Configuration Data

The Hamming distance, i.e., the number of different bits, between R' and the read PCS value is determined. The read configuration data are accepted if the number of different bits is below a given threshold value.

When writing modified configuration data CD' by the device, the device performs similar steps: The device computes the hash value of the modified configuration data CD' that is to be written to the serial EEPROM. Depending on the hash value, a challenge value is determined.

The device PUF is used to determine the corresponding response as checksum PCS'. The configuration data CD' and the checksum PCS' are written to the serial EEPROM.

This usage of a PUF allows the device to check the integrity of configuration data read from a serial EEPROM. It is ensured that the configuration data has in fact been written by the device. If an attacker should have modified the configuration data on the EEPROM, the checksum would not match the manipulated configuration data. The device would reject the read configuration data, and go into an error state or use internal default values. In this use case, a PUF is used in a similar way as a keyed hash function to determine respectively to check a message authentication code over a given data.

In a similar way as the computation of a message authentication code, a PUF may be used also as part of a cryptographic key derivation function for a cryptographic key *K*. Thereby, a hardware-bound key derivation function is realized. Depending on the cryptographic key *K*, challenge values are determined. The PUF response value(s) are used to determine a (derived) key.

C. PUF Tamper Sensor and PUF Built-In Self Test

Challenge response pairs of the PUF are typically stored as reference data internally within a device. The integrated circuit uses the PUF and the reference data to check whether the PUF circuit is working correctly.

This approach can be used for different purposes:

- A PUF-based tamper-sensor can be realized: The PUF is used as digital sensor to determine a tampering information. When a tampering of the device occurred, the PUF provides different response value with a certain probability. Here, the result of the PUF is not used directly for an authentication or for determining a cryptographic key, but to generate information about the tamper status of a device. If a malfunction is detected, the device can e.g., block a functionality of the device, or it could zeroize stored cryptographic keys.
- A PUF-based device degradation sensor can be realized: Besides physical tampering, also other physical reasons like degradation affect the PUF behavior. A degradation of a device, e.g. a semiconductor IC, can be detected by a changing PUF behavior. The PUF allows detecting such degradations before a regular digital circuit realized on the same semiconductor shows a malfunction. So hardware defects can be detected early, i.e., before the devices shows a failure (predictive maintenance).
- A built-in PUF self-test functionality can be realized. Before a PUF is used, e.g., for authentication or key extraction, its correct operation is verified. Only if the PUF works as expected, the self-test succeeds. The main

function of the PUF, i.e., authentication or key extraction, is performed only when the PUF self-test has succeeded.

Figure 8 shows a realization option where reference data (RD) are used to check the PUF. Only if the PUF provides responses sufficiently similar to the reference data, access to the PUF is enabled by the PUF self-test unit PST. So, an integrated self-test functionality is realized for the PUF. It can be used, e.g., for key extraction or authentication, only if the PUF has passed the self-test successfully.

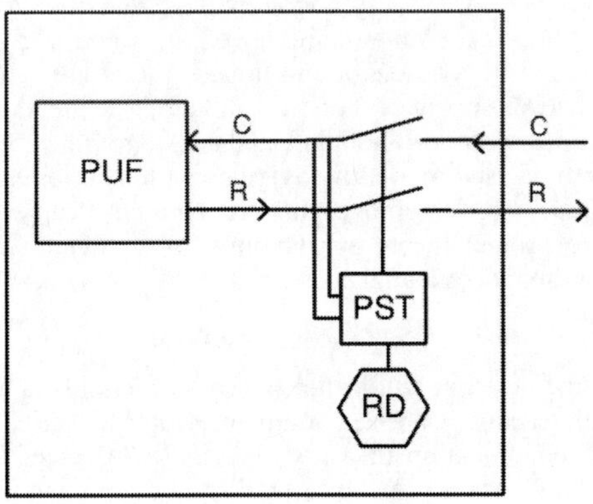

Figure 8. PUF Built-In Self Test

D. *Identifying Communication Sender*

A PUF can be used to derive a serial number of a device. This PUF derived serial number or a derivation of thereof can be used to determine an identifier for data communication.

For example, an IPv6 stateless address auto configuration can be performed using a PUF. Aura defines how an IPv6 address can be created cryptographically [28]. Similarly, a PUF can be used to determine an IPv6 address. The challenge can be determined based on network part of the IPv6 address assigned by an IPv6 router. The host part is created depending on the PUF response output.

Figure 9 shows a different variant where the PUF-based identifying information is not included in the sender address. Instead, if a wireless spread spectrum transmission system is used, a spreading code is build or modified respectively depending on the PUF response. Hence, the PUF is used to realize a kind of "stream cipher" as spreading code.

A PUF can be used to determine a watermarking information also for digital media, not only for a wireless transmitted information stream. For example, a PUF-based identifying noise signal can be created using a PUF. The noise signal is embedded in a picture, or a video stream as physical watermarking information. Here, a PUF is used to determine the spread spectrum watermarking signal. Instead of a cryptographic signature based watermark as known from [29], a PUF-based identifying watermark is embedded in the digital media. So, a hardware-bound watermarking information can be created, e.g., to prove the originating device that created the media.

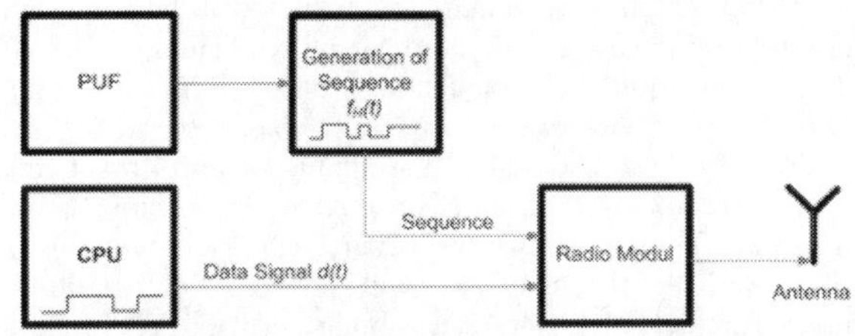

Figure 9. PUF-based Spread-spectrum Transmission

E. *PUF-helper Data as License File (license key)*

A fuzzy key extractor allows determining a given cryptographic key using a PUF and stored helper data. The helper data has two purposes: it allows correcting random errors of the PUF response, and it transforms the device-specific PUF response to a given cryptographic key. These properties can be used to realize a licensing mechanism, e.g., for feature activation on an embedded device.

In a licensing scheme, a license code, or license key, is required to use a certain, software-based feature. The license code/key can be checked to determine whether a certain feature is allowed to be used, or a cryptographic key to decrypt executable code can be determined based on the license key.

With PUF helper data being required to determine a certain cryptographic key, the license code/key can be provided in the form of helper data: as long as the required helper data is not available, the license key cannot be built by a certain device. However, if helper data to reconstruct a certain license code/key is provided, the device can determine the license code/key. As a PUF is used, the helper data can be processed only on the single intended target device to reconstruct the license information. So, the helper data that is used as license information is valid only on a certain device.

During manufacturing, the executable code for several licensable features would be stored on the device in encrypted form. Without a license, the features cannot be used. To enable the usage of a feature as part of a feature activation procedure, a license code is provided to the device and stored: The license code in the form of helper data enables the device to determine the cryptographic key required to decrypt and execute the code for a certain licensable feature. As different features can be encrypted with a different cryptographic key, the features can be activated independently.

During manufacturing, the PUF of a certain device would be measured. Parameters of the PUF or challenge response pairs would be stored in a device database of the manufacturer. When a certain feature shall be activated for a certain device, the manufacturer uses the stored PUF data to compute offline helper data for the target device. The helper data is constructed in such a way that the resulting cryptographic key is the one needed to decrypt the code for the feature to be activated. So the helper data is not computed by the device itself, but offline by the manufacturer.

F. PUF based Credential Bootstrapping

Cryptographic credentials, as a symmetric or asymmetric cryptographic key, can be used to authenticate a device. The device authentication credentials have to be configured initially by a bootstrapping process (also called enrollment).

Automated credential bootstrapping or enrollment refers to the initial configuration of devices including the key material. This is shown in Figure 10. Field devices are connected to the network, and contact the public key infrastructure (PKI) server to obtain certified key material. Here, the field devices generate their public/private key pairs locally, and send a Certificate Signing Request (CSR) for the public key to the PKI server. Part of the CSR may be a serial number of the device, against which the PKI server can check a configured list of devices allowed to be enrolled. This authorization may also be realized by other means like one-time passwords.

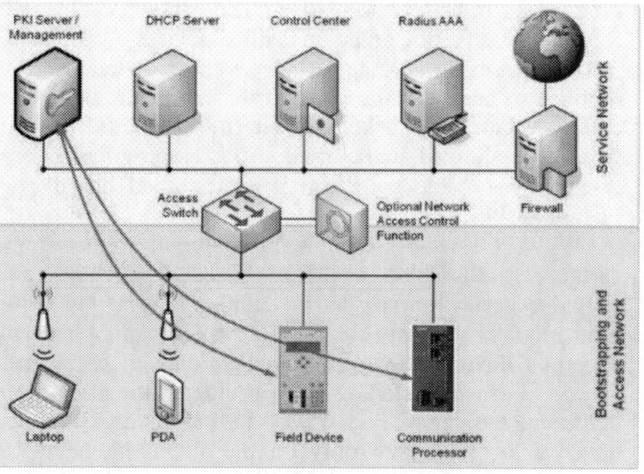

Figure 10. Automated distribution using management protocols

The initial credential bootstrapping is protected usually by organizational and personal security measures. For example, the credential bootstrapping of cryptographic device credentials can be performed during the manufacturing within a secure manufacturing area. Credentials are typically provisioned at the end of a production line. So during the manufacturing and testing of a device, often no credentials are available yet. The manufacturing can be performed at a single manufacturing site, or across different manufacturing sites.

In early manufacturing phases, e.g., directly after the assembly of a digital circuit board, no cryptographic credentials are available yet. However, the device can already be identified using its PUF fingerprint, anyhow. A PUF can be used to identify a manufactured device during the manufacturing process securely along different manufacturing steps *before* cryptographic device credentials have been provisioned. At later steps of the production, or at delivery time to a customer, it can be verified that a certain device is still the same device as intended by checking its PUF fingerprint. So here, a PUF is used not during the regular operation of the device, but during the manufacturing until initial set of cryptographic device credentials have been provisioned.

The provisioning of device certificate using a certificate management protocol like the simple certificate enrolment protocol (SCEP) [30], enrollment over secure transport (EST) [31], or the certificate management protocol CMP [32], a PUF-based device authentication may be used to protect a certificate request message.

In a similar way, a PUF may still be used when cryptographic credentials are not available anymore or are not valid anymore during the lifetime of a device: The validity period of cryptographic credentials may have expired, or credentials may have been zeroized when a device has been decommissioned. A PUF, which is intrinsically available on a device independently on provisioned configuration data and cryptographic credentials, may still be used to identify a device with a certain reliability independently of cryptographic credentials. It can be used as basis to protect the re-provisioning of a device with fresh cryptographic credentials.

V. RELATED WORK

Authentication within the Internet of Things is an active area of research and development. Gupta described multi-factor authentication of users towards IoT devices [33][33]. The Cloud Security Alliance published recommendations on identity and access management within the IoT [34]. Ajit and Sunil describe challenged to IoT security and solution options [35]. Authentication systems for IoT where analyzed by Borgohain, Borgohain, Kumar and Sanyal [36].

Al Ibrahim and Nair have combined multiple PUF elements into a combined system PUF [37].

Host-based intrusion detection systems (HIDS) as SAMHAIN [38] and OSSEC [39], analyze the integrity of hosts and report the results to a backend security monitoring system.

VI. CONCLUSION

Physical unclonable functions have been investigated extensively by both research, and industry. The work focuses much on design constructions to realize a PUF, analyzing their statistical, and security properties, and on key extraction. Although being known for at least 10 years, one limited number of examples for commercial applications exists. Besides the classical usages, object authentication, and key extraction, a PUF can be specific new usages can be realized based on a PUF. This paper described several new possible applications for PUFs in different systems, either self-contained, like a PUF-based tamper sensor or degradation sensor, or in conjunction with other parts of target solutions like in the case of licensing of credential provisioning. These new applications are discussed as abstract concepts and need to be integrated as security solution element in an overall security solution.

Issues for the practical application of PUFs are the stability over time (ageing), and under harsh environmental conditions. As PUFs are still a relatively new security feature that is not yet broadly applied in practice, careful analysis of the actual security level as to be performed (e.g., modeling attacks, physical attacks, side channel attacks). A PUF may be used as one security element in an overall security solution design. The security management of a PUF-based security solution has to be designed (e.g., enrollment of key material or helper data, building and maintaining databases comprising challenge/response pairs, update and revocation of security management data along the lifecycle).

However, PUFs show unique properties that make them interesting for practical usage: they allow "storing" a cryptographic key in a protected way without requiring physical non-volatile memory. Low-cost authentication solutions can be built that do not require implementations of cryptographic algorithms. They may be used when conventional cryptographic security mechanisms cannot be applied, or in combination with such security mechanisms. PUFs may be used on low-end devices that do not support cryptographic mechanisms, as additional protection mechanism complementing cryptographic security measures (defense in depth), or during lifecycle phases of a device in which cryptographic credentials are not available. Such lifecycles may occur during production before device credentials have been provisioned or during the lifetime of a device when it is decommissioned or re-provisioned.

REFERENCES

[1] R. Falk and S. Fries, "New Directions in Applying Physical Unclonable Functions," The Ninth International Conference on Emerging Security Information, Systems and Technologies (SECURWARE), 23-28 August 2015, Venice, Italy, Thinkmind, pp. 31-36, available from: https://www.thinkmind.org/index.php?view=article&articleid=securware_2015_2_20_30028, last access: January 2016

[2] IEC 62443, "Industrial Automation and Control System Security" (formerly ISA99), available from: http://isa99.isa.org/Documents/Forms/AllItems.aspx, last access: January 2016

[3] B. Gassend, "Physical Random Functions", Masters Thesis, MIT, February, 2003, available from: http://csg.csail.mit.edu/pubs/memos/Memo-458/memo-458.pdf, last access: January 2016

[4] C. Herder, Y. Meng-Day, F. Koushanfar, and S. Devadas, "Physical Unclonable Functions and Applications: A Tutorial," Proceedings of the IEEE, Vol.: 102 No. 8, Aug. 2014, pp. 1126-1141, available from: http://ieeexplore.ieee.org/stamp/stamp.jsp?arnumber=6823677, last access: January 2016

[5] S. Devadas, "Physical Unclonable Functions and Applications, Presentation Slides," available from: http://people.csail.mit.edu/rudolph/Teaching/Lectures/Security/Lecture-Security-PUFs-2.pdf, last access: January 2016

[6] G. E. Suh and S. Devadas, "Physical Unclonable Functions for Device Authentication and Secret Key Generation," DAC 2007, June 4-8, 2007, pp. 9-14 ACM, available from: http://www.verayo.com/pdf/2007_PUF_dac.pdf, last access: January 2016

[7] S. Katzenbeisser, Ü. Kocabas, V. Rožic, A. Sadeghi, I. Verbauwhede, and C. Wachsmann, "PUFs: Myth, Fact or Busted? A Security Evaluation of Physically Unclonable Functions (PUFs) Cast in Silicon," IACR eprint 2012/557, Sep. 2012. Online]. Available from: https://eprint.iacr.org/2012/557.pdf, last access: January 2016

[8] Intrinsic ID Technology, available from: https://www.intrinsic-id.com/technology/, last access: January 2016

[9] Verayo, "Physical Unclonabel Functions (PUF)," available from: http://verayo.com/tech.php, last access: January 2015

[10] Verayo, "Introduction to Verayo," available from: http://www.rfidsecurityalliance.org/docs/Verayo_Introduction_RFIDSA_July_9_08.pdf, last access: January 2016

[11] Microsemi, "SmartFusion2," available from: http://www.microsemi.com/products/fpga-soc/soc-fpga/smartfusion2, last access: January 2016

[12] NXP Semiconductors, "PUF - Physical Unclonable Functions Protecting next-generation Smart Card ICs with SRAM-based PUFs," February 2013, available from: http://www.nxp.com/documents/other/75017366.pdf, last access: January 2016

[13] C. Böhm and M. Hofer, "Physical Unclonable Functions in Theory and Practice," Springer, 2012

[14] Y. Dodis, L. Reyzin, and A. Smith, "Fuzzy Extractors: How to Generate Strong Keys from Biometrics and Other Noisy Data," Eurocrypt 2004, LNCS 3027, Springer, 2004, pp. 523-540, available from: http://www.iacr.org/archive/eurocrypt2004/30270518/DRS-ec2004-final.pdf, last access: January 2016

[15] B. Škorić, P. Tuyls, and W. Ophey, "Robust key extraction from Physical Uncloneable Functions," Applied Cryptography and Network Security, LNCS 3531, Springer, 2005, pp 407-422, available from: http://members.home.nl/skoric/security/PUF_KeyExtraction.pdf , last access: January 2016

[16] Y. Alkabani and F. Koushanfar, "Active Hardware Metering for Intellectual Property Protection and Security," 16th USENIX Security Symposium, 2007, pp. 20:1-20:16, available from: http://www.usenix.org/event/sec07/tech/full_papers/alkabani/alkabani.pdf, last access: January 2016

[17] M. Gora, A. Maiti, and P. Schaumont, "A Flexible Design Flow for Software IP Binding in FPGA," IEEE Transactions on Industrial Informatics, vol. 6, issue 4, Nov. 2010, pp. 719-728

[18] R. Nithyanand and J. Solis, "Theoretical Analysis: Physical Unclonable Functions and the Software Protection Problem," IEEE Symposium on Security and Privacy Workshop, 2012, pp. 1-11 available from: http://www.ieee-security.org/TC/SPW2012/proceedings/4740a001.pdf, last access: January 2016

[19] U. Rührmair, F. Sehnke, J. Sölter, G. Dror, S. Devadas, and J. Schmidhuber, "Modeling Attacks on Physical Unclonable Functions," Proc. of the 17th ACM conference on Computer and communications security, 2010, pp. 237-249, , available from: http://people.idsia.ch/~juergen/attack2010puf.pdf, last access: January 2016

[20] K. Rosenfeld, E. Gavas, and R. Karri, "Sensor Physical Unclonable Functions," IEEE International Symposium on Hardware-Oriented Security and Trust (HOST), June 2010, pp. 112-117, available from: http://isis.poly.edu/~kurt/papers/sensorpuf.pdf, last access: January 2016

[21] W. Bares, S. Devadas, V. Khandelwal, Z. Paral, R. Sowell, and T. Zhou, "Soft message signing," patent application, WO2012154409, Nov. 2012

[22] S. Devadas and T. Ziola, "Securely field configurable device," patent application, US2010/0272255, Oct. 2010

[23] M. van Dijk and U. Rührmair, "Physical Unclonable Functions in Cryptographic Protocols: Security Proofs and Impossibility Results," Cryptology ePrint Archive: Report

2012/228, April 2012, available from: https://eprint.iacr.org/2012/228.pdf, last access: January 2016

[24] M. Majzoobi, M. Rostami, F. Koushanfar, D. Wallach, and S. Devadas, "Slender PUF Protocol: A lightweight, robust, and secure authentication by substring matching," IEEE CS Security and Privacy Workshop, 2012, pp. 33-44, available from: http://www.ieee-security.org/TC/SPW2012/proceedings/4740a033.pdf, last access: March 2015

[25] D. Merli, D. Schuster, F. Stumpf, and G. Sigl, "Side-Channel Analysis of PUFs and Fuzzy Extractors," Conference on Trust and Trustworthy Computing (TRUST 2011), LNCS 6740, Springer, 2011, pp. 33-47

[26] A. Mahmoud, U. Rührmair, M. Majzoobi, and F. Koushanfar, "Combined Modeling and Side Channel Attacks on Strong PUFs," Cryptology ePrint Archive, Report 2013/632, 2013, available from: http://eprint.iacr.org/2013/632, last access: January 2016

[27] C. Helfmeier, C. Boit, D. Nedospasov, S. Tajik, and J.-P. Seifert, "Physical Vulnerabilities of Physically Unclonable Functions," Proceedings of the conference on Design, Automation & Test in Europe (DATE'14), Dresden, Germany, 24-28 March 2014, available from: http://www.date-conference.com/files/proceedings/2014/pdffiles/12.2_5.pdf, last access: January 2016

[28] T. Aura, "Cryptographically Generated Addresses (CGA)," RFC3972, March 2005, available from: https://www.ietf.org/rfc/rfc3972.txt, last access: January 2016

[29] U. Fiore and F. Rossi, "Embedding an Identity-Based Short Signature as a Digital Watermark," Future Internet 2015, 7(4), pp. 393-404, available online: http://www.mdpi.com/1999-5903/7/4/393, last access: January 2016

[30] P. Gutman and M. Pritikin, "Simple Certificate Enrolment Protocol SCEP," draft-gutmann-scep-01.txt, Internet draft, work in progress, September 2015, available from: https://tools.ietf.org/html/draft-gutmann-scep-01, last access: January 2016

[31] M. Pritikin, P. Yee, D. Harkins, "Enrollment over Secure Transport," RFC7030, October 2013, available from: https://www.ietf.org/rfc/rfc7030.txt, last access: January 2016

[32] C. Adams, S. Farrell, T. Kause, T. Mononen, "Internet X.509 Public Key Infrastructure Certificate Management Protocol (CMP)," RFC4210, September 2005, available from:, available from: https://www.ietf.org/rfc/rfc4210.txt, last access: January 2016

[33] Udit Gupta, "Application of Multi factor authentication in Internet of Things domain: multi-factor authentication of users towards IoT devices", Cornell university arXiv:1506.03753, 2015, available from: http://arxiv.org/ftp/arxiv/papers/1506/1506.03753.pdf , last access: April 2016

[34] Arlene Mordeno and Brian Russel, "Identity and Access Management for the Internet of Things - Summary Guidance," Cloud Security Alliance, 2015, available from: https://downloads.cloudsecurityalliance.org/assets/research/internet-of-things/identity-and-access-management-for-the-iot.pdf , last access: April 2016

[35] Jha Ajit and M.C. Suni, "Security considerations for Internet of Things," L&T Technology Services, 2014, http://www.lnttechservices.com/media/30090/whitepaper_security-considerations-for-internet-of-things.pdf , last access: April 2016

[36] T. Borgohain, A. Borgohain, U. Kumar, S. Sanyal, "Authentication Systems in Internet of Things," Int. J. Advanced Networking and Applications, vol. 6, issue 4, pp. 2422-2426, 2015, available from http://www.ijana.in/papers/V6I4-11.pdf , last access: April 2016

[37] O. Al Ibrahim and S. Nair, "Cyber-Physical Security Using System-Level PUFs," 7th International Wireless Communications and Mobile Computing Conference (IWCMC), 2011, available from http://lyle.smu.edu/~nair/ftp/research_papers_nair/CyPhy11.pdf , last access: April 2016

[38] R. Wichmann, "The Samhain HIDS," fact sheet, 2011, available from http://la-samhna.de/samhain/samhain_leaf.pdf , last access April 2016

[39] OSSEC, "Open Source HIDS SECurity," web site, 2010 - 2015, available from http://ossec.github.io/ , last access April 2016

Implementation and Evaluation of Intrinsic Authentication in Quantum Key Distribution Protocols

Stefan Rass
Department of Applied Informatics, System Security Group
Universität Klagenfurt, Universitätsstrasse 65-67
9020 Klagenfurt, Austria
email: stefan.rass@aau.at

Sandra König, Stefan Schauer, Oliver Maurhart
Digital Safety & Security Department
Austrian Institute of Technology, Klagenfurt, Austria
email: {sandra.koenig, stefan.schauer, oliver.maurhart}@ait.ac.at

***Abstract*—We describe a method to authenticate the qubit stream being exchanged during the first phases of the BB84 quantum key distribution without pre-shared secrets. Unlike the conventional approach that continuously authenticates all protocol messages on the public channel, our proposal is to authenticate the qubit stream already to verify the peer's identity. To this end, we employ a second public channel that is physically and logically disjoint from the one used for BB84. This is our substitute for the otherwise necessary assumption on the existence of pre-shared secrets. To practically verify the expected improvement in terms of bandwidth consumption during the public discussion part of BB84, we implemented the scheme within an existing BB84 framework, and emulated the additional public channel used by Bob with the help of additional messages on the same channel. On this implementation, simulations were conducted that confirm the efficiency, bandwidth improvements and to illustrate the difficulties in forging an authentication based on the qubit streams only (as a person-in-the-middle attack is already detected before the public discussion part in our variant of BB84).**

Keywords*–*Quantum Key Distribution; Authentication; BB84; QKD Implementation; Experimental Quantum Key Distribution

I. INTRODUCTION

It is a well recognized requirement of any quantum key distribution protocol to employ an authenticated public channel for the key distillation. This channel can be constructed in various ways, for example by embedding pseudorandom bits in the initial qubit streams to authenticate, as we already showed in [1]. In this extended version of the article, we will show how this method can be implemented and described its benefits.

Most existing QKD protocols use information-theoretically secure authentication based on universal hashing [2] to continuously attach message authentication codes (MACs) to all data being exchanged during the public discussion. Thus, an interception of the qubit streams is not detected until the public discussion starts. This continuous authentication [3] shall thwart person-in-the-middle attacks by an eavesdropper sitting in between Alice and Bob, running BB84 [4] with both of them. In that sense, quantum key distribution does not really create keys from nothing, but is rather a method of key expansion. The question discussed in this work relates to whether we can cast BB84 into a protocol that in fact *does* create keys from nothing, while retaining the security of "conventional BB84".

To this end, observe that it may already be sufficient for Alice to verify Bob's identity, if she can somehow verify that Bob is really the person from which her received qubit stream originated. One possibility to do so is to ask Bob for the way in which he created the stream, say as a pseudorandom sequence, so as to prove his identity. Of course, it is neither viable nor meaningful in our setting to let Bob create his entire qubit stream pseudorandomly, but it may indeed be useful to have him embed pseudorandom bits at a priori unknown places, while leaving the rest of the stream truly random. Alice, in an attempt to verify Bob as the "owner" of the qubit stream, may ask Bob for the seeds to recover the pseudorandom bits and their positions.

An eavesdropper, on the other hand, cannot reasonably pre-compute Bob's response to Alice's inquiry, if the pseudorandom bits cannot be recognized (distinguished from) the truly random bits. While this apparently induces a flavour of computational security (indistinguishability of pseudorandom from really random sequences), we can almost avoid threats by computationally unbounded adversaries. To see why, assume that the pseudorandom sequence originates via iterative bijective transformations from a uniformly distributed and truly random seed. If so, then all pseudorandom bits will themselves enjoy a uniform distribution. As being embedded inside another sequence of independent uniformly distributed bits, the distribution of the pseudorandom bits is identical to that of the truly random bits. Despite the correlation that inevitably exists among the pseudorandom bits, the distributions are nevertheless indistinguishable, except in case when the positions of the pseudorandom bits are known a priori. However, since these positions are chosen secretly and independently of any publicly available information, the attacker has no hope better than an uninformed guess about which positions matter.

Organisation of the paper: The following Sections III-A and II give details on BB84 to the extent needed in the following, and relate the proposal to other solutions in the literature. Section IV expands the technique how we embed pseudorandom bits into the qubit stream during BB84. Section V discusses the security of our modified version of BB84, and Section VII draws conclusions.

II. STATE OF THE ART

There have been several approaches to replace the authentication protocol for the classical channel by quantum approaches. For example, an authentication scheme is presented in [5], which provides an increased conditional entropy for the seed of the adversary and which is optimized for scenarios where the shared symmetric key used in the authentication becomes extremely short.

Other protocols entirely eliminate the classical channel thus also eliminating the need for classical authentication [6]. Such protocols make use of quantum authentication, a topic that has been studied for more than 15 years and which has already been formally defined in 2002 [7]. Quantum authentication protocols perform the task of authentication with little or no help of classical cryptography solely using quantum mechanical sources. Hence, some of these protocols combine QKD protocols with authentication [8][9][10] or use quantum error correction for the authentication of the communication parties [11]. Other quantum authentication protocols also use entanglement as a source for authentication (e.g., [12][13][14][15][16] to name a few), or employ a third party [17].

Entangled states consist of two or more particles, which have the specific property that they give completely correlated results when the respective particles are measured separately. As it has been shown by Bell [18], as well as Clauser et al. [19], this correlation can be verified if the measurement results violate some special form of inequalities. In some QKD protocols, for example the Ekert protocol [20] (among others [21]), this argument is used to generate a secure key (cf. the next section), but these protocols still require an authenticated classical channel (cf. [20]).

III. Quantum Key Distribution Protocols

In this section, we will provide a short overview on basic QKD protocols together with their key concepts. We will focus on the so-called "prepare and measure" protocols describing the BB84 protocol [4] (which we will use later on as an example for the implementation of our methodology), the B92 protocol [22], the six-state protocol [23] as well as the BBM92 protocol [24]. There are, of course, more advanced versions of QKD protocols, like the SARG protocol [25], but we will not look at them in the scope of this article and will refer the interested reader to the literature.

A. BB84 Protocol

The BB84 protocol has first been presented by Bennett and Brassard [4]. It allows two communication parties, Alice and Bob, to generate a classical key between them by using the polarization of single photons to represent information. Therefore, Alice is in possession of a single photon source and prepares the photons randomly according to the horizontal/vertical basis (Z-basis) and the diagonal basis (X-basis), i.e., for each photon she prepares one of states $\{|0\rangle, |1\rangle\}$ and $\{|x+\rangle, |x-\rangle\}$, respectively. After Alice choses the basis, the qubit is sent to Bob, who performs a measurement on it. Since Bob does not know which basis Alice used for the preparation he does not know which measurement basis he should use and thus he will not be able to retrieve the full information from each qubit. Hence, the best strategy for him is to randomly choose between the Z- and X-basis for his measurement himself. In this case Bob will choose the correct basis half of the time – but he does not know in which cases he has guessed right. Thus, Alice and Bob compare the choice of their bases in public after Bob measured the last qubit.

During the *sifting phase* [26], Alice and Bob eliminate their measurement results for those measurements where they used different bases. The remaining measurement results are converted into classical bits using the mapping

$$\begin{aligned} \{|0\rangle, |x+\rangle\} &\longrightarrow 0 \\ \{|1\rangle, |x-\rangle\} &\longrightarrow 1. \end{aligned} \tag{1}$$

At this stage, Alice and Bob should have identical classical bit strings if the channel is perfect (noiseless channel, no eavesdropper). In reality, a certain error rate is introduced in the protocol due to physical limitations (lossy and noisy channels, imperfect devices, no single photon sources, etc.). To estimate this error rate, Alice and Bob publicly compare a fraction of their results in public to check whether they are correlated. Then, classical error correction protocols are used to identify and eliminate the differences in their bit strings. Such a procedure that has been heavily used for error correction is the *CASCADE* algorithm first introduced by Bennett et al. [27]. Due to the fact that Alice and Bob publicly compare some information during the error correction, an adversary is able to obtain further information about the secret bit string (assuming Eve's presence has not been detected during error correction). Therefore, a last process called *privacy amplification* [28] performed by Alice and Bob uses *strongly-universal$_2$ hash functions* (as presented in [29] and recently discussed in [30]) to minimize the amount of information leaked to the adversary. After all, the security of QKD protocols has been discussed in depth and various security proofs have been provided, for example, in [31] or [32]. A main result of these proofs shows that Alice and Bob are still able to establish a secret key, if the error rate is below a maximum value of $\simeq 11\%$ [31].

B. B92 Protocol

In 1992 Charles Bennett pointed out that two non-orthogonal states instead of four would be enough to perform the BB84 protocol [22]. The idea is that two non-orthogonal states can not be perfectly distinguished but they can be distinguished without making a wrong decision using positive operator-valued measurement (POVM) [33]. That means when Bob measures the state sent by Alice he will never make a wrong decision but sometimes he will not be able to make any decision at all.

Alice prepares one of the states $|\varphi\rangle$ and $|\psi\rangle$, where $|\varphi\rangle$ codes for a classical 0 and $|\psi\rangle$ for a classical 1. She sends the qubit to Bob, who uses three POVM operators, which are designed to distinguish between $|\varphi\rangle$ and $|\psi\rangle$ in one-half of the cases. In detail, when Bob measures the qubit coming from Alice he obtains a correct result half of the time. For the other half he obtains an intetermінate result and both parties have to eliminate that qubit. Similarly to the BB84 protocol, Bob announces where his measurements were indeterminate and the corresponding measurement results must be discarded in the end. For the remaining results, Alice and Bob publicly announce a fraction of them to check whether they are really correlated. If the error rate is above some predefined threshold, they have to assume that it is due to the presence of an eavesdropper rather than a noisy quantum channel or imperfect devices and they restart the protocol.

C. Six-State Protocol

A natural extension of the BB84 protocol is the *six state protocol* [23]. In this protocol, additionally to the Z- and the

X-basis the third complementary basis, i.e., the Y-basis is introduced, having

$$|y+\rangle = \frac{1}{\sqrt{2}}\Big(|0\rangle + i|1\rangle\Big), \qquad |y-\rangle = \frac{1}{\sqrt{2}}\Big(|0\rangle - i|1\rangle\Big). \tag{2}$$

This extension is called "natural" because in this case all three dimensions of the Bloch sphere are used. Alice chooses randomly one of the six states and sends it to Bob. Bob has to select one out of three (instead of two as in the BB84 protocol [4]) bases and performs a measurement on the received qubit. Hence, his choice will correspond to Alice's preparation only in $1/3$ of the cases such that they will have to discard a greater amount of qubits when they publicly compare their measurement bases. As in the other protocols described above, Alice and Bob choose a certain fraction of the remaining measurement results and compare them in public to check if an eavesdropper is present. The major advantage of the six state protocol is that it is more sensitive to attacks and an adversary will have a smaller chance to stay undetected.

D. BBM92 Protocol

Whereas the BB84 protocol just discussed above is based on single photon sources, Ekert presented a protocol in 1991 [20], which uses a source emitting maximally entangled qubit pairs, i.e., the Bell states $|\Phi^{\pm}\rangle, |\Psi^{\pm}\rangle$. In principle, this source is located between Alice and Bob and one qubit of the entangled state is flying to Alice and the other one to Bob. In practice, when looking at implementations of the Ekert protocol it will be more common that one of the communication parties is in possession of the source.

In the Ekert protocol, Alice and Bob also randomly measure the polarization of their qubit, but they use different angles at Alice's and Bob's side. These angles are non-orthogonal and are later used to violate the CHSH-inequalities [19]. The CHSH-inequalities provide an indication that the quits are originally coming from an entagled state, i.e., the inequalities are violated if an entangled state is present.

In 1992 Bennett, Brassard and David Mermin presented a variant of the Ekert protocol where they show that a test of the CHSH-inequalities is not necessary for the security of the protocol [24]. Instead, Alice and Bob use two complementary measurement bases as in the BB84 protocol and randomly apply them on the received qubits. In detail, Alice and Bob receive qubits coming from the source located in the middle of them (as pointed out above, the protocol does not change if the source is in possession of Alice or Bob). Again, the qubits are parts of a Bell state, e.g., $|\Psi^-\rangle$. After receiving both qubits, Alice and Bob randomly and independently choose either the Z- or the X-basis to measure the qubit. Due to the entanglement of the qubits, Alice's measurement completely determines the state of Bob's qubit, i.e., if Alice measures a $|1\rangle$, Bob's qubit is in the state $|0\rangle$, and vice versa. If Bob measures in a different basis than Alice he destroys the information carried by the qubit and thus will not obtain the same result as Alice. Therefore, after the measurements are finished, both parties publicly compare their measurement bases and discard their results where they used different bases (i.e., similar to the BB84 protocol).

The remaining results should be perfectly correlated and the communication parties compare a randomly chosen fraction in public. If there is too much discrepancy between their

Figure 1. Channel configuration of our enhanced protocol

results they have to assume that an adversary is present and they start over the protocol. It has also been shown by Bennett et al. in this paper that the security of this version of the protocol is equal to the security of the BB84 scheme [24].

IV. Assembling Authentication into the Protocol

In a standard person-in-the-middle scenario, we have Eve sitting in between Alice and Bob, executing BB84 with both of them simultaneously.

Alice and Bob, to authenticate one another, make contact *out of band*, by contacting the other on a physically and logically separate channel that Eve has not intercepted. In that sense, we augment the usual picture of BB84 by another channel, shown dashed in Figure 1.

The key point here is that during the public discussion phase of BB84, Alice and Bob both reveal to each other their entire random sequence of polarization settings, along which their – so far private – random sequences are disclosed. Within these private random sequences, Alice will embed a pseudorandom subsequence that is indistinguishable from the truly random rest of the sequence, but for which she can tell Bob the way in which she constructed the bits and their positions. Our intuition behind this is that Alice, running BB84 with Eve, and Eve in turn running BB84 with Bob, Eve will not know (nor can determine) which of the transmitted bits are pseudorandom, and which are not. In turn, she cannot reproduce or relay these specific bits to her communication with Bob, in order to mimic Alice's behavior correctly.

Upon authentication, which happens after the public discussion phase and before the final key is distilled, Bob will get the information required to reproduce Alice's pseudorandom sequence on his own. If he were talking to Eve instead, his recorded bitstream will – with a high likelihood – not match what he received from Eve, thus revealing her presence.

Now, let us make this more rigorous. In the following, let $|x|$ denote the bitlength of a string x, and let $t \in \mathbb{N}$ be a security parameter. By the symbol $x \xleftarrow{r} \Omega$, we denote a uniformly random draw of an element x from the set Ω. Let $\mathcal{H} = \left\{H_k : \{0,1\}^t \to \{0,1\}^t \,|k \in \{0,1\}^t\right\}$ be a family of *permutations*, which will act as uniform hash-functions in our setting (note that our scenario permits this exceptional assumption, as our goal is not as usual on hashing arbitrarily long strings, but on producing pseudorandom sequences by iteration). Furthermore, let m be an integer that divides 2^t.

Under this setting, let us collect some useful observations: take $x \xleftarrow{r} \{0,1\}^t$, then for any k, the value $H_k(x)$ must again be uniformly distributed over $\{0,1\}^t$, since H_k is a permutation. Likewise, since m divides 2^t, the value $H_k(x)$ mod m is uniformly distributed over $\{0, 1, \ldots, m-1\}$.

To embed authentication information in her bit stream, Alice secretly chooses two secret values $k_v, k_p \xleftarrow{r} \{0,1\}^t$ define a permutation H_{k_v} on $\{0,1\}^t$ and a function $h_k(x) := 1 + [H_{k_p}(x) \mod m]$ on $\{1, 2, \ldots, m\}$. Using these two functions, she produces a pseudorandom sequence of *values* $v_{n+1} = H_{k_v}(v_n)$ and another (strictly increasing) pseudorandom sequence of *positions* $p_{n+1} = p_n + h_{k_p}(p_n)$, with starting values $v_0, p_0 \xleftarrow{r} \{0,1\}^t$.

Within the first phase of BB84, i.e., when the randomly polarized qubits are being transmitted, Alice uses the pseudorandom information $f(v_i)$ whenever the p_i-th bit is to be transmitted, and true randomness otherwise. In other words, Alice constructs the bitstream

$$(b_n)_{n\in\mathbb{N}} = (b_0, b_1, \ldots, b_{p_i-1}, b_{p_i} = f(v_i), b_{p_i+1}, \ldots) \quad (3)$$

with truly random b_i whenever $i \notin \{p_0, p_1, \ldots\}$ and inserts a pseudorandom value v_i at each position p_i for $i = 1, 2, \ldots$. This sequence determines the respective qubit stream upon polarizing photons according to $(b_n)_{n\in\mathbb{N}}$.

A. Authentication

To authenticate, Bob calls Alice on a separate line and asks for k_p, k_v, v_0, p_0, which enables him to reproduce the pseudorandom sequence and bits and to check if these match what he has recorded. He accepts Alice's identity as authentic if and only if all bits that he recorded match what he expects from the pseudorandom sequence. The converse authentication works in the same way.

B. The Auxiliary Public Channel

We stress that the auxiliary public channel does not need to be confidential. However, some sort of authenticity is assumed, but without explicit measures for it. This is because authenticity in our proposal relies on the assumption that the adversary is unable to intercept *both* public channels at the same time (otherwise, a person-in-the-middle attack is impossible to counter in the absence of pre-shared secrets).

The assumption of an auxiliary public channel puts security to rest on Eve not intercepting now two public channels simultaneously. If more such channel redundancy is available, then known techniques of multipath transmission allow to relax our assumption towards stronger security (by enforcing Eve to intercept > 2 paths in general). We believe this approach to practically impose only mild overhead, since many reference network topologies and multi-factor authentication systems successfully rely on and employ multiple independent and logically disjoint channels, at least for reasons of communication infrastructure availability. Suitable multipath transmission techniques [34] are well developed and successfully rely on exactly this assumption (although pursuing different goals [35]). Moreover, a common argument against multipath transmission (which technically offers an entirely classical alternative to quantum key distribution with very similar security guarantees) that relates to the blow-up of communication overhead does not apply to our setting here. The amount of information being exchanged over the auxiliary (multipath) channel is very small, thus making the additional overhead negligibly small. Therefore, the only physical obstacle that remains is a topology permitting the use of multiple channels; however, many physical network reference topologies are at least bi-connected graphs and thus offer the assumed additional channel (besides the usually valid assumption on the co-existence of independent communication infrastructures besides the quantum network).

V. Security

First, observe that endowing Eve with infinite computational power could essentially defeat any form of authentication, since Eve in that case could then easily intercept Alice and Bob's communication by a two-stage attack: First, she would let Alice and Bob do a normal run of BB84, sniffing on the authenticated public discussion and doing passive eavesdropping to make Alice and Bob abort the protocol and abandon the key. Before Alice and Bob restart again, Eve can – thanks to unlimited computing power – extract or simply guess-and-check the authentication secret, so as to perfectly impersonate Alice and Bob as person-in-the-middle during their next trial to do BB84. If Alice and Bob decide to use another authentication secret this time, Eve will fail the authentication but will have further data to learn more authentication secrets, until Alice and Bob eventually run out of local keys. Thus, Eve has a good chance to succeed ultimately.

Even if a universal hash function is in charge (see [36] for a recent proposal), the universality condition and the fact that strings of arbitrary length are hashed, both guarantee the existence of more than one possible key (hashes) that would produce the given result. Thus, the residual uncertainty about the authentication secret remains strictly positive. However, this residual uncertainty is not necessarily retained in cases where consistency with three or more MACs is demanded.

Therefore, it appears not too restrictive to assume that Eve cannot recognize the pseudorandom part in $(b_n)_{n\in\mathbb{N}}$ from the truly random portion, as neither the number nor the position of the pseudorandom bits is known. In other words, if N bits have been used, then Eve would have to test all 2^N subsets against their complements. However, even if she succeeds and recognizes which bits are the pseudorandom ones and how they have been created (i.e., if she finds the proper keys and preimages to the hash-values), this information becomes available too late, as the relevant protocol phase has been completed by this point.

Let us compute the likelihood for Alice to tell Bob the correct values, although Bob ran BB84 with Eve who impersonated Alice. Hence, the chances for Eve to remain undetected equal the likelihood for Alice's and Bob's pseudorandom sequences to entirely match by coincidence. We compute this probability now.

Let $X_1, \ldots, X_n$ be the random variables (position *and* value) corresponding to Alice's pseudorandom part in $(b_n)_{n\in\mathbb{N}}$. Likewise, let $y_1, \ldots, y_n$ be what Bob expects these values to be upon Alice's response to his authentication request. Define the random indicator variable $\chi_k = 1 :\iff X_k = y_k$, for $1 \leq k \leq n$. Bob buys Alice's claimed identity if and only if $\sum_{k=1}^{n} \chi_k = n$. Hence, we look for a tail bound to $S_n := \sum_{k=1}^{n} \chi_n$ in terms of n.

By construction, the sequence $X_1, \ldots, X_n$ is identically but not independently distributed. More precisely, each realization x_k of X_k points to a position p_k and value $v_k = b_{p_k}$ expected at this position, where position and value are stochastically independent.

So, let us compute the likelihood that Bob finds the expected bit at the told position, i.e.,

$$\Pr[X_k = y_k] = \mathbb{E}[\chi_k] = \Pr[b_{p_k} = v_k] \quad (4)$$

Since each b_i in the sequence $(b_i)_{i=1}^n$ is uniformly distributed irrespectively of its particular position, we get $\Pr[b_{p_k} = v_k] = 1/2$. Hence, as $\mathbb{E}[\chi_k]$ is bounded within $[0,1]$ and the expectations of all $\mathbb{E}[\chi_k]$ are independent (although the χ_k's themselves are indeed dependent as emerging from a deterministic process), we can apply Smith's version [37] of the Hoeffding-bound to obtain

$$\Pr[S_n - \mathbb{E}[S_n] \geq \varepsilon] \leq \exp\left(-\frac{2\varepsilon^2}{n}\right). \quad (5)$$

Applied to the event $S_n \geq \varepsilon + \mathbb{E}[S_n] = n$ and considering $\mathbb{E}[S_n] = \sum_{k=1}^n \mathbb{E}[\chi_k] = n/2$ we may set $\varepsilon = n/2$ to conclude that a pseudorandom sequence constructed from random, i.e., incorrect, authentication secrets, will make Bob accept with likelihood

$$\Pr[\text{all } X_n \text{ match}|\text{incorrect seeds}] = \Pr[S_n \geq n] \leq e^{-n/2}. \quad (6)$$

Now, we can compute the overall probability of a successful impersonation from the law of total probability. Eve will successfully convince Bob to be Alice, if any of the following two events occur:

E_1: She correctly guesses the authentication secrets, in which case Bob's reconstructed pseudorandom sequence matches his expectations. Thus, $\Pr[\text{all } X_n \text{ match}|\text{correct seeds}] = 1$, obviously. However, $\Pr[E_1] = 2^{-O(t)}$, since the authentication secrets are chosen independently at random and have bitlength t (implied by the security parameter).

E_2: She incorrectly guesses the authentication secrets, and thus presents a "random" pseudorandom sequence to Bob. The likelihood of success is bounded by (6), and the likelihood for E_2 to occur is $1 - 2^{-O(t)}$.

The law of total probability then gives

$$\Pr[\text{Bob accepts}] = \Pr[\text{all } X_n \text{ match}] = \quad (7)$$
$$= \Pr[\text{all } X_n \text{ match}|E_1]\Pr[E_1]$$
$$+ \Pr[\text{all } X_n \text{ match}|E_2]\Pr[E_2] \quad (8)$$
$$\leq e^{-n/2}(1 - 2^{-O(t)}) + 2^{-O(t)} \leq 2^{-O(t+n)}, \quad (9)$$

where n is the number of pseudorandom bits embedded, and t is the security parameter (bitlength of authentication secrets).

VI. EVALUATION

For the evaluation we used two common low level machines, each one Intel i5-3470 CPU, having four cores running at 3.20GHz, 3GB memory, 48 GB hard disk and Debian 8.2 as operating system. The machines have been connected using standard Ethernet with an average round trip time of 0.017 milliseconds.

We implemented the proposed protocol on a branch of the current available AIT QKD R10 software stack V9.9999.7 [38]. This Open Source software contains a full featured QKD post processing environment containing BB84 sifting, error correction, privacy amplification and other steps necessary.

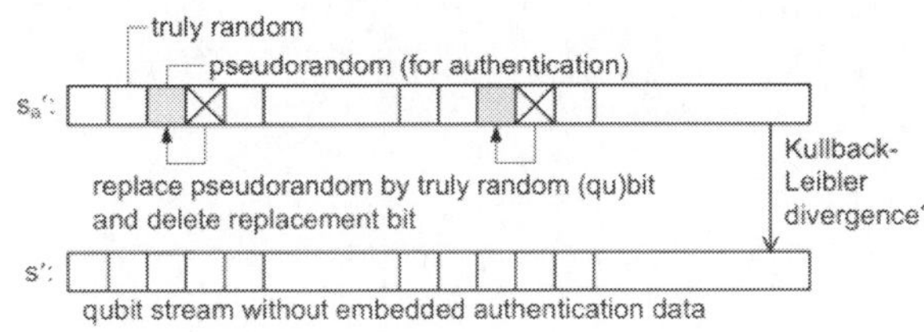

Figure 2. Comparison of BB84 with and without authentication data

For the development at hand the protocol was built full-duplex, i.e., BB84 basis comparison is run with with separately added authentication bits both ways: Alice and Bob choose their v_i, p_i independently and add this information to their base strings before transmission to their peer. A second message exchange emulates the second auxiliary channel by sending k_v, k_p, v_0, p_0 to the peer.

We used a $GF(2^{32})$ with $P(x) = x^{32} + x^7 + x^3 + x^2 + 1$ as irreducible polynomial to construct a universal hash family $\mathcal{H}$, with members H_k acting on this finite field. For hashing a message M under a secret $k = (k_1, k_2) \in \{k_p, k_v\}$, we split into chunks of equal size $M = m_1\|m_2\|\ldots\|m_n$ with $|m_i| = 32$. Using the partial key k_1, we calculate a tag t as $t = m_1k_1 + m_2k_1^2 + \ldots + m_nk_1^n$ within the finite field using polynomial multiplication. For the message, we take the current values p and v, respectively, and the result of the hashing under k is $H_k(M) = t \oplus k_2$, where $\oplus$ denotes the bitwise XOR (cf. [39]).

The experiment has been done with raw data grabbed from the current setup of the AIT's QKD-Telco project [40]. The QKD-TELCO aims to integrate quantum key distribution in telecom networks to provide a modern, trustworthy ICT infrastructure. This is an approach to use DWDM (Dense Wavelength Division Multiplexing) communication as an seamless integration of QKD systems in existing and next-generation metro-access architectures. The measurement data consisting of 64 Bit photon detector timestamps sums up to 4.7 GB data covering a timespan of nearly 5465 seconds.

For a practical evaluation, we drained a total of $3,272,234$ bits from the BB84 implementation, including a total of $375,142$ pseudorandom authentication bits embedded in the string. Call s_a a bitstring with authentication data in it, as opposed to s denoting a bitstring without such data (e.g., as obtained from a plain BB84 execution). From our experiment, we directly obtained s_a, and constructed the string s by replacing the pseudorandom bits (at the known positions) with truly random ones picked from the same string (to have these obey the same randomness in terms of distribution as the remaining string). The replacement bits were removed from both strings later on, to obtain strings s'_a and s' of equal length, which differ only in those positions where pseudorandom bits were inserted in s'_a. So, the only differences between s'_a and s' are due to the pseudorandom bits. Figure 2 summarizes the details.

To measure how much difference is noticeable in information-theoretic terms, we evaluated the Kullback-Leibler divergence $KL(s'_a[1:n], s'[1:n]) = K(n)$, where the notation $s[1:n]$ denotes the first n bits of the string n. Figure 3 shows the plot, illustrating that the difference comes

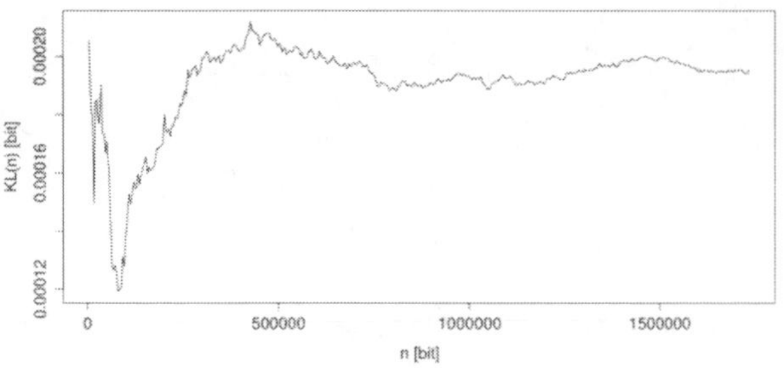

Figure 3. Kullback-Leibler divergence $KL(s'_a, s')$ (for the first n bits)

to ≈ 0.00019 bits near the end of the plot.

For a second experiment, we divided the total string s'_a and s' into consecutive chunks of 70 bits (after additionally removing bits that were marked as measurement errors). From the so-obtained set of strings of 70 bits each, we computed the empirical joint distribution of 70 bits with and without authentication data in them. Let $b_a[i]$ and $b[i]$ for $1 \leq i \leq 70$ denote the i-th bits from the chunk/string with and without authentication data, respectively, then the difference was measured by $\max_{1\leq i\leq 70} |\Pr(b_a[i] = 1) - \Pr(b[i] = 1)| \approx 0.01414979 < 1/70 \approx 0.01428571$. Thus, the change in the empirical distribution due to the pseudorandom authentication data is numerically less than 1 bit different over 70 trials (consequently, both empirical distribution seemingly converge to the uniform mass function $1/70$ as the number of chunks approaches infinity). However, even if distinguishing a plain from an authenticated BB84 would be effective based on empirical distributions, the problem of *where* the pseudorandom bits are located remains; based on the quality of the universal hash function being used, this problem should remain practically infeasible.

VII. Conclusion

a) Application to other QKD Protocols: The methodology that we described in this article is integrating pseudorandom sequences into the randomly chosen bit strings defining the basis choice for Alice and Bob. Thus, the technique is partly unrelated to the protocol executed between Alice and Bob. We focused on the BB84 protocol in sections IV, V, and VI but the general idea can, in principle, also be applied to other QKD protocols described in Section III.

For the B92 protocol, the number of quantum states representing classical bits is reduced, compared to the BB84 protocol, from four to two states. As pointed out in Section III-B, this leads to indeterminate outcomes, which have to be deleted before Alice and Bob can perform the error correction and privacy amplification. Thus, our methodology can in principle also be applied for the non-orthogonal states of the B92 protocol. Nevertheless, one challenge comes up when results have to be deleted, which corresponds to the pseudorandom bits required for authentication. Since no measurement result is available in this case, Alice and Bob have to compensate somehow for the missing bit.

Additionally, an application of the third orthogonal basis, as in the six-state protocol (cf. Section III-C), does not represent a big change to our authentication scheme. The choice of all three bases is still relying on a random sequence where additional pseudorandom elements can be integrated. Due to the fact that Alice and Bob have to choose between three bases instead of two, simple bit strings representing the basis choice will not be sufficient any more (i.e., one bit can only represent two different bases). Under the obvious changes, our authentication method can be applied as described in this article. It remains to investigate whether the reduced efficiency of the six-state protocol [23], which is due to the three bases, also affects the efficiency of our authentication process.

Finally, our authentication scheme can also be integrated into "prepare and measure" protocols using entangled states instead of single photon sources. This explicitly holds for the BBM92 protocol, since the measurement bases are the same as in the BB84 protocol. Hence, the introduction of additional pseudorandom bits in to the bit string defining the basis choice analogously follows the way described in Section IV and all computations can be performed alike.

b) Summary and Outlook: Authentication is a crucial issue for quantum key distribution and can be tackled in several ways. Traditionally, this matter is handled by authentication based on strong symmetric cryptography, which makes shared secrets necessary in the standard setting. These shared secrets can, however, be replaced by assumptions on the availability of additional communication channels, similarly as in multipath communication. Indeed, by having the peers in a BB84 protocol embed pseudorandomness in their qubit stream, we can use out of band authentication in a straightforward form to secure a BB84 execution. Our treatment here so far does not account for measurement errors, say when a pseudorandom qubit goes lost (recovery from measurement errors may be easy upon simply discarding lost qubits from the check; at the cost of taking more pseudorandom bits accordingly). These would have to be discarded from both lists (Alice's and Bob's pseudorandom sequence) upon the checking of the authentication data. For the experiments, we discarded erroneously measured bits for simplicity.

As the experimental evaluation showed, there was no noticeable difference between an authenticated and a non-authenticated BB84 qubit stream in the first phases. However, our variant of BB84 detects person-in-the-middle attacks at a much earlier stage than competing schemes, which do that along the public discussion phase. Thus, efficiency is also gained by earlier termination of the protocol. The most important aspect of our proposed variant is the avoidance of pre-shared secrets, however, which technically turns BB84 from quantum key *growing* into quantum key *establishment*.

References

[1] S. Rass, S. König, and S. Schauer, "Bb84 quantum key distribution with intrinsic authentication," in Proc. of Ninth International Conference on Quantum, Nano/Bio, and Micro Technologies (ICQNM), 2015, pp. 41–44.

[2] D. R. Stinson, "Universal hashing and authentication codes," in CRYPTO '91: Proceedings of the 11th Annual International Cryptology Conference on Advances in Cryptology. London, UK: Springer, 1992, pp. 74–85.

[3] G. Gilbert and M. Hamrick, "Practical quantum cryptography: A comprehensive analysis (part one)," 2000, (last accessed: June, 2015). [Online]. Available: http://arxiv.org/abs/quant-ph/0009027

[4] C. Bennett and G. Brassard, "Public key distribution and coin tossing," in IEEE International Conference on Computers, Systems, and Signal Processing. Los Alamitos: IEEE Press, 1984, pp. 175–179.

[5] F. M. Assis, A. Stojanovic, P. Mateus, and Y. Omar, "Improving Classical Authentication over a Quantum Channel," Entropy, vol. 14, no. 12, 2012, pp. 2531–2549.

[6] N. Nagy and S. G. Akl, "Authenticated quanntum key distribution without classical communication," Parallel Processing Letters, vol. 17, no. 03, 2007, pp. 323–335.

[7] H. Barnum, C. Crepeau, D. Gottesman, A. Smith, and A. Tapp, "Authentication of Quantum Messages," in Proceedings of the 43rd Annual IEEE Symposium on the Foundations of Computer Science (FOCS'02). IEEE Press, 2002, pp. 449–458.

[8] M. Dušek, O. Haderka, M. Hendrych, and R. Myska, "Quantum Identification System," Phys. Rev. A, vol. 60, no. 1, 1999, pp. 149–156.

[9] Y. Chang, C. Xu, S. Zhang, and L. Yan, "Controlled quantum secure direct communication and authentication protocol based on five-particle cluster state and quantum one-time pad," Chinese Science Bulletin, vol. 59, no. 21, 2014, pp. 2541–2546. [Online]. Available: http://dx.doi.org/10.1007/s11434-014-0339-x

[10] T. Hwang, Y.-P. Luo, C.-W. Yang, and T.-H. Lin, "Quantum authencryption: one-step authenticated quantum secure direct communications for off-line communicants," Quantum Information Processing, vol. 13, no. 4, 2014, pp. 925–933. [Online]. Available: http://dx.doi.org/10.1007/s11128-013-0702-x

[11] J. G. Jensen and R. Schack, "Quantum Authentication and Key Distribution using Catalysis," quant-ph/0003104 v3, 2000, (last accessed: June, 2015). [Online]. Available: http://arxiv.org/abs/quant-ph/0003104

[12] H. N. Barnum, "Quantum Secure Identification using Entanglement and Catalysis," quant-ph/9910072 v1, 1999, (last accessed: June, 2015). [Online]. Available: http://arxiv.org/abs/quant-ph/9910072

[13] Y.-S. Zhang, C.-F. Li, and G.-C. Guo, "Quantum Authentication using Entangled State," quant-ph/0008044 v2, 2000, (last accessed: June, 2015). [Online]. Available: http://arxiv.org/abs/quant-ph/0008044

[14] M. Curty and D. J. Santos, "Quantum Authentication of Classical Messages," Phys. Rev. A, vol. 64, no. 6, 2001, p. 062309.

[15] Y. Chang, S. Zhang, J. Li, and L. Yan, "Robust EPR-pairs-based quantum secure communication with authentication resisting collective noise," Science China Physics, Mechanics & Astronomy, vol. 57, no. 10, 2014, pp. 1907–1912. [Online]. Available: http://dx.doi.org/10.1007/s11433-014-5434-0

[16] T.-Y. Ye, "Fault-tolerant authenticated quantum dialogue using logical bell states," Quantum Information Processing, vol. 14, no. 9, 2015, pp. 3499–3514. [Online]. Available: http://dx.doi.org/10.1007/s11128-015-1040-y

[17] W.-M. Shi, J.-B. Zhang, Y.-H. Zhou, and Y.-G. Yang, "A novel quantum deniable authentication protocol without entanglement," Quantum Information Processing, vol. 14, no. 6, 2015, pp. 2183–2193. [Online]. Available: http://dx.doi.org/10.1007/s11128-015-0994-0

[18] J. Bell, "On the Einstein Podolsky Rosen Paradox," Physics, vol. 1, 1964, pp. 403–408.

[19] J. F. Clauser, M. A. Horne, A. Shimony, and R. A. Holt, "Proposed Experiment to Test Local Hidden-Variable Theories," Phys. Rev. Lett., vol. 23, no. 15, 1969, pp. 880–884.

[20] A. Ekert, "Quantum Cryptography Based on Bell's Theorem," Phys. Rev. Lett., vol. 67, no. 6, 1991, pp. 661–663.

[21] G. L. Long and X. S. Liu, "Theoretically efficient high-capacity quantum-key-distribution scheme," Phys. Rev. A, vol. 65, Feb 2002, p. 032302. [Online]. Available: http://link.aps.org/doi/10.1103/PhysRevA.65.032302

[22] C. H. Bennett, "Quantum Cryptography using any Two Nonorthogonal States," Phys. Rev. Lett., vol. 68, no. 21, 1992, pp. 3121–3124.

[23] D. Bruss, "Optimal Eavesdropping in Quantum Cryptography with Six States," Phys. Rev. Lett, vol. 81, no. 14, 1998, pp. 3018–3021.

[24] C. H. Bennett, G. Brassard, and N. D. Mermin, "Quantum Cryptography without Bell's Theorem," Phys. Rev. Lett., vol. 68, no. 5, 1992, pp. 557–559.

[25] V. Scarani, A. Acin, G. Ribordy, and N. Gisin, "Quantum Cryptography Protocols Robust Against Photon Number Splitting Attacks for Weak Laser Pulses Implementations," Phy. Rev. Lett., vol. 92, no. 5, 2004, p. 057901.

[26] B. Huttner and A. Ekert, "Information Gain in Quantum Eavesdropping," J. Mod. Opt., vol. 41, no. 12, 1994, pp. 2455–2466.

[27] C. H. Bennett, F. Bessette, G. Brassard, L. Salvail, and J. Smolin, "Experimental Quantum Cryptography," J. Crypt., vol. 5, no. 1, 1992, pp. 3–28.

[28] C. H. Bennett, G. Brassard, and J. M. Robert, "Privacy Amplification by Public Discussion," SIAM Journal of Computing, vol. 17, no. 2, 1988, pp. 210–229.

[29] M. N. Wegman and J. L. Carter, "New Hash Functions and their Use in Authentication and Set Equality," Journal of Computer and System Science, vol. 22, 1981, pp. 265–279.

[30] T. Tsurumaru and M. Hayashi, "Dual Universality of Hash Functions and Its Applications to Quantum Cryptography," IEEE Transactions on Information Theory, vol. 59, no. 7, 2013, pp. 4700–4717.

[31] P. Shor and J. Preskill, "Simple Proof of Security of the BB84 Quantum Key Distribution Protocol," Phys. Rev. Lett., vol. 85, no. 2, 2000, pp. 441–444.

[32] R. Renner, "Security of quantum key distribution," Ph.D. dissertation, Dipl. Phys. ETH, Zurich, Switzerland, 2005.

[33] A. Peres, "How to Differentiate Between Non-orthogonal States," Phys. Lett. A, vol. 128, no. 1-2, 1988, p. 19.

[34] M. Fitzi, M. K. Franklin, J. Garay, and S. H. Vardhan, "Towards optimal and efficient perfectly secure message transmission," in 4th Theory of Cryptography Conference (TCC), ser. Lecture Notes in Computer Science LNCS 4392, S. Vadhan, Ed. Springer, 2007, pp. 311–322.

[35] H. Han, S. Shakkottai, C. V. Hollot, R. Srikant, and D. Towsley, "Multi-path TCP: a joint congestion control and routing scheme to exploit path diversity in the internet," IEEE/ACM Trans. Netw., vol. 14, December 2006, pp. 1260–1271.

[36] M. Hayashi and T. Tsurumaru, "More efficient privacy amplification with less random seeds via dual universal hash function," vol. 62, 2016, pp. 2213–2232.

[37] W. D. Smith, "Tail bound for sums of bounded random variables," scorevoting.net/WarrenSmithPages/homepage/imphoeff.ps, April 2005, (last accessed: June, 2015).

[38] C. Pacher and O. Maurhart, "AIT QKD R10 Software," 2015, https://sqt.ait.ac.at/software/projects/qkd, (last accessed: Feb.23, 2016).

[39] T. Johansson, G. Kabatianskii, and B. Smeets, "On the relation between A-Codes and codes correcting independent errors," in Advances in Crypology (EuroCrypt), ser. LNCS 765, T. Helleseth, Ed. Berlin Heidelberg: Springer, 1994, pp. 1–11.

[40] Austrian Institute of Technology, "QKD-Telco – practical quantum key distribution over telecom-infrastructures," 2015, http://www.qkd-telco.at/, (last accessed: Feb.23, 2016).

Practical Use Case Evaluation of a Generic ICT Meta-Risk Model Implemented with Graph Database Technology

Stefan Schiebeck, Martin Latzenhofer, Brigitte Palensky, Stefan Schauer
Digital Safety & Security
Austrian Institute of Technology
Vienna, Austria
e-mail: {stefan.schiebeck.fl | martin.latzenhofer | brigitte.palensky | stefan.schauer}@ait.ac.at

Gerald Quirchmayr
Research Group Multimedia Information Systems
Faculty of Computer Science
University of Vienna
Vienna, Austria
e-mail: gerald.quirchmayr@univie.ac.at

Thomas Benesch
Research & Development
s-benesch
Vienna Austria
e-mail: thom@s-benesch.com

Johannes Göllner, Christian Meurers, Ingo Mayr
Department of Central Documentation & Information
National Defence Academy of the Austrian Federal Ministry of Defence and Sports, Vienna, Austria
e-mail: {johannes.goellner | christian.meurers | ingo.mayr}@bmlvs.gv.at

***Abstract*— Advanced Persistent Threats impose an increasing threat on today's information and communication technology infrastructure. These highly-sophisticated attacks overcome the typical perimeter protection mechanisms of an organization and generate a large amount of damage. In this article, we introduce a generic ICT meta-risk model implemented using graph databases. Due to its generic nature, the meta-risk model can be applied on both the complex case of an APT attack as well as on a conventional physical attack on an information security management system. Further, we will provide details for the implementation of the meta-risk model using graph databases. The major benefits of this graph database approach, i.e., the simple representation of the interconnected risk model as a graph and the availability of efficient traversals over complex sections of the graph, are illustrated giving several examples.**

Keywords*— *risk management; APT; ICT security; physical security; graph databases; interconnected risk model.

I. INTRODUCTION

Based on a practical use case of a real-life Advanced Persistent Threat (APT) lifecycle, we showed in a recent article [1] how this type of attack can be tackled by a generic information and communication technology (ICT) meta-risk model using graph databases. In the present article, we will extend our preliminary work and show how the meta-risk model can be applied in a different context, i.e., a physical attack scenario.

Although internal attacks can be seen as today's biggest threat on information security [2], in practice, information security officers still put great emphasis on perimeter control. The internal area of a company's ICT network, e.g., the demilitarized zone (DMZ) or the intranet, is secured based on standard technical guidelines demanding, e.g., the logical separation of a network into subnetworks according to specific security requirements [3]. Nevertheless, the effort invested in monitoring the internal network is moderate. Intrusion detection and prevention systems are cost and time consuming and require a large amount of administration. Recent attack strategies like APTs take advantage of this lack of internal control.

The term APT summarizes a family of highly sophisticated attacks on an ICT network or infrastructure. Usually, an APT runs over an extended period of time with the objective to steal data and maintain presence indefinitely without being detected. A continuous access allows collecting new data as it emerges, extending the achieved foothold over time, and using the site as a jumping point for the attack on other facilities. The adversary – usually a group of people – has a large amount of resources at hand and applies the whole range of digital, physical and social attack vectors to gain access to a system. The attack is specifically designed for a particular victim, i.e., a company or an organization, such that common security measures can be circumvented effectively. Thus, the adversary stays undetected over a long period of time. One particular technique recurrently used in APTs is social engineering, which exploits the human factor as a major vulnerability of an ICT system. Potential countermeasures, like increasing the staff's awareness concerning ICT security threats via training courses, are not very common. According to a Ponemon study [4], about 52% of the interviewed organizations do not offer respective training courses for their employees.

In the course of the last decade, APTs became one of the most significant kinds of threats on information security, causing a great number of security incidents all over the world [5]. Besides the most prominent APT attack, the application of the malware Stuxnet in an Iranian nuclear power plant, a number of other APT attacks have become known, e.g., Operation Aurora, Shady Rat, Red October or MiniDuke [6][7][8]. As it is shown in the Mandiant Report [5], some adversaries even have a close connection to governmental organizations. The former director of the US cyber command, General Keith Alexander, referred to the currently occurring industrial espionage and theft of intellectual property as "the greatest transfer of wealth in history" [9]. In Europe, the disclosures of Edward Snowden [10] have drawn great attention to this issue. Based on current numbers from cyber-crime reports, which show the growing amount of damage [11][12], it is distressing how poorly evolved today's countermeasures seem to be.

This article focuses on the implementation of a generic ICT meta-risk model that can deal both with the described issues and can be applied on conventional ICT security use cases as well – e.g., a physical attack on a building with the aim to gain access to some information. The implementation of the meta-risk model is based on graph databases and social network analysis concepts to provide a perspective that can focus on a specific aspect (node) and its influences (relationships). From a technological perspective, the advantages of the chosen approach are demonstrated, in particular concerning aggregation of exposures, risks, etc.. Therefore, different types of assets, e.g., organizational aspects like processes and personnel, ICT components like IT systems and logical networks, and physical infrastructure objects, serve as examples of assets that are attacked in fictitious, but realistic ways.

In detail, after a short overview of related work on graph-based models in Section II, Section III sketches the different steps of an APT attack for a fictitious scenario to illustrate the basic principles of this family of threats. Section IV introduces the theoretical background and the development of the generic ICT meta-risk model depicted as a graph model. The subsequent Section V shortly discusses the pros and cons of an implementation via graph databases vs. relational databases. Sections VI and VII show the modeling of the two use cases introduced in this article, the APT and the physical attack scenario. Section VIII provides a detailed description of how the generic risk model is implemented using a graph database. Finally, Section IX summarizes the results.

II.□ RELATED WORK

Whereas the internationally widely spread ISO 31000 standard [13] provides generic guidelines for the design, implementation and maintenance of risk management processes throughout an organization, the ISO/IEC 27005 standard [14] specifically focuses on information security risk management. In [15], this standard is taken as a basis and extended by the introduction of iteratively calculated management measures, indicators and expert knowledge, as well as the possibility to integrate sensors for automation purposes. The resulting continuous information security risk management model (cf. Figure 1) is also demonstrated and verified by a prototype and provides a framework for extendable sensors. This framework can be used to continuously gather security relevant attributes having a high impact on the overall model, derive security metrics and indicators based on ISO/IEC 27004 [16] and enable adaptable knowledge management approaches to infer risk factors of a risk assessment model. In the KIRAS project MetaRisk [17], the approach of [15] is connected with meta-models for organization planning and control to derive a comprehensive enterprise risk management system referred to as meta-risk model. Additionally, a graph-based implementation has been introduced, which allows the visualization and semi-heuristic handling of complex relationships in a schema-free form.

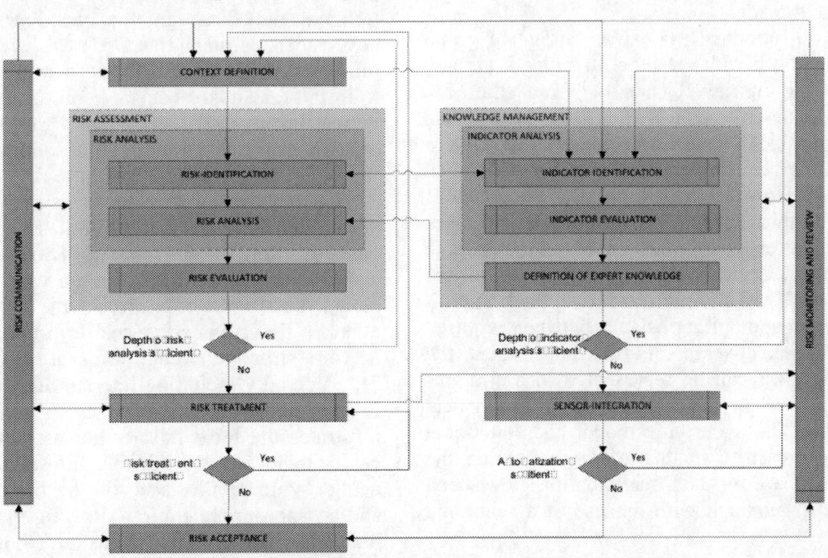

Figure 1. Extended ISO/UEC 27005 risk management process.

In general, graph-based models are used to capture relations among system entities at various abstraction levels. In [18], Chartis Research advises the introduction of graph analytics (based on graph databases) to the risk management activities of financial institutions so that they can discover so far unknown risks by revealing interconnected risk patterns. In [19], graph-based representations are applied in the area of risk management for critical infrastructures (CI). Bayesian Networks are used to learn (or simply estimate) CI service risks and their interdependencies. Additionally, a risk prediction is introduced and a case study to validate the model is carried out. However, some of the model's features, like risk prediction and the handling of cyclic dependencies, could not be verified because they simply did not occur during the run-time of the case study. In contrast to the work presented in this article, the main goal of the approach in [19] is to identify an abstract set of variables and their dependencies based on system measurements and it is for this purpose that graph-based representations are introduced. The direct use of graph databases is not foreseen or discussed in [19].

The continuous risk management process depicted in Figure 1 essentially consists of four main steps, which are performed iteratively (cf. in particular with the additional parts to the standard version on the right side of Figure 1 referred to as Knowledge Management). These steps are the business value analysis, the scenario analysis, the threat analysis and the relation analysis (further described in Section IV. All risk-relevant measures and events available within an organization can be integrated in the continuous risk assessment process by repetitively identifying these measures (categorized and compressed according to ISO/IEC 27004 [16]) and evaluating them with respect to indicators. The input of formally defined expert knowledge ensures a continuous update of the used risk factors and their corresponding indicators. The development and application of sensors for an ongoing collection of relevant data leads to a higher degree of automation.

In this article, we introduce the explicit usage of graph databases and combine it with the aforementioned, already existing risk scheme retrieved mainly from the IT-Grundschutz catalog described in [15]. This approach has initially been shown in [1] and is extended here with a conventional use case implementation for physical information security. However, many important extensions have been made to this scheme to derive a much more generic model. The presented approach enables a measurable iterative increase of the depth of the risk analysis on all the analysis levels as well as an improved risk treatment. It enables the setup of an appropriate balance between required effort and obtained risk coverage. Furthermore, using the approach, cascading risks can be represented in a straight-forward way that allows us to run easily through a typical APT attack scenario. The underlying model and functional assessment concept presented in this article, excluding the usage of a graph database for data manipulation, have been demonstrated in [20], although with the use of a relational database.

Before going into more detail on the description of the meta-risk model in Section IV and its implementation in Section V, we will present the general APT use case scenario we will rely our further discussion on.

III. APT SCENARIO

In [5], the US security company Mandiant describes the typical lifecycle of an APT attack based on an analysis of how a Chinese cyber espionage group infiltrated several companies in the US and worldwide. In the following, the different steps in this APT lifecycle are briefly sketched to give an overview on the basic operations of an APT attack (cf. Figure 2). To provide a better illustration of the scenario, a fictional research facility, *Biomedical Research,* is used. It consists of four research laboratories with increasing degrees of security requirements (*Biosafety Level 1-4*) located in physically separated buildings. Additionally, the research facility runs two data centers, one located in the research building itself, and the other, which works as a backup, located at a distant administrative building. The information most valuable for an attacker is assumed to be hosted in Research Laboratory FL4, which is the one with the highest security level, or in one of the data centers. Based on this setting, a generalized APT attack can be outlined in eight steps.

As a first step, *Initial Recon*, the adversary tries to gain access to the organization's ICT infrastructure. Since the terminals in Research Laboratory FL1 are the only ones having full connection to the internet, a user in FL1 would be a primary target for a spear phishing attack (cf. (1) in Figure 1) in order to place a remote backdoor on either of these terminals. A potential user to be attacked can be identified for example using social engineering. In the second step, *Initial Compromise*, a user in FL1 receives a spear phishing mail and opens the infected attached file (e.g., a ZIP-file). During the execution of the ZIP-file, a basic backdoor (beachhead backdoor, cf. (2) in Figure 2) is installed on the terminal W1. Through this backdoor, a connection to the adversary's command and control server is established. In a third step, *Establish Foothold*, this initial connection is used to install a standard backdoor on the compromised terminal, giving the adversary an increased set of possibilities. Hence, the adversary is able to gain foothold at the application server S1 in FL1 (cf. (4) in Figure 2).

The following four steps (steps 4 to 7) are usually performed more than once, until the adversary acquires the desired information. In step 4, *Escalate Privileges*, the adversary gathers information on valid combinations of user names and passwords inside the internal networks. The attacker also gains additional information about the internal network structure (step 5 – *Internal Recon* – cf. (5) in Figure 2), potentially including internal authentication information. In the following step 6, *Move Laterally*, the adversary infiltrates the local data center as well as the backup data center to locate the valuable information. This is achieved using a vulnerability scan on the file servers S7.1 and S7.2 and an appropriate exploit allowing the compromise of both identically configured systems (cf. (6) in Figure 2). As a final step of this recurrent loop, *Maintain Presence*, all tracks are covered up and the adversary silently stays in the victim's system with an extended foothold (cf. (7) in Figure 2).

The final step, *Complete Mission*, starts when all the target information is collected. Covert channels are established (e.g., using cryptography/steganography) to extract the sensitive information from the file servers (cf. (8) in Figure 2). Afterwards, all traces of the attack are erased.

IV. SETUP OF THE ICT META-RISK MODEL

The risk analysis process of the continuous information security risk management model presented in [15] (cf. Section II above) incorporating the knowledge management parts comprises of the following layers or steps:

- *business value analysis* for the systemic representation of all the assets that need to be protected,
- *scenario analysis* (optional) for the representation of high-level dependencies between assets,
- *threat analysis* (optional) for the specific modeling of low-level threat cascades,
- *relation analysis* (automatic) which delivers a combined risk overview over all the modeled scenarios for each asset.

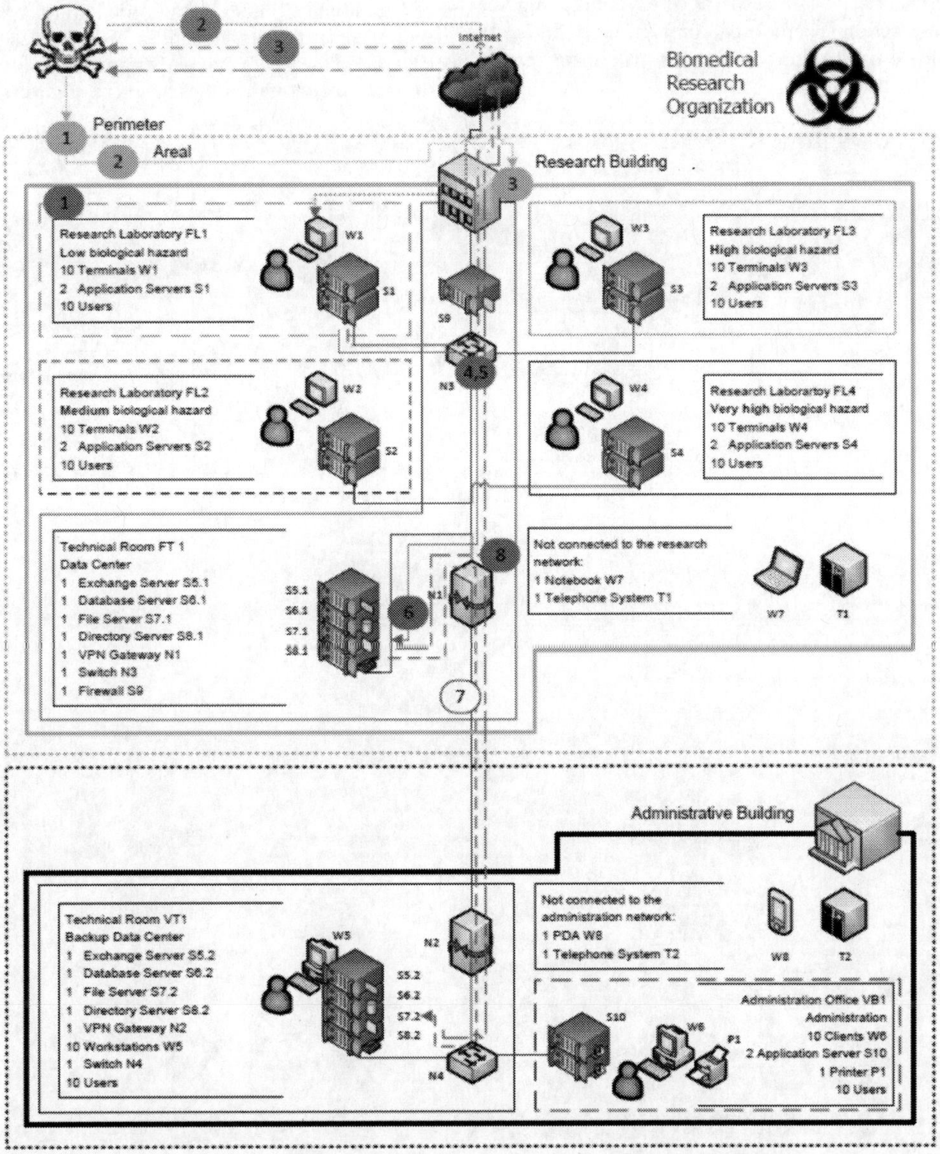

Figure 2. Sample scenarios: APT attack (red), physical security attack (blue).

The Business value, scenario and threat analysis can be modelled with iterative increase of modelling depth and detail, while the relation analysis automatically incorporates all asset instances modeled. So far, the implementation of the prototype of the proposed general model and thus also of the risk-analysis is largely based on the standards, catalogues and cross references from the BSI's IT-Grundschutz [15]. The advantage of using the IT-Grundschutz approach is that it delivers an extensive list of IT-related threats, which are already connected with assets, together with safeguards against these threats and roles that are responsible for planning and implementation of these safeguards. Although using it as a basis, our model extends the BSI approach in several aspects, e.g., concerning the view on the protection criteria (i.e., confidentiality, integrity and availability), or the introduction of risk management aspects. In the following, we will describe the four steps of the risk analysis process of our model (cf. also Figure 3).

A. *Business Value Analysis*

In the first step, all assets of an organization requiring protection have to be identified. This can be done, for example, using the IT-Grundschutz catalog. In this case, the business assets are represented by one or more modules from the IT-Grundschutz. In this context, standard assets are, for example, applications, IT-systems, networks, rooms, and buildings. Additionally, in more complex models also legal entities, organizational divisions, or processes can be taken into account by representing them in the form of modules. In any case, each module has several protection criteria (e.g., confidentiality, integrity, and availability) and is associated with various threats, which, in turn, are related to protection criteria on the one hand, and appropriate security measures to mitigate them on the other hand (cf. Figure 4).

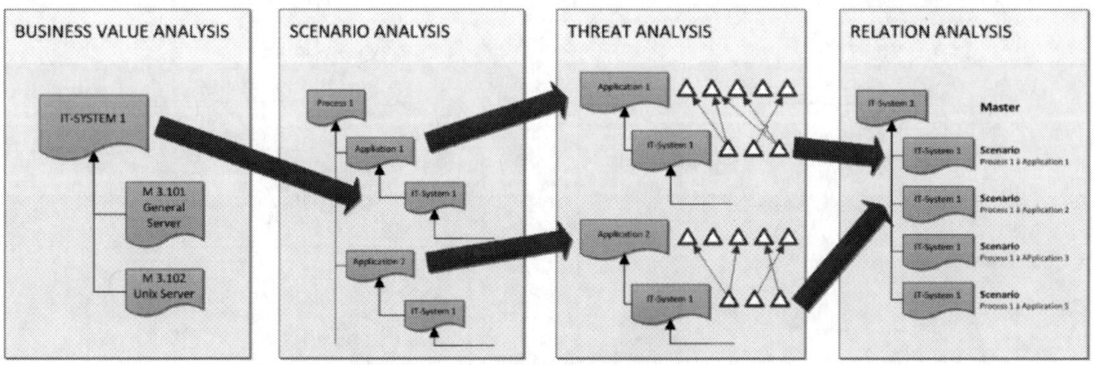

Figure 3. Analysis layers of the overall model.

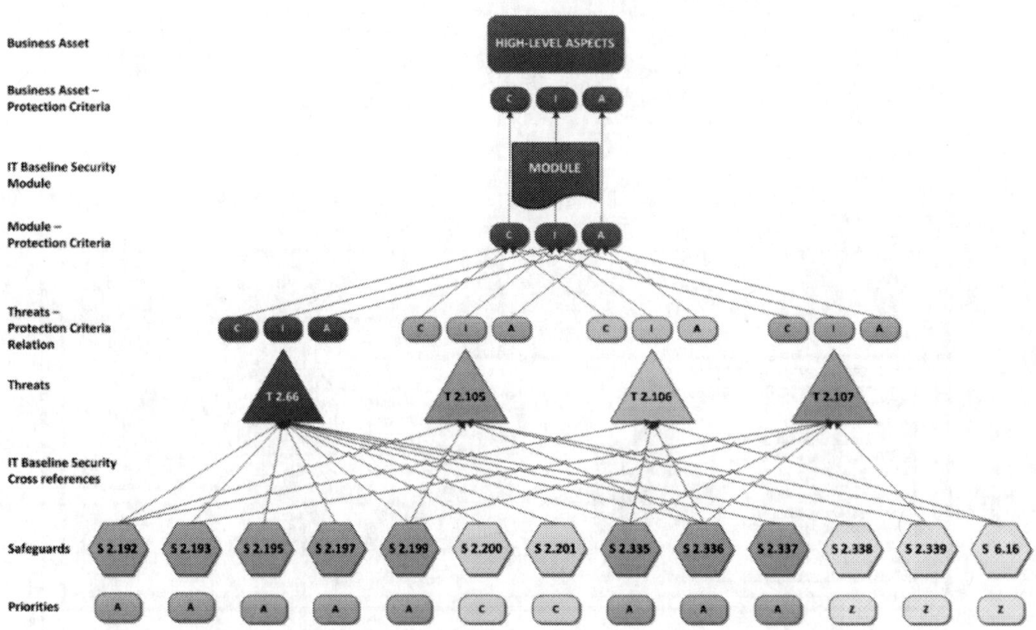

Figure 4. Business Asset Analysis.

The information contained in the interrelations between modules, threats, and security measures is used for the calculation of a value for the exposures of an asset. Thereby, the threat exposure is a function of the likelihood of an attack and the vulnerability of the threatened asset (which largely depends on the maturity levels of the related security measures). Higher level exposures (e.g., module exposure, asset exposure) are aggregated using generic estimation functions (e.g., maximum, sum, energetic sum, etc.). At the asset level, each protection criteria (e.g., confidentiality, integrity, availability, etc.) has an associated requirement level which corresponds with the maximum tolerable impact. By multiplication of protection criterion impact of an asset with its distinct exposure, , an asset risk value is obtained for this protection criterion (e.g., availability risk). An overall asset risk value can, for example, be estimated based on the sum of its protection criteria risks.

B. Scenario Analysis

In the scenario analysis [21], the identified business assets are connected with each other. This is done in a structural way, starting from high-level assets (e.g., legal entities or business processes) and going down to more and more specific assets they depend on (e.g., applications, IT systems and networks, buildings and personnel) (cf. Figure 5). Based on the determined dependencies between assets the necessary risk inheritance functions between assets can be set up. Moreover, with the obtained structural knowledge, a business impact analysis [22] can be carried out to identify the protection criteria requirements of each of the assets in various scenarios. In the course of the business impact analysis, a choice of inheritance functions for the protection criteria associated with assets also takes place.

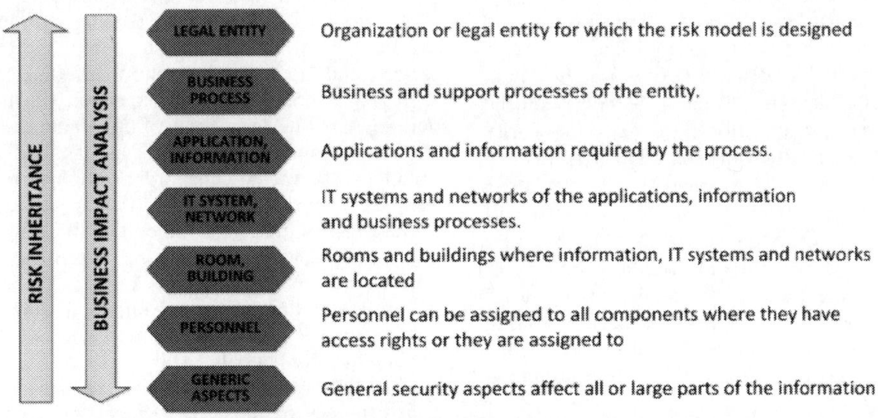

Figure 5. Generalized structure of a scenario analysis.

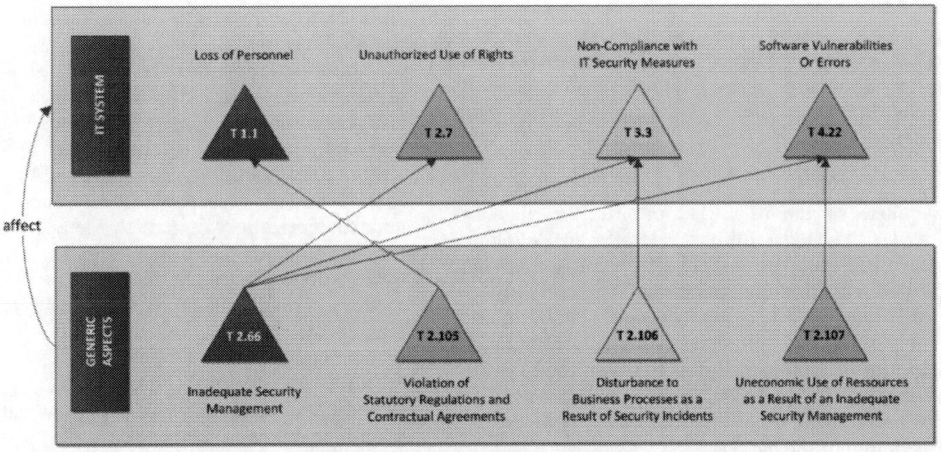

Figure 6. Representation of threat cascades.

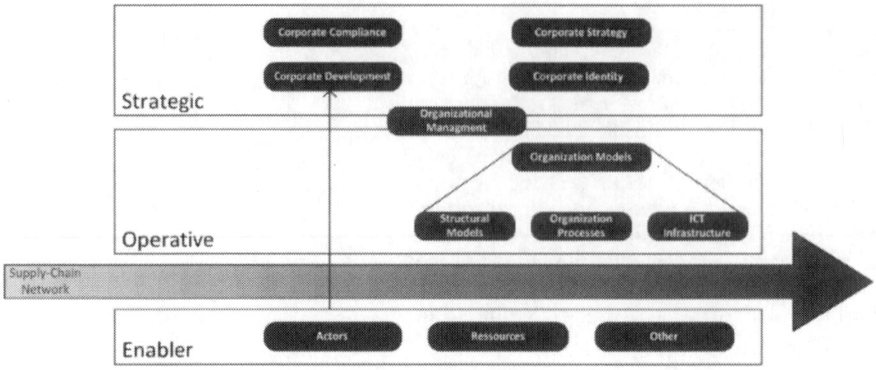

Figure 7. Meta-model of an organization [23].

C. *Threat Analysis*

Building on the aforementioned structural relations describing the risk inheritance between different business assets, a representation of how different threats affect each other can be obtained. Figure 6 schematically presents several such threat cascades between two assets. In detail, the first asset is an ICT system ("Generic Server") and the second one is an organizational entity ("Security Management") [24]. From this representation it is easy to see that an "Inadequate Security Management" (T2.66) can lead to several other threats, i.e., "Unauthorized Use of Rights" (T2.7), "Non-Compliance with IT Security Measures" (T3.3), and "Software Vulnerabilities or Errors" (T4.22). By iteratively extending the model of low-level threat cascades between the assets connected during scenario analysis, the estimation model gains knowledge about adapted threat exposures based on required threat predecessors.

D. *Relation Analysis*

As a final step, to get an estimation of the threat exposure per asset additionally to the scenario-based threat picture, all the risk carrying scenarios that affect a specific asset are aggregated. Further, the protection criteria values coming from the various scenarios are combined per asset. The negative effects of unwanted events on the protection criteria of an asset are a measure of their impact on that asset. By combining the threat exposure with the impact, a risk value can be calculated.

E. *ICT Meta-Risk Model*

In the course of the MetaRisk project, the approach described above has been further extended to develop a comprehensive ICT meta-risk model. Derived in a combined bottom-up/top-down way, this generic ICT meta-risk model subsumes all the typical components of common risk management models, tools, processes, and control logic. Its central component is a meta-model of an organization, which aims at describing an organization in a holistic way (cf. Figure 7 for a schematic representation and [23] for a more detailed description of the model).

This meta-model of an organization builds upon three layers: a strategic layer, an operative layer, and a layer that subsumes the enablers of the organization. It also includes the organization's supply chain network. On the strategic level, the overall strategy of the organization is described, together with the corporate compliance, the corporate identity and the development of the organization. These four topics influence the risk management on the highest level, defining the long-term goals of the organization.

On the operative layer, more detailed models can be found. These include the organization's structural models, i.e., the general setup of the organization, including buildings, machines and other tangible objects, as well as process models describing the activities and day-to-day business of the organization. A special focus is laid on the ICT infrastructure of the organization, since it represents a core feature of every organization and is crucial to achieve the organization's goals.

The third layer describes the enablers, i.e., all the actors and resources required to perform the organization's daily business. In this context, actors are usually divided into several groups and types of actors, often specific to the underlying organization, together with their respective roles according to knowledge management. The enablers have to be seen as key factors in the overall risk management process since they can represent threats, targets, and safeguards (i.e., mitigation actions).

Starting from the described generic model of an organization, several standard processes and frameworks for risk assessment and risk management are combined in a bottom-up approach to derive the ICT meta-risk model. Therein, the plan-do-check-act (PDCA) cycle defined in the ISO 31000 [13] represents the reference for the basic process and categorization model. A detailed analysis of several further standards and frameworks has shown that the PDCA cycle works as a robust basis for their integration. Generic modelling requirements outlined in ISO 31000, ISO 27000, ISO 28000 and, e.g., OCTAVE have been used to perform completeness checks on the ICT meta-risk model. Furthermore, several frameworks, primarily the IT-Grundschutz catalogues, COBIT 5 as well as the respective control mappings and goal cascade information, have been integrated as modelling catalogs.

The resulting ICT meta-risk model (cf. Figure 8) can be represented by a graph. It integrates all information required for the modeling and computation of risk objects within an organization. The intended purpose of the generic graph-based ICT meta-risk model is to provide an easy-to-extend and schema-less representation with the ability to interrelate different types of nodes and to aggregate information across affected relationships.

V. Prototype Implementations

In the following, we will describe the implementation details of the ICT meta-risk model in graph databases. The underlying approach covers semi-quantitative analysis steps usually used within risk models applying ISO 27005 [14]. We focus on the interconnections in the graph-based meta-model (cf. Figure 8), their representation in the graph database, and the relation to the implementation of the APT attack scenario and the physical attack scenario therein.

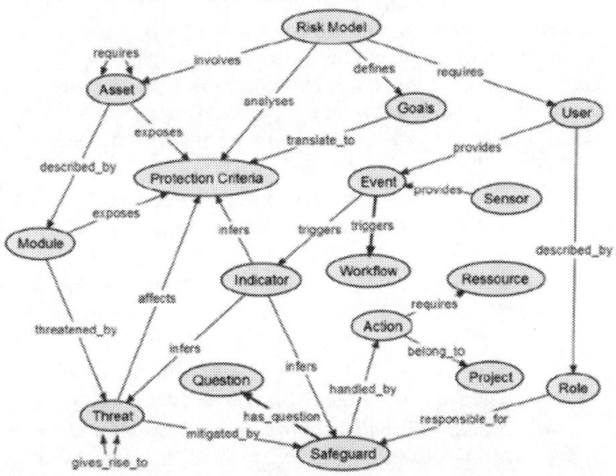

Figure 8. Graph-based meta-risk-model.

A. Graph Databases

In this work, as architectural background for the implementation of the model, the graph database Neo4j [25] is used instead of a relational database. Graph databases provide the advantage of being able to perform near-real-time traversals and aggregations, efficient topology analyses, and the optimal finding of node neighbors [26]. The retrieval time of graph databases is usually significantly less than that of relational databases [27][28]. Moreover, the graph-based implementation ensures more flexibility for defining relationships between datasets. Whereas relational databases are difficult to extend, in graph databases only a few edges and nodes have to be added to extend the graph. Thus, the adaption and extension capabilities of the generic ICT meta-risk model are supported by the schema-less definition of data in graph databases. For instance, additional information on customer and competitor intelligence, responsibilities, or other quantifiable business data can be easily integrated in the database schema. When using Neo4j, the integrated declarative query language CYPHER [25] supports most of the work. Thus, analysis models with extended and adapted functionality are greatly simplified and the graph-based approach is more efficient than business code migration on the software backend.

In situations, where the data set is quite homogenous and rarely changed, other architectural designs, like relational databases or in-memory databases, may be more appropriate. They also offer more support as well as advantages in the field of maturity. Regarding security, MySQL has an extensive security support based on access control lists. In contrast, graph databases like Neo4j expect a trusted environment.

B. Graph-based ICT Meta-Risk Model

The starting point for the graph-based ICT meta-risk model is the node *Risk Model*. This risk model contains narrative information on the scope of the risk analysis, the goals as well as its requirements. Each risk model has several goals relevant for the analysis attached to it (*Risk Model defines Goals*). For the categorization of these goals we will use the taxonomy coming from the IT-Grundschutz. In detail, the following categories are distinguished:

- *Modules*: applications, IT systems, networks, infrastructure, high-level aspects, etc.
- *Threats*: elementary risks, force majeure, organizational deficiencies, human failure, technical failure, intentional actions, etc.
- *Safeguards*: infrastructure, hard- and software, emergency planning, organization personnel, communication, etc.

The integration of several frameworks into the ICT meta-risk model allows us to use the taxonomy of COBIT 5.0 and to deduce COBIT-specific goals, e.g., stakeholder needs, enterprise goals, IT-related goals. These goals correlate to the exposure of the components in the risk model and therefore affect the relevant protection criteria, e.g., confidentiality, integrity, availability (*Goals translate_to Protection Criteria*). Furthermore, the ICT meta-risk model also allows evaluating these protection criteria separately (*Risk Model analyses Protection Criteria*).

Users can be associated to the risk model (*Risk Model requires User*) in specific roles (*User described_by Role*) regarding the planning, implementation, and audit of required safeguards (*Role responsible_for Safeguard*). Users as well as automatable sensors using pre-aggregated data from external support systems (e.g., security information management solutions or security incident and event management (SIEM) systems) can provide measurements and events to the framework (*User/Sensor provides Event*). Events can be used to trigger workflows (*Event triggers Workflow*), e.g., when a new IT system is detected. The framework also provides a possible inference option between objective measurements and related subjective risk factors using fuzzy indicators (*Event triggers Indicator*) and an expert knowledge system. There might be the following interferences:

- Protection criteria (*Indicator infers Protection Criteria*) meaning that the indicators refer to the estimated damage

- Threats (*Indicator infers Threat*) meaning that the indicators refer to probabilities of occurrence
- Safeguards (*Indicator infers Safeguard*) meaning that the indicators refer to the exploitation potential of vulnerabilities.

In context of some events it can be useful to trigger workflows (*Event triggers Workflow*), e.g., integrating new vulnerabilities of IT systems into the risk model, which were discovered during scans. In order to support basic risk management functionalities, safeguards can be summarized as organizational actions (*Safeguard handled_by Action*), which can be combined with resources, e.g., personnel, finance, etc. (*Action requires Resource*) or projects (*Action belong_to Project*). By integrating priorities, return on security investment models can be feed with the results from cost and availability information analyses.

Pre-existing information including goals, boundaries, and requirements are narratively documented within the nodes of the risk model. Risk identification is carried out by the definition of organizational assets (*Risk emergency planning,Model involves Asset*) that are depicted by modules (*Asset described_by Module*), threats (*Module threatened_by Threat*), safeguards (*Threat mitigated_by Safeguard*), and roles (already introduced: *Role responsible_for Safeguard*). Goals can be defined based on the usual protection criteria (confidentiality, integrity, availability), as well as on requirements derived from other taxonomies. IT-Grundschutz [15] defines a respective risk catalog, providing a categorization by module type (applications, IT systems, networks, infrastructure, common aspects), threat type (basic, force majeure, organizational shortcomings, human error, technical failure, deliberate acts), and safeguard type (infrastructure, organization, personnel, hardware and software, communications, contingency planning). Moreover, additional goals and requirements (e.g., stakeholder needs, enterprise goals, IT-related goals, etc.) coming from different frameworks like COBIT [29] can be integrated using cross-references with IT-Grundschutz. The defined goals correlate with the respective exposure of the components within the risk model, which translate to several risk dimensions *Risk Model analyses Protection Criteria*).

Risk estimation is based on the determination of safeguard maturities (supported by additional control questions, *Safeguard has_question Question*), threat likelihoods, and impacts on protection criteria. As a result of estimation, exposures are calculated for assets, modules, and threats separately (*Asset/Module exposes Protection Criteria; Threat affects Protection Criteria*) (cf. Section 0).

Assets can optionally be related to each other during scenario analysis in order to depict their dependencies (*Asset requires Asset*). This supports business impact analysis and the option to perform risk propagation between scenario assets. Another optional step is to perform a detailed threat analysis by modeling threat cascades [30] (*Threat gives_rise_to Threat*) based on the relationships of the pre-structured scenario model (*Asset requires Asset*).

VI. MODELING THE APT SCENARIO

In the following, the graph-based model of the APT use case scenario described in Section III is discussed in detail (cf. Figure 9). Assets (blue ovals) are modeled by *_requires_* dependencies, which can be identified by a scenario analysis. The resulting structure defines the top-down inheritance between sub-systems and, at the same time, serves as default path for potential bottom-up threat cascades (*_gives rise to_*). Assets are connected to IT-Grundschutz modules (yellow hexagons) [15], where the referring relation is *described_by*. Threats (red trapezia) are linked to assets by *threatened_by* relations and associated with security measures (green rectangles) by *mitigated_by* relations. For the purpose of a detailed analysis, available threats can be combined to threat cascades via *gives_rise_to* relations. The business impact analysis model (*described_by*) and the IT-Grundschutz taxonomy itself indicate how these cascading paths might look like. This approach of modeling cascades might not address all of the potentially existing correlations, but it provides an easy way of dealing with chained probabilities.

When looking in detail at the APT attack scenario as described in Section III, we see that initially a user opens a spear phishing mail at the Terminal W1 (*Module M 3.201 General client*). This is an exploitation of the organizational threat *T 3.3 Non-compliance with IT security measures*, which is connected with the following security measures:

- *S 2.23 Issue of PC Use Guidelines*
- *S 4.3 Use of virus Protection Programs*
- *S 4.41 Use of appropriate security products for IT systems*

Afterwards, at the corresponding terminal server S1 (*Module M 3.305 Terminal servers*) a standard backdoor is installed. This is possible because of the threat *T 2.36 Inappropriate restriction of user environment*, which could have been addressed by the following security measures:

- *S 2.464 Drawing up a security policy for the use of terminal servers*
- *S 4.365 Use of a terminal server as graphical firewall*
- *S 4.367 Secure use of client applications for terminal servers*

Having gained access to the Terminal server S1, a software vulnerability scan is performed, helping the attacker to exploit the threat *T 4.22 Software vulnerabilities or errors* at the File server S 7.1 and, later on, at the file server S 7.2 (*Module 3.109 Windows Server 2008*). In the analyzed use case, the following security measures were not properly implemented:

- *S 2.32 Establishment of a restricted user environment*
- *S 2.491 Use of roles and security templates under Windows Server 2008*
- *S 4.417 Patch Management with WSUS under Windows Server 2008 and higher*
- *S 4.419 Application control in Windows 7 and higher by means of AppLocker*

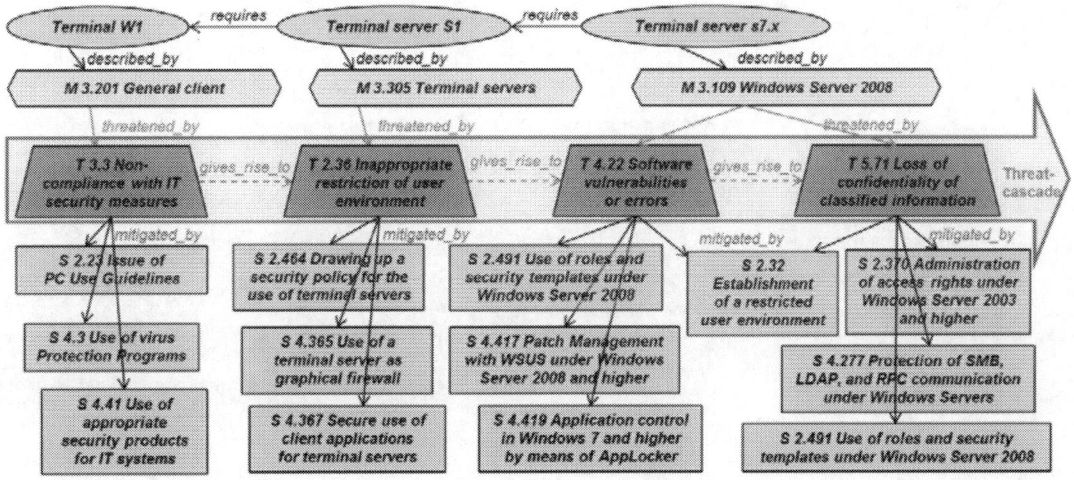

Figure 9. Graph-based illustration of the APT scenario.

At the same module, the follow-up threat *T 5.71 Loss of confidentiality of classified information* can be triggered, which is addressed by the following security measures:

- *S 2.32 Establishment of a restricted user environment*
- *S 2.370 Administration of access rights under Windows Server 2003 and higher*
- *S 2.491 Use of roles and security templates under Windows Server 2008*
- *S 4.277 Protection of SMB, LDAP, and RPC communication under Windows Servers*

In order to perform quantitative analyses, the risk inheritance between different components can be modeled by appropriate functions, e.g., maximum, sum, product, or minimum. More complex normalized, weighted, or bounded variants are also applicable. Possible candidates for the latter are weighted weakest link or prioritized sibling [20][31].

VII. Modeling the Physical Scenario

In this section, it is shown that in an analog way to the ATP attack example, the ICT meta-risk model can also be used to describe and evaluate a physical attack scenario. Therefore, the use case discussed below models a typical physical environment of an ICT infrastructure. This scenario is also depicted in Figure 2. A layered architecture is assumed, i.e., the relevant ICT infrastructure is located within a building, the building is located on the grounds of a company, and the company is protected by a specific perimeter.

A graph-based illustration of this scenario, similar to the one of the APT scenario in Figure 9, is given in Figure 10. Therein, the relevant assets are represented by blue ovals and modeled by *_requires_* dependencies. The associated modules (yellow hexagons) do not correspond to modules from the IT-Grundschutz anymore, but can still be treated as such by the ICT meta-risk model. Thus, each module is linked to threats (red trapezia) by the *_threatened_by_* relations, and threats themselves are linked to mitigation actions (green rectangles) using the *_mitigated_by_* relation.

In the physical security use case, just as in the APT use case, the ICT meta-risk model allows the representation of threat cascades using the *_gives_rise_to_* relations. Thus, the cascading effects of a threat as well as different attack variants affecting various assets (physical objects) can be modeled. Accordingly, not only the analysis of unrelated individual risks of single objects can be achieved but also that of threat cascades and the risks of whole attack chains.

As shown in Figure 10, an attacker who wants to enter a building has to overcome the perimeter protection first. This can be mitigated, for example, by the following safeguards:

- *Protection against climbing over* (e.g., using a barbed wire on top of a fence)
- *Patrols* (i.e., security guards walking around the area to spot trespassing

If no physical barrier is present, an attacker could simply *cross the perimeter* line. This could be mitigated for example by the security measures

- *Surveillance* (e.g., using CCTV cameras at the perimeter line)
- *Guard* (e.g., located at a gate to the area)

If the perimeter is not well-protected by these security measures, both above mentioned threats will give rise to the threat *Crossing the grounds.* To mitigate this threat, two possibilities are given

- *Identity badges*
- *Patrols* (as described above)

If an attacker can overcome the area around the building, there are several ways to enter it. Thus, the threat *Crossing the grounds* gives rise to five new threats, i.e.,

- *Unauthorized entry into building (via door)*
- *Break-in door*
- *Break-in ground floor*
- *Break-in upper floor*
- *Break in lower ground floor*

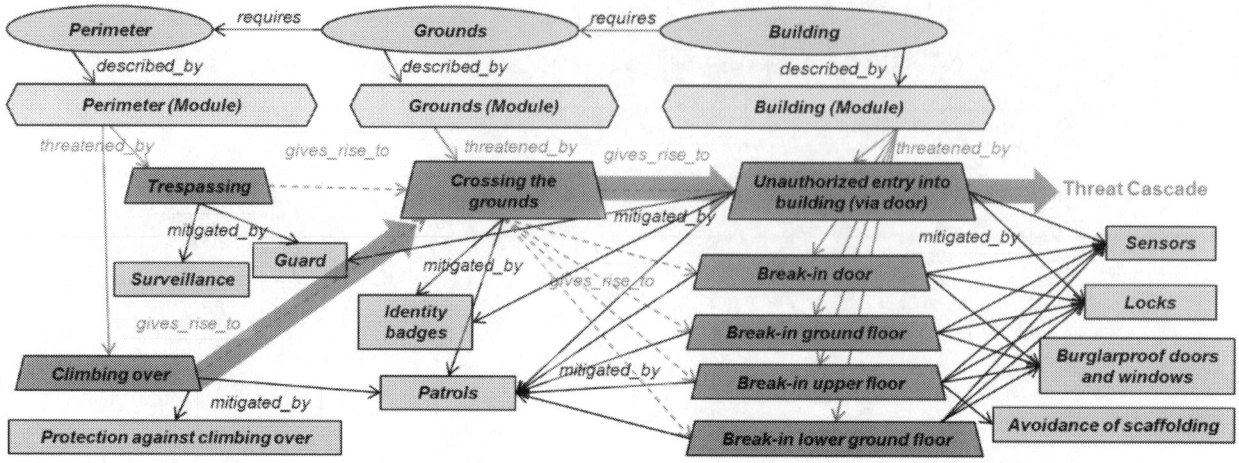

Figure 10. Graph-based model for the physical environment use case (excerpt).

For each of these threats, a number of safeguards are exemplarily given. One safeguard can be used to mitigate several of the above threats. For example, the safeguard Patrol is effective against all the threats. Other security measures could be

- *Sensors*
- *Locks*
- *Burglarproof doors and windows*
- *Avoidance of scaffolding*

Usually, the representation of the threatened objects (assets/modules, threats, safeguards) follows a risk inheritance model based on an instantiated structure similar to a fault tree. Such an implementation is based on master-scenario assets and the dependencies representation of the different branches of the attack tree is done as a nested set of a relational database. This approach described above is appropriate for the representation of different scenarios.

However, the physical scenario requires an individual definition and maintenance of the attack vectors, following separate paths for each variant. Consequently, such attack variants like trespassing/crossing the perimeter on the ground floor must be defined and maintained separately for the upper floors of the building.

To overcome this problem as well as to solve the basic requirement for a simple combination of risk information, the advantages of an implementation in a graph database (as described in Section V above), where nodes, relationships and attributes are provided, can be used. Additionally, the schema-less representation of a graph database simplifies extensions of the model. By applying graph operations, structures, traversals and aggregations can be easily extended as well. These advantages can only be achieved by switching to a representation within a graph database.

Based on the described threats within the physical security example and following the *_gives_rise_to_* relations of the ICT meta-risk model, the model will not only indicate one single but several potential threat cascades for the physical security use case (in Figure 10, we highlighted only one of them). Thus, due to the graph-based nature of the model, a large number of attack vectors can be described in a rather simple way. To compute a quantitative score for the risk analysis, the risk inheritance has to be modeled by appropriate functions (as already described in Section IV above).

VIII. RESULTS

In this section, it is demonstrated how the presented risk analysis approach can be used to derive (semi-)quantitative results (e.g., annualized loss expectancy (ALE) risk) based on semi-quantitative inputs (e.g., safeguard maturity levels according to the Capability Maturity Model Integration (CMMI) framework: 0.. Incomplete, 1.. Initial, 2.. Managed, etc.). By using graph databases as model environment, the writing of complex business code for risk estimation can be avoided by performing the required assessments using CYPHER statements.

The outlined risk estimation method is a simplified variant of the method defined in [20]. The general view is that vulnerabilities of assets can be exploited by threat sources resulting in negative impacts on protection criteria. Thus, for risk estimation, the vulnerabilities of assets are explicitly taken into account; however, instead of using them directly, they are substituted by maturity gaps of safeguards.

This results in risk as a function of the likelihood of the occurrence of a threat, the maturity gap of an associated safeguard, and the impact that the unwanted event has on protection criteria (cf. (1)).

$$R := f\,(T_{likelihood}, S_{maturity\ gap}, I_{protection\ criteria}) \qquad (1)$$

In an initial step, the safeguard requirements are derived from goals and estimated using maturity levels (from [0…5]). The product of the maturity gap (i.e., 1+maturity gap to evade division by zero) and the safeguard priority (from [1…4]) gives an estimation of the *safeguard exposure* (from [1…24]) (2). Additionally, the relation to the potential maximum exposure (based on the current goal definitions) is also calculated (cf. (3) (4) and Figure 11).

$$\textbf{\textit{safeguard exposure}} = (1+ \textit{maturity goal} - \textit{estimated maturity}) * \textit{safeguard priority} \tag{2}$$

$$\textbf{\textit{safeguard exposure max}} = (1+ \textit{maturity goal}) * \textit{safeguard priority} \tag{3}$$

$$\textbf{\textit{safeguard exposure \%}} = \textit{safeguard exposure} / \textit{safeguard exposure max}*100 \tag{4}$$

```
match (a:USE_CASE:Asset{name_de:'x'})
-[r1:described_by]->(b:USE_CASE:Module{name_de:'x'})
-[r2:threatened_by]->(c:USE_CASE:Threat)
-[r3:mitigated_by]->(d:USE_CASE:Safeguard)
with (1+r3.target_maturity-r3.maturity)*r3.priority as
  exposure, (1+r3.target_maturity)*r3.priority as
  exposure_max, r3
set r3.exposure = exposure
set r3.exposure_max = exposure_max
set r3.exposure_rel = r3.exposure/r3.exposure_max*100
return r3
```

Figure 11. Listing for the calculation of safeguard exposures.

After all safeguard exposures are calculated for each asset, the threat likelihoods are estimated for a specific timeframe (from [0…1], however, to simplify the CYPHER code, the null value is excluded to avoid a potential division by zero).

In a next step, the *threat exposures* are calculated. The threat exposure (from [0…20]) depends on the estimated likelihood (from [0…1]) and a function of its safeguard exposures (cf. (5)(6)(7) and Figure 12). For reasons of simplicity, here, the maximum function is used. In order to assess estimation variances, it may be appropriate to estimate the threat likelihood risk-averse (likelihood high) and risk-affine (likelihood low). Based on the calculation of current and potential maximum events, the risk factors within the model can be described either absolutely or relatively.

$$\textbf{\textit{threat exposure}} = \textit{likelihood(low)} * \textit{MAX(safeguard exposure)} \tag{5}$$

$$\textbf{\textit{threat exposure max}} = \textit{likelihood (high)} * \textit{MAX (safeguard exposure max)} \tag{6}$$

$$\textbf{\textit{threat exposure \%}} = \textit{threat exposure} / \textit{threat exposure max} * 100 \tag{7}$$

```
   match (a:USE_CASE:Asset{name_de:'x'})
   -[r1:described_by]-
>(b:USE_CASE:Module{name_de:'x'})-[r2:threatened_by]-
>(c:USE_CASE:Threat)
   -[r3:mitigated_by]->(d:USE_CASE:Safeguard)
with max(r3.exposure) as safeguard_exposure,
 max(r3.exposure_max) as safeguard_exposure_max, c
   set c.exposure = c.likelihood*safeguard_exposure
set c.exposure_max =
 c.likelihood*safeguard_exposure_max
   set c.exposure_rel = c.exposure/c.exposure_max*100
   return c
```

Figure 12. Listing for the calculation of threat exposures.

The threat exposures of all threats that have no incoming *gives_rise_to*-relationships are calculated first. The reason why the exposures of all uninfluenced threats are calculated initially is because no other threats have an effect on them (business impact analysis does not allow cyclic models).

After having calculated the threat exposures of all uninfluenced threats, the threat likelihood of all influenced threats (*gives_rise_to*-relations) can be updated based on the likelihood of their predecessors (chained likelihood). The calculation will be triggered as soon as all predecessors have been calculated. For reasons of simplicity, this is done by a simple multiplication of the original likelihood of the threat and the maximum of the likelihoods of its predecessors. Of course, a more complex function (weighting) representing the relative exposure of the threat to its influences can be used. In the following example (cf. Figure 13), the originally estimated likelihood of threat *'y'* is multiplied with the maximum of all its incoming *gives_rise_to*-likelihoods.

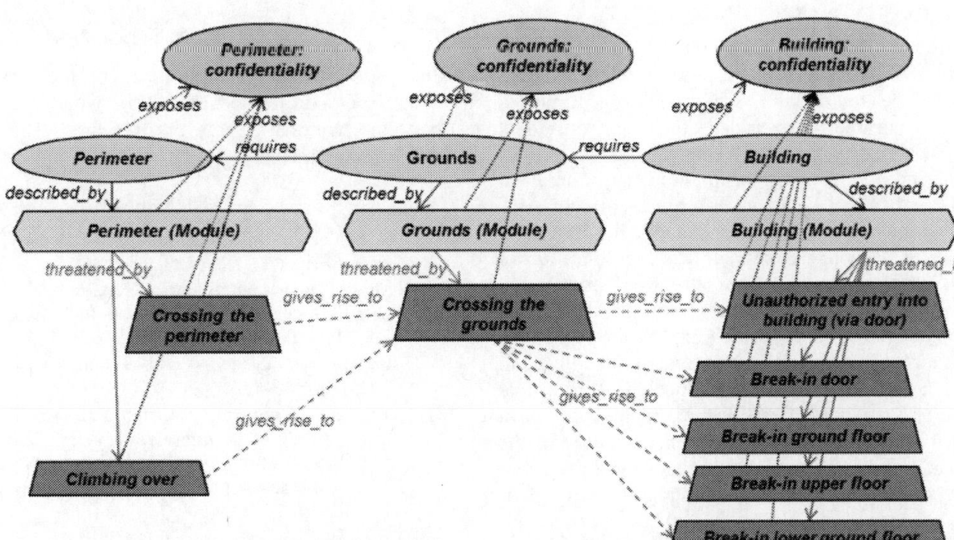

Figure 13. Possible aggregation of exposures on asset-specific protection criteria (here: confidentiality).

```
match (a:USE_CASE:Asset{name_de:'x'})
-[r1:described_by]->(b:USE_CASE:Module{name_de:'x'})
-[r2:threatened_by]->(c:USE_CASE:Threat)
-[r3:gives_rise_to]->(d:USE_CASE:Threat{name_de:
  'Threat y', module_id:2})
with max(c.likelihood) as trigger_likelihood,
  d.likelihood as original_likelihood, d
set d.original_likelihood = original_likelihood
set d. likelihood = d. likelihood *trigger_ likelihood
return d
```

Figure 14. Listing for the likelihood update of influenced threats.

After the likelihood update of all threats with incoming *gives_rise_to*-relations is finished, the remaining threat exposures can be calculated.

Depending on the desired level of detail, threats can be assessed individually or as generalized protection criteria related to assets (*asset exposures*), as illustrated in Figure 14. By extending the graph model, arbitrary aggregation layers can be defined. Here, to simplify the outlined use case, asset exposures are aggregated based on the maximum principle and risk is estimated based on the annualized loss expectancy (ALE) formula (cf. (8) and Figure 15). Again, additional lower and upper bounds could be integrated to express variance.

$$\textbf{\textit{asset risk}} = \textit{estimated impact} * \textit{MAX (threat exposure \% / 100)} \quad (8)$$

```
match (a:USE_CASE:Asset{name_de:'x'})
-[r1:described_by]->(b:USE_CASE:Module{name_de: 'x'})
-[r2:threatened_by]->(c:USE_CASE:Threat)
with max(c.exposure) as threat_exposure,
  max(c.exposure_max) as threat_exposure_max, a
set a.exposure = threat_exposure
set a.exposure_max = threat_exposure_max
set a.exposure_rel = a.exposure/a.exposure_max*100
set a.ale_risk = a.impact*a.exposure_rel/100
return a
```

Figure 15. Listing for the calculation of asset exposures and annualized loss expectancy (ALE) risks.

IX. CONCLUSION

This article describes how a generic ICT meta-risk model benefits from the qualities of a graph-based implementation, especially from the features of schema-less information, which can be parametrized based on the individual requirements of the organization, near-real-time traversals and flexible definitions of relationships between nodes, and the ability of easy model extension. A representative APT scenario is described to demonstrate a practical application of the presented ICT meta-risk model. The consideration of cascading risk effects, including human-based information system vulnerabilities, is a necessary prerequisite for an effective defense against APTs, which exploit the full range of attack vectors, from social over digital to physical. Consequently, a second use case introduced in this article illustrates an application of the ICT meta-risk model on a physical security attack. In general, the generic nature of the model allows addressing all kinds of threats - from the cyber over the physical to the business realm - and their dependencies.

The presented approach shows the application of a combination of several analysis steps and different parts of existing methods, e.g., morphological matrices, fault-tree- and event-tree-analysis, scenario analysis, threat analysis, system decomposition, and functional relationships [32]. The advantages of the presented combined approach are, for example, the possibility to focus on special requirements of information security and to cover a broader range of analysis depth and detail. These features cannot be achieved by using the previously mentioned methods on their own. The introduced scenarios are represented as a particular instance of a graph-based implementation of the generic ICT meta-risk model. The relevant risk components, which can be easily integrated into the graph-based ICT meta-risk model, are provided by widely-accepted ICT risk frameworks, most importantly by IT-Grundschutz. The defined relations between relevant risk components within this framework give an excellent starting point for possible paths that potential cascading risk effects might take.

From a technical point, for modeling and inference analysis of threat cascades, the graph-oriented database Neo4j with its query language CYPHER was used. Threat cascades and their relations can be visualized by graph databases in a more optimized way compared to relational databases. The schema-less data model of graph databases allows an easier adaption during the modeling process and the application of traversals to integrate calculations without modifications of the business code. However, with regard to the correctness of the results, the domain has to be specified and defined with a low level of uncertainty, and the level of detail of the risk factors has to correlate with the granularity of the results to guarantee a consistent distribution of risk values. Within the discussed use cases, uncertainty resulting from subjective assessments, or inconsistencies and errors in modeling depth is not dealt with explicitly. It can be addressed, like any other aspect, by introducing semi-quantitative descriptors (e.g., assessment uncertainty, etc.), which can be aggregated within the graph model similar to other variables.

ACKNOWLEDGEMENT

This work is party supported by the research project "MetaRisk" (Project-Nr. 840905), which is funded by the Austrian National Security Research Program KIRAS (http://www.kiras.at/).

REFERENCES

[1] S. Schiebeck, M. Latzenhofer, B. Palensky, S. Schauer, G. Quirchmayr, T. Benesch, J. Göllner, C. Meurers, and I. Mayr, "Implementation of a Generic ICT Risk Model using Graph Databases," presented at the SECURWARE 2015, 9th International Conference on Emerging Security Information, Systems and Technologies, Venice, Italy, 2015, pp. 146–153.

[2] T. W. Coleman, "Cybersecurity Threats Include Employees," *International Policy Digest*. [Online]. Available: http://www.internationalpolicydigest.org/2014/05/12/cybersecurity-threats-include-employees/. [Accessed: 19-Mar-2015].

[3] SANS Institute, "Critical Security Controls: Guidelines." [Online]. Available: http://www.sans.org/critical-security-controls/guidelines. [Accessed: 19-Mar-2015].

[4] Ponemon Institute, "Exposing the Cybersecurity Cracks: A Global Perspective Part 2: Roadblocks, Refresh and Raising the Human Security IQ," Traverse City, Michigan, USA, 2014.

[5] Mandiant Intelligence Center, "APT1. Exposing One of China's Cyber Espionage Units," Mandiant, Alexandria, Washington, DC, Feb. 2013.

[6] D. Moon, H. Im, J. Lee, and J. Park, "MLDS: Multi-Layer Defense System for Preventing Advanced Persistent Threats," *Symmetry*, vol. 6, no. 4, pp. 997–1010, Dec. 2014.

[7] C. Tankard, "Advanced Persistent threats and how to monitor and deter them," *Netw. Secur.*, vol. 2011, no. 8, pp. 16–19, Aug. 2011.

[8] I. Friedberg, F. Skopik, G. Settanni, and R. Fiedler, "Combating advanced persistent threats: From network event correlation to incident detection," *Comput. Secur.*, vol. 48, pp. 35–57, Feb. 2015.

[9] The Commission on the Theft of American Intellectual Property, "The IP Commission Report," National Bureau of Asian Research, May 2013.

[10] G. Greenwald, *No Place to Hide: Edward Snowden, the NSA, and the U.S. Surveillance State*. Metropolitan Books, 2014.

[11] Internet Crime Complaint Center, "2013 Internet Crime Report," Federal Bureau of Investigation, 2013.

[12] BMI, "Polizeiliche Kriminalstatistik 2013," Bundesministerium des Innern, Berlin, 2013.

[13] International Organization for Standardization (ISO), Ed., *ISO 31000:2009 Risk management - Principles and guidelines*. ISO, Geneva, Switzerland, 2009.

[14] ISO International Organization of Standardization, *ISO/IEC 27005 - Information technology -- Security techniques -- Information security risk management*. 2011.

[15] BSI, "IT-Grundschutz-catalogues 13th version 2013," Bundesamt für Sicherheit in der Informationstechnik - Federal Office for Information Security, Bonn, Germany, 2013.

[16] International Standards Organization (ISO), *IEC 27004: 2009 Information Technology - Security Techniques - Information Security Management - Measurement*. Geneva, Switzerland: ISO, 2009.

[17] Federal Ministry for Transport, Innovation and Technology (BMVIT) and Austrian Research Promotion Agency (FFG), "KIRAS Security Research: MetaRisk," 2016. [Online]. Available: http://www.kiras.at/. [Accessed: 17-Feb-2016].

[18] T. Schaberreiter, "A Bayesian Network Based On-line Risk Prediction Framework for Interdependent Critical Infrastructures," Dissertation, University of Oulu, Oulu, Finlande, 2013.

[19] Chartis Research, "Looking fo Risk. Applying Graph Analytics to Risk Management. Leading practices from YarcData," 2013.

[20] S. Schiebeck, "An Approach to Continuous Information Security Risk Assessment focused on Security Measurements," Dissertation, University of Vienna, Wien, 2014.

[21] B. Williams and R. Hummelbrunner, *Systems concepts in action: a practitioner's toolkit*. Stanford University Press, 2010.

[22] S. Radeschütz, H. Schwarz, and F. Niedermann, "Business impact analysis—a framework for a comprehensive analysis and optimization of business processes," *Comput. Sci.-Res. Dev.*, vol. 30, no. 1, pp. 69–86, 2015.

[23] J. Göllner, T. Benesch, S. Schauer, K. Schuch, S. Schiebeck, G. Quirchmayr, M. Latzenhofer, and A. Peer, "Framework for a Generic Meta Organisational Model," in *Abstract Proceedings for the 14th FRAP Conference - Oxford*, Oxford, United Kingdom, 2014.

[24] R. McCrie, *Security operations management*. Butterworth-Heinemann, 2015.

[25] Neo4j Graph Database, "Intro to Cypher - Neo4j Graph Database." [Online]. Available: http://neo4j.com/developer/cypher-query-language/. [Accessed: 25-Mar-2015].

[26] R.-G. Urma and A. Mycroft, "Source-code queries with graph databases—with application to programming language usage and evolution," *Sci. Comput. Program.*, vol. 97, pp. 127–134, Jan. 2015.

[27] C. Batra and C. Tyagi, "Comparative Analysis of Relational And Graph Databases," *Int. J. Soft Comput. Eng.*, vol. 2, no. 2, pp. 509–512, May 2012.

[28] C. T. Have and L. J. Jensen, "Are graph databases ready for bioinformatics?," *Bioinformatics*, vol. 29, no. 24, pp. 3107–3108, Dec. 2013.

[29] ISACA, "COBIT 5 - Enabling Processes," Rolling Meadows, Illinois, 2012.

[30] T. UcedaVelez and M. M. Morana, *Risk Centric Threat Modeling: Process for Attack Simulation and Threat Analysis*. John Wiley & Sons, 2015.

[31] C. Wang and W. A. Wulf, "Towards a Framework for Security Measurement," in *Proc. of 20th National Information Systems Security Conference*, Baltimore, Maryland, 1997.

[32] Federal Aviation Administration (FAA), Ed., "FAA System Safety Handbook." 30-Dec-2000.

Secure Vehicle-to-Infrastructure Communication: Secure Roadside Stations, Key Management, and Crypto Agility

Markus Ullmann* †, Christian Wieschebrink*, Thomas Strubbe*, and Dennis Kügler*
* Federal Office for Information Security
D-53133 Bonn, Germany
Email: {markus.ullmann christian.wieschebrink thomas.strubbe dennis.kuegler}@bsi.bund.de
† University of Applied Sciences Bonn-Rhine-Sieg
Institute for Security Research
D-53757 Sankt Augustin, Germany
Email: markus.ullmann@h-brs.de

***Abstract*—With the rising interest in vehicular communication systems many proposals for secure vehicle-to-vehicle communication were made in recent years. Also, several standardization activities concerning the security and privacy measures in these communication systems were initiated in Europe and in US. Here, we discuss some limitations for secure vehicle-to-infrastructure communication in the existing standards of the European Telecommunications Standards Institute. Next, a vulnerability analysis for roadside stations on one side and security and privacy requirements for roadside stations on the other side are given. Afterwards, a proposal for a multi-domain public key architecture for intelligent transport systems, which considers the necessities of road infrastructure authorities and vehicle manufacturers, is introduced. The domains of the public key infrastructure are cryptographically linked based on local trust lists. In addition, a crypto agility concept is suggested, which takes adaptation of key length and cryptographic algorithms during PKI operation into account.**

Keywords*–*Vehicular Ad hoc Networks; Vehicle-to-Vehicle Communication; Vehicle-to-Infrastructure Communication; Intelligent Transport System; Public Key Infrastructure

I. Introduction

Vehicle-to-vehicle (V2V) and vehicle-to-infrastructure communication (V2I) (consolidated V2X) has been discussed intensively in recent years. To specify use cases and prepare the necessary standardizations for the V2X communication, the Car2Car Communication Consortium was initiated by European vehicle manufacturers, equipment suppliers, research organisations and other partners.

The wireless communication technology for cooperative V2X communication is based on the IEEE 802.11p standard. A frequency spectrum in the 5.9 GHz range has been allocated on a harmonized basis in Europe in line with similar allocations in US. The neccessary specification and standardization in Europe is done by the European Telecommunications Standards Institute (ETSI). This includes the security standardization as well.

The ETSI standards for intelligent transport systems (ITS) specify a basis set of applications, like emergency vehicle warning, traffic light optimal speed advisory or co-operative local services (e.g., automatic access control and parking management). Different types of messages are defined for information exchange to support these use cases (see Section III). According the ETSI specifications messages shall be digitally signed by the sender (vehicles or roadside stations) to guarantee message integrity and authenticity. In order to issue and authenticate the corresponding cryptographic keys a suitable public key infrastructure (PKI) has to be established.

A first analysis of the current ETSI specifications and a proposal for a PKI, which regards the needs of infrastructure authorities and vehicle manufacturer was given in [1].

The first milestone in applying this technology in a realistic setting was the SimTD project with more than 100 vehicles equipped with V2V communication technology in the Frankfurt area in Germany in 2012 and 2013, see [2]. In a next step, the V2X technology will be deployed in large scale intelligent mobility infrastructure projects, for example, SCOOP@F [3] in France and the C-ITS corridor Rotterdam-Frankfurt-Vienna [4]. The main objective of the C-ITS corridor project is to increase road safety and provide the basis for an improved traffic flow.

In the C-ITS project roads work warning trailers are equipped with a digital gateway (RWWG) to communicate with the bypassing vehicles.

Two services are planned in the C-ITS corridor project:

- Send warning information via the road works warning gateway to the vehicles within the radio range. This message can be displayed in the infotainment device of the vehicle to inform the driver about the existing road works. So, the driver will be informed about the existing road works much earlier than today.
- Collect short range messages of bypassing vehicles by the RWWG to establish a traffic situation overview.

The purpose of the SCOOP@F project is to enhance the road safety and the travel quality. Therefore, five tests sites are established (e.g., Paris-Strasbourg highway, Bordeaux and its by-pass road) to examine V2X communication and to evaluate new services. In this project 3000 vehicles and 2000 km of streets will be equipped with ITS communication technology. This communication infrastructure facilitates the communication between vehicles and roadside stations to exchange

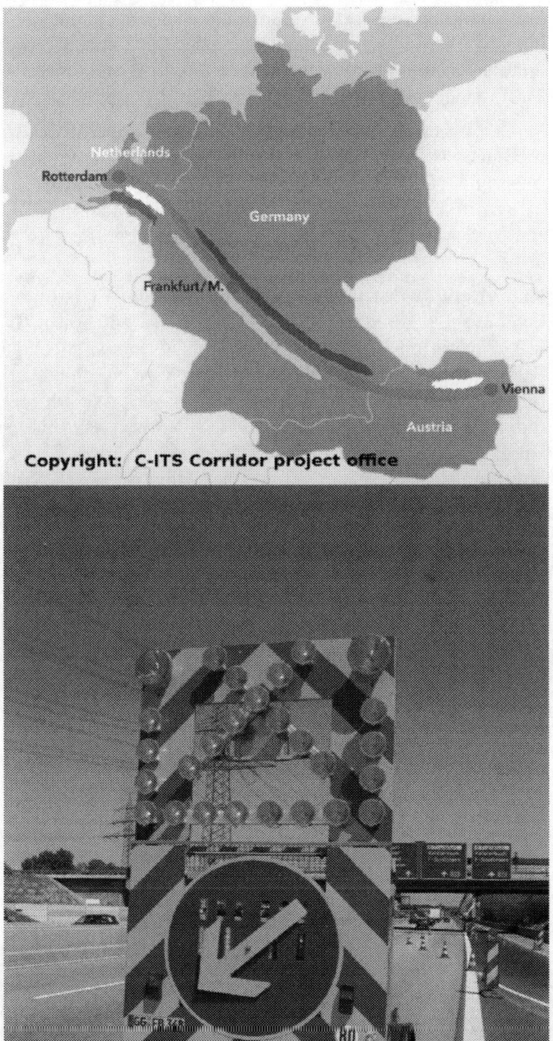

Figure 1. Road works warning trailer with digital road works warning gateway to communicate with the bypassing vehicles within the motorway C-ITS corridor Rotterdam-Frankfurt-Vienna

information. Vehicles communicate their geographic position, speed, obstacles, etc. while ITS roadside stations broadcast information concerning traffic conditions, works, speed limit, etc.

These projects mark only the very beginning of ITS technology deployment in Europe. Further plans like the integration of V2X gateways in roadside emergency telephones, sign gantries, etc. are already made.

The establishment of exhaustive V2X communication requires that existing physical infrastructure components (road works warning, road signs, lights, emergy telephones, etc.) are replaced by digitalized versions or upgraded with ITS communication gateways. However, ITS roadside stations (IRS) are often located in untrusted environments. If no effective security measures are taken physical manipulation of IRS in order to distribute false messages is easy. Therefore, the question arises which attacks are conceivable and which security measures has to be chosen so that vehicles can trust messages originating from ITS roadside stations. The importance of trust in V2X messages of ITS roadside stations will increase over time especially if automated vehicles will use the electronic information for vehicle control (e.g., adapt vehicle speed according to traffic light state).

In this paper, we regard the secure V2X communication especially from an infrastructure perspective. We identify measures that are needed so that a vehicle can trust V2X messages sent by ITS roadside stations. Therefore, we present results of a risk analysis for ITS roadside stations and derive security requirements. The security requirements adress the architecture of an IRS as well as the key management. Due to the specified usage of asymmetric cryptography (digital signature algorithms) a public key infrastructure is required. A number of practical considerations has to be taken into account when designing such a PKI.

- Many different stakeholders like vehicle manufacturers, transportation infrastructure authorities, etc. participate in ITS, especially in multi-national (e.g., European) systems. The PKI should provide flexibility to support different operators managing the vehicles and ITS roadside stations in their respective responsibilities.
- Requirements on cryptographic algorithms, domain parameters, key lengths, etc. may change over time due to new weaknesses and attacks or the increase of computer performance. In general, this means that a PKI needs a crypto agility concept to switch to a new cryptographic setting during its (possibly long) lifetime.
- Revocation of certificates and distribution of certificate revocation lists in time to all entities may turn out to be challenging in complex ITS scenarios. A simple alternative should be used to avoid distribution of certificate revocation lists.

Moreover, we introduce a multi-domain PKI for intelligent transport systems based on Local Trust Lists (LTL). This concept considers a PKI domain for vehicles (ITS vehicle stations) and different PKI domains for infrastructure components (ITS roadside stations). A PKI domain for ITS roadside stations is slightly different from the PKI concept proposed by [5]. Our approach guarantees that the infrastructure components remain under control of the particular infrastructure authority. In the ITS literature certification authorities are termed very different. Due to ongoing and trend-setting work of the security working group of the C-ITS platform we will use the naming conventions of this group. Certification authorities, which issue long term valid certificates are termed Enrolement Authority (EA). Certification authorities, which issue credential - or pseudonymous certificates are termed Authorization Authority (AA).

The PKI for ITS roadside stations (IRS PKI) is interoperable with the PKI for vehicles (IVS PKI). The IRS PKI for ITS roadside stations consists of two parts: an Enrolement Authority (EA) for issuing certificates for the identification of IRS gateways and an Authorization Authority (AA) for issuing authorization certificates to IRS gateways. With the

AA we take the hostile environment of IRS gateways into account. Although a PKI alone can not prevent local attacks on ITS roadside stations, it can mitigate their effects to a certain degree.

Our PKI proposal for ITS roadside stations supports cryptographic agility in the sense that modifications of cryptographic keys and algorithms during lifetime of the PKI are possible.

Finally, we derive necessary modifications of the existing ETSI certificate format [6] to be compatible to our concept because mechanisms for the delegation of rights and a crypto agility approach are missing to date. Here, we address only modifications to the ETSI certificate format, which are motivated from an infrastructure perspective.

The following sections are organized as follows: Section II is a description of related work. Section III provides a brief overview of the secure V2V communication specified in the according ETSI standards. Also, the suggested PKI architecture for ITS vehicle stations (IVS PKI), specified in [5], is described. Here, we state the problems if this IVS PKI is used for issuing certificates for IRS gateways, too. Security and privacy requirements for ITS roadside stations are given in Section IV. In the next Section V, the multi-domain PKI approach, the PKI concept for IRS gateways and the crypto agility proposal are introduced. Finally, in Section VI we summarize our results.

II. Related Work

Security and privacy issues in vehicular ad-hoc networks (VANETs) are addressed in many research papers. A detailed overview of attacks in VANETs is given by Ghassan Samara et al. in [7]. A security and privacy architecture for pseudonymous message signing is described in [8]. Here, a public key infrastructure is regarded, too. In [9], Julien Freudiger et al. suggested mix zones for location privacy in vehicular networks. Giorgio Calandriello et al. propose on-board, on-the-fly pseudonym certificate generation and self-certification. The authors developed this approach to alleviate one of the most significant limitations of the pseudonym-based approach: the need for complex management. To achieve this, the use of group signatures is proposed. Panagiotis Papadimitratos reports the research status of secure vehicular communication in the year 2008 [10]. Ma Di and Gene Tsusik give an overview about security and privacy in emerging wireless networks including VANETs [11]. Overall, a good overview concerning security and privacy in V2X communication can be found in [12].

More technical research results are archieved in public co-founded research projects. Here, we mention EVIVA [13] and OVERSEE [14], both co-founded by the european union. EVIVA addresses secure in-vehicle communication whereas the main objectives of the OVERSEE platform are techniques for strong isolation between independent applications to ensure that vehicle functionality and safety cannot be harmed by any other application.

A detailed analysis of privacy requirements and a comparison with the security requirements in VANETs is given in [15]. Further security and privacy concepts are presented in [16], [17], [18], [19], and [20]. Wiedersheim et al. [21] analyzed the location privacy in a specific communication scenario. Vehicles send beacon messages periodically. The beacons only carry the geographic position and an identifier. To support location privacy, the vehicles use pseudonymous identifier that are changed regularly. Assuming a passive attacker who is able to eavesdrop the communication in a specific region the attacker is able to track the vehicles with an accuracy of almost 100% if he uses the approach in [21].

A first analysis of vehicular data in cooperative awareness messages (CAM) and dezentralized environmental notification messages (DENM) messages like geographic position, speed, etc. from a data protection perspective is given in [22]. In this report CAM and DENM messages are regarded as *personal data*.

Different trust models for multi-domain PKIs on a generic level are described in [23], [24]. Here, we will follow the naming convention of [24]. It distinguishes between end entities (EE), that are subject of a certificate, Certification Authorities (CAs), that issue certificates, and root CAs, which are on top of a hierarchy of CAs. In [5] Norbert Bissmeyer et al. suggest a PKI for securing V2X communication. The Car2Car communication consortium adopted this proposal. We outline this IVS PKI in the following section.

III. Brief Overview on Secure V2X Communication

A. Communication

First, the ETSI specifications define a basic set of applications for ITS, like

- Active road safety (e.g., emergency vehicle warning, slow vehicle indication),
- Co-operative traffic effiency (e.g., regular speed, limits notification),
- Co-operative local services (e.g., automatic access control and parking management), and
- Global internet services (e.g., fleet management, loading zone management).

ITS applications are distributed among ITS stations that can be equipped with multiple communication capabilities. To date for V2X only broadcast communication based on IEEE 802.11p is provided. So, V2X is a short range communication technology with a communication range of about 600 m in open space.

The ETSI ITS architecture [25] distinguishes 4 different ITS roles termed ITS station types:

- ITS roadside stations, typically termed road side unit (RSU),
- ITS vehicle stations,
- ITS central stations, e.g., traffic operator or service provider, and
- ITS personal stations, e.g., a handheld device of a cyclist or pedestrian such as a smart phone.

The ITS stations exchange information mainly based on two different specified message types:

- Cooperative Awareness Message (CAM), and
- Dezentralized Environmental Notification Message (DENM).

CAMs are comparable with beacon messages. They are broadcasted periodically with a packet generation rate of 1 to

Complete Message			
	Header		Signer_Info
			Generation_Time
			its_aid ITS-AID for CAM
	CAM Information	Basis Container	ITS-Station Type
			Last Geographic Position
		High Frequency Container	Speed
			Driving Direction
			Longitudinal Acceleration
			Curvature
			Vehicle Length
			Vehicle Width
			Steering Angle
			Lane Number
			...
		Low Frequency Container	Vehicle Role
			Lights
			Trajectory
		Special Container	Emergency
			Police
			Fire Service
			Road Works
			Dangerous Goods
			Safety Car
			...
	Signature		ECDSA Signature of this Message
	Certificate		According Certificate for Signature Verification

Figure 2. Examplary message format of a CAM. The CAM consists of a header, different data containers, e.g., the basis container, a signature and the appropriate certificate

Complete Message			
	Header		Signer_Info
			Generation_Time
			its_aid ITS-AID for DENM
	DENM Information	Management Container	Last Vehicle Position (GPS)
			Event Identifier
			Time of Detection
			Time of Message Transmission
			Event Position (GPS)
			Validity Period
			Station Type (Motor Cycle, Vehicle, Truck)
			Message Update / Removal
			Relevant Local Message Area (geographic)
			Traffic Direction (forward, backwards, both)
			Transmission Interval
			....
		Situation Container	Information Quality (low -high, tbd)
			Event Type (Number)
			Linked Events
			Event Route (geographical)
		Location Container	Event Path
			Event Speed
			Event Direction
			Road Type
		A la carte Container	Road Works (Speed Limit, Lane Blockage....)
			....
	Signature		ECDSA Signature of this message
	Certificate		According Certificate for Signature Verification

Figure 3. Examplary message format of a DENM. The DENM consists of a header, different data containers, e.g., the management container, a signature and the appropriate certificate.

10 Hz. Based on received CAM messages, ITS vehicle stations can calculate a local dynamic traffic map of their environment. It is not planned to forward CAM messages hop-to-hop. Figure 2 illustrates the structure of a CAM. The CAM is specified in detail in [26].

In contrast, the second message type, DENM, is event-driven and indicate a specific safety situation, e.g., road works warning (from an ITS roadside station) or a damaged vehicle warning (from an ITS vehicle station). The DENM message format is specified in detail in [27]. DENM messages can be transmitted hop-by-hop. RWWGs in the C-ITS project transmit DENM messages. Figure 3 illustrates the structure of a DENM.

B. Security and Privacy Architecture for Secure V2V Communication

*1) **Security**:* The designed security architecture [5] fulfills following security requirements:

1) Entity authentication: For entity authentication, each vehicular gateway has to be equipped with a *long term valid key pair* (secret key and corresponding public key E_{PK}) and a corresponding *long term valid certificate* E_{cert}. The key pair is generated at the gateway and the long term valid certificate E_{cert} is issued to a vehicle by the so called Enrolement Authority (EA) at the beginning of the vehicle's lifetime. The EA is part of the PKI described below. For the signatures ECDSA based on the NIST P-256 elliptic curve is applied. Certificates have to be structured according the defined ETSI format, see [6]. The validity period of a E_{cert} is not specified to date. That is to be specified within the common ITS PKI policy, which is in progress. Its final version is planned for publication in autumn 2016.
2) Message integrity and authentication: To realize message integrity and authentication the CAMs and DENMs are digitally signed using ECDSA, see Figures 2 and 3.
3) Message freshness and location protection: Assuming that ITS stations know their genuine geographic position and genuine current time they can detect replayed messages, because the geographic position and the transmission time are part of CAMs and DENMs.

Long term certificates and pseudonymous certificates are implemented based on the ETSI certificate format [6]. This certificate format was designed for the automotive domain and is still not widely applied yet. Primary design principle is shortness of the certificate format due to the necessary transmission over the wireless IEEE 802.11p channel.

*2) **Privacy**:* CAMs and DENMs should not reveal the identity of the vehicle (sender anonymity). Furthermore, it should not be possible to link messages of a vehicle (message unlinkability) over a longer period of time. Both requirements shall be sufficient to assure location privacy of the vehicle and his driver. Due to these privacy requirements, CAMs and DENMs are signed using pseudonymous certificates, which are not linked to an ITS vehicle station. Moreover, the used key and the according certificates are changed periodically. Therefore, an ITS vehicle station needs a set of pseudonymous certificates valid for some period of time. The set size and the pseudonym change frequency are not specified in [5] and will also be specified within the common ITS PKI policy.

An Authorization Authority (AA) is responsible for the

issuing of pseudonymous certificates ($A_{cert_1}, \ldots, A_{cert_N}$) to the vehicles. Pseudonymous certificates will only be issued to authenticated vehicles.

AA and EA operate under a root CA called ITS vehicle station root CA (IVS-RCA). To date, following revocation operations are provided: revocation of an EA and AA authorization certificate and revocation of vehicular long term certificates E_{cert}. The architecture of the IVS PKI domain is shown in Figure 4.

*3) **Shortcomings of this approach**:* As mentioned above the ETSI certificate format provides only elliptic curve cryptography based on the NIST prime curve P-256, [28]. No mechanism is provided to securely adapt key length or ECC domain parameter or cryptographic algorithms if necessary. In the meantime, the US National Security Agency (NSA) does not recommend to use this elliptic curve any more, [29].

Unfortunately, no detailed argumentation on this issue, only a hint of needed quantum resistant algorithms in a not too distant future, is given by NSA. N. Koblitz and A. Menezes attempt an evaluation of the various theories, speculations, and interpretations that have been proposed for this sudden change of course by the NSA [30].

The discussion shows that a crypto agility concept also for V2X communication is required.

In the final report of the C-ITS platform of the European Commission the data elements of CAM and DENM messages are rated as *personal data*, see [22]. This means, each vehicle broadcasts periodically with its CAMs digitally signed private data. Shortly spoken, each vehicle leaves a signed location trace. Every entity within the communication range can receive the data.

From our point of view, the pseudonym concept does not solve the vehicular privacy requirements. However, a detailed description of the V2V privacy problem is outside of the scope of this paper.

C. Using the IVS PKI for IRS Roadside Stations

The IVS PKI domain shown in Figure 4 has been proposed for issuing certificates to IRS gateways as well [5]. However, security and privacy requirements for vehicles and infrastructure components are not necessarily identical. In contrast to ITS vehicle stations, ITS roadside stations (road works warning, traffic lights, etc.) do not involve persons during operation comparable to a motorist. Usually, they operate without any human supervision. That is the reason that from our point of view, IRS gateways do not have to regard any privacy concerns. More details are given to this issue in Section IV-C. As consequence, IRS gateways do not really need a set of valid pseudonymous certificates at each time as it is designed for vehicles. Instead, we propose that IRS gateways need only one *Authorization Certificate* with a specific subject name identifying the IRS for each time frame. Due to the security considerations for IRS gateways, see Section IV-B, the validity period of authorization certificates for ITS roadside stations should be rather short. This means the requirements for certificates for vehicles and roadside stations are different.

Moreover, arising security weaknesses of the used security technology may be asessed differently by vehicle manufacturers on one side and infrastructure authorities on the other side. However, the rules of operation for a PKI domain are defined

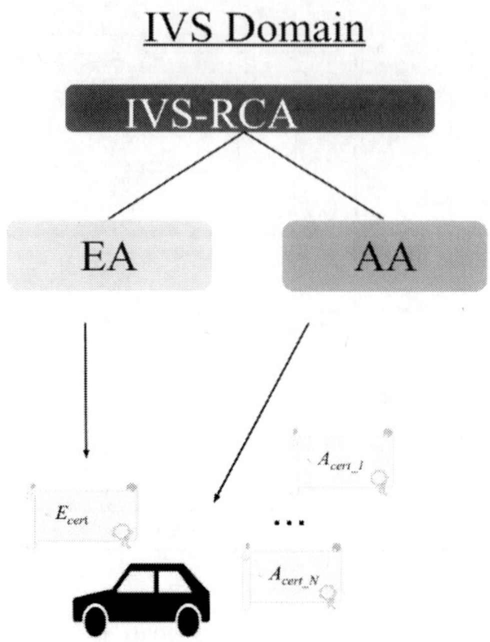

Figure 4. IVS PKI architecture promoted by the car2car communication consortium for ITS vehicle stations. This PKI consists of the Root Certification Authority (IVS-RCA), the Enrolement Authority (EA) and the Authorization Authority (AA)

in a single PKI policy, which will be specified by the root certification authority. For this reason, we propose a multi-domain PKI architecture: individual ITS PKIs under control of infrastructure autorities and an IVS PKI under control of the vehicle manufacturers, which are cryptographically linked to each other based on local trust lists (LTLs). The purpose of local trust lists is described in Section V-D.

So, each individual PKI domain can specify its own PKI policy for their specific needs. In addition, this multi-domain PKI architecture ensures that IRS unit gateways remain under control of the particular infrastructure authority. The idea of the common ITS PKI policy in progress in the security working group of the C-ITS platform of the EC DG MOVE is that individual PKI requirements can be specified in *Certificate Practise Statements*.

The concept of a multi-domain PKI architecture without any superior root CA is not new and already mentioned in [24]. It has been applied globally for electronic passports for many years. Here, each country operates its own root certification authority and has its own local trust list. The different national root certification authorities are cryptographically linked based on local trust lists. This concept works quite well and seems to be a good architecture approach for intelligent transport systems, too. The benefit of this approach is the possibility to configure PKI domains as needed. A drawback of the multi-domain PKI concept based on local trust lists is that each

PKI domain has to securely mange is own LTL. More details concerning this issue can be found in Section V-C.

IV. Security - and Privacy Requirements for ITS Roadside Stations

A. Vulnerability Analysis

In this section, we give a brief vulnerability analysis and formulate some security requirements for ITS roadside stations. When analysing possible threats to an IRS the operational environment has to be taken into account. Different types of ITS roadside stations operate in different environments with different degrees of trustworthiness. For example, one may assume that when a roadworks warning gateway is deployed at a construction site it is more or less under constant supervision of the (trustworthy) roadworks personnel. On the other hand, an IRS attached to traffic lights may be located in an unsupervised environment. In consequence, a traffic lights IRS may be subject to stronger attacks like hardware manipulation and thereby must match stronger security requirements. In the following, we take the conservative viewpoint and consider a hostile environment.

In [31], several threats towards vehicles and ITS roadside stations are analysed and corresponding (abstract) countermeasures are proposed. Summarizing the most important points of [31] (and somewhat extending the analysis), starting from the generic security goals availability, authenticity, integrity and confidentiality the following threats targeted at ITS roadside stations can be identified. The security goals may refer to incoming or outgoing messages.

- Threats to availability
  - jamming,
  - injection of a large number of forged or replayed messages.
- Threats to authenticity
  - masquerading (for example, as an legitimate IRS),
  - injection of forged messages or other data.
- Threats to integrity
  - injection of forged messages or other data,
  - altering of messages previously sent by vehicles,
  - replay of messages,
  - spoofing of GNSS information (or other sensor data),
  - spoofing time information.
- Threats to confidentiality
  - extraction of sensitive information (for example, cryptographic keys or other management data).

Attacks can either be facilitated locally or remotely. For example, forged messages can be either be transmitted via the wireless interface or they can be injected via some hardware interface at the IRS. Depending on the operational environment of the IRS both attack locations have to be accounted for.

In the setting of ITS applications the data sent out by an IRS is generally not considered confidential since it is intended to be used by any traffic participant. (As seen above from the perspective of data protection however the identity of vehicles or at least motorist is considered sensitive information.) On the other hand some cryptographic key material like signature keys stored on an IRS must remain confidential.

When implementing cryptographic mechanisms, these have to protected themselves in particular when considering a local attacker. For example, the keys for signing outgoing messages have to be stored in such a manner that they cannot be extracted since otherwise it can used by an attacker to masquerade as a legitimate IRS and to forge outgoing messages. Furthermore, it should not be possible to circumvent integrity and authenticity checks on an IRS.

More generally, an important factor to ensure the above security requirements is correct implementation. It should not be possible to introduce false traffic data or extract secret keys by exploiting weaknesses in the software (including the operating system) or hardware. In particular, it has to prevented that malicious software is installed on an IRS (for example, by an unprotected update procedure).

Cryptographic mechanisms themselves can be abused to facilitate denial of service attacks. For example, digital signatures require considerable computational effort for verification. An attacker (without the signing key) could produce and send out a large number of correctly formatted messages containing incorrect signatures. While checking these signatures the IRS may be unable to verify messages from legitimate senders.

As shown in [32], with some effort it is possible to simulate the signal of a Global Navigation Satellite System (GNSS) such that a wrong location is determined. This threatens the integrity of the data transmitted by an IRS. A wrong location of a roadworks site may be announced for example. It the GNSS signal is used to adjust the internal clock wrong time information may also be introduced. This can be possibly used by an attacker to mount replay attacks where old (already sent) messages are then accepted by the IRS.

B. Security Requirements

In addition to the security requirements in Section III-B the following security requirements are derived from the above vulnerability analysis.

- Since IRS possibly are located in hostile environments they should be equipped only with time restricted authorization to limit the timeframe for possible misuse.
- In order to protect secret key material the use of a secure hardware element is proposed. This secure element is hardened against side-channel and invasive attacks so that key extraction becomes very difficult. Secret key material is generated on this device.
- Only authentic and integrity protected (i.e., signed) software or firmware updates shall be accepted by the IRS.

Of course the connection of the IRS to the back-end system also has to be protected in particular regarding authenticity and integrity.

Attacks on the availability can be mitigated to some extent by non-cryptographic means. For example, jamming can be impeded by spread spectrum techniques like frequency hopping [33]. In order to mitigate attacks exploiting the computational overhead of cryptographics mechanisms fast implementations in particular of the signature verification algorithm are required.

To counter GNSS attacks on ITS roadside stations the geographic location of IRS with a fixed geographic location should be statically coded. Also, for time synchronization a secure alternative to GNSS time synchronization should be used.

The analysis given here should only be considered as a starting point for more detailed security assessments for different types of ITS roadside stations. Security requirements for IRS gateways should be carefully specified in depth, e.g., in form of a Protection Profile (PP) according to Common Criteria.

If IRS gateways are verifiably resistant to active attacks they can play an import role as separate trust anchors in a cooperative ITS system, e.g., for implementing secure time synchronization, distribution of CRLs, etc.

C. *Privacy Requirements*

Current vehicles are controlled by the driver. Due to this issue, privacy concerns have to be regarded by the vehicular broadcast communication. In contrast to vehicles, ITS roadside stations are not directly controlled by a user. They operate without any direct personal reference. So, during the sending of messages of an IRS no personal data is revealed. Therefore, no privacy requirements are needed.

But if ITS roadside stations receive and process vehicular CAMs and DENMs privacy requirements may have to be fulfilled because vehicular CAMs and DENMs are regarded as personal data, see [22].

The main privacy requirement is to erase the personal reference of the data on the ITS roadside station immediately after the reception of it. If some use cases have to transmit data from ITS roadside stations to traffic control center, only anonymized data should be send, e.g., realized by data aggregation. Following this main requirement, we can isolate the privacy problem on ITS roadside stations and do not regard backend systems as well. If some use cases require the storage of CAM respective DENM messages on an IRS, e.g., to calculate a traffic situation overview, the stored data should be erased immediately after the processing of the data.

V. IRS PKI CONCEPT

A. *Role of Authorization Certificates for ITS Roadside Stations*

The primary use case for IRS gateways is the transmission of local traffic information. Due to integrity and authenticity reasons, these messages have to be signed. Therefore, the IRS gateways need signature keys and according certificates. ITS roadside stations do not have to regard any privacy concerns, as explained in Section IV-C. Technically, this means that IRS gateways do not have to have pseudonymous keys and certificates. Instead, we propose that IRS gateways have only one valid authorization key pair and one corresponding authorization certificate at a time. Only in the transition phase between two certificate validity periods an IRS gateway two valid authorization certificates $C_{cert_{N-1}}$ and C_{cert_N} may be necessary.

The IRS gateway should be implemented in such a way that it acts in his designated role and transmits DENM messages only if it owns a valid authorization certificate. By this a possible misuse of IRS gateways is made more difficult.

B. *IRS PKI Architecture*

As mentioned above, we propose that ITS roadside stations have only one authorization key pair and one corresponding authorization certificate A_{cert} at each time. The secret key corresponding to such a A_{cert} is used for signing outgoing messages, e.g., DENM messages. For this reason, these certificates have to be implemented according to the ETSI certificate format. Since it is technically challenging to distribute certificate revocation lists (CRLs) to vehicles in time, authorization certificates should have a short validity period, for example, one day. Thereby implicit revocation of A_{cert} becomes possible by not issuing new authorization certificates to IRS gateways. The exact validity period of authorization certificates have to be specified according to a detailed risk assessment concerning the addressed IRS type. For example, RWWG are deployed for road works sites, which are usually established for one or two days. It may be good practice then to issue an authorization certificate with a maximal validity period of two days to a RWWG shortly before it is deployed.

For authentication purposes, e.g., to obtain authorization certificates (for example, on a daily basis) an infrastructure component requires a long term identification certificate E_{cert}. These long term certificates E_{cert} are issued by an Enrolement Authority (EA) during the enrolment of the IRS gateway. A long term certificate E_{cert} is used within a certificate request for authorization certificates towards the AA. We suggest that the authorization key pair is generated within the secure element of the IRS gateway and the authorization certificate is only issued after mutual authentication of IRS gateway and AA and only if the E_{cert} of the IRS gateway is not revoked. Therefore, the EA has to maintain a CRL for revoked long term certificates E_{cert}.

A long term identification certificate E_{cert} is only visible inside the IRS PKI and is not transmitted to vehicles. In particular, it is not communicated over the IEEE 802.11p channel. For this reason, we suggest to implement the long term identification certificates E_{cert} of ITS roadside stations according to the X.509 v3 certificate profile. This profile is widely applied and provides all necessary certificate services like time stamping, issuing CRLs, etc. The validity period of a E_{cert} should be at the order of years, e.g., five to six years for IRS gateways like RWWGs. A timeframe of five to six years seems to be reasonable considering progress in cryptanalysis or hardware security vulnerabilities. Due to different certificate issuing policies and certificate formats the EAs and the AAs are attached to different root certification authorities, which are called E-RCA and A-RCA respectively here, see Figure 5.

Due to the long validity periods of long term certificates, certificate revocation, implemented as a CRL according to X.509 v3, is suggested. Once a long term certificate is revoked, no authorization certificates are issued to the IRS gateway any more.

Due to the short validity period of authorization certificates of IRS gateways, the IRS gateways require an online communication channel, e.g., via GSM, LTE, etc. to receive new authorization certificates.

C. *Crypto Agility*

Figure 6 shows how the validity periods of the certificates within the IRS PKI domain relate to each other. The validity

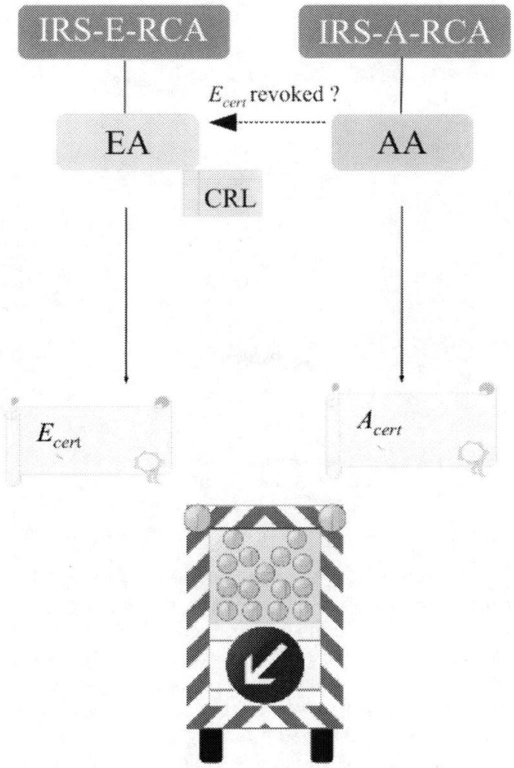

Figure 5. IRS PKI domain architecture. An IRS PKI domain consists of an EA for issuing long term certificates E_{cert} and an AA for issuing authorization certificates A_{cert}.

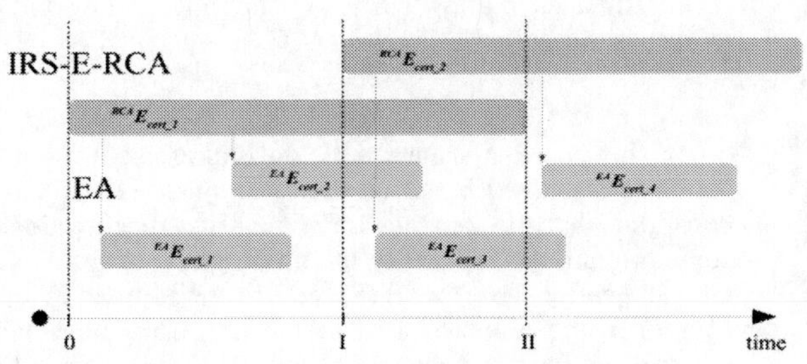

Figure 6. Certificate shell model. The validity period of a certificate is within the validity period of the issuing Certification Authority. E.g., the validity period of ${}^{EA}E_{cert\_1}$ is within the validity period of ${}^{RCA}E_{cert\_1}$

periods follow the shell model, i.e., the validity periods of certificates are enclosed in the validity periods of superior certificates.

1) A certificate of a certification authority (CA) is in one of three states: *active*, *passive* or *expired*. After generation of a key pair the according certificate is in state *active*. Over time the certificate state changes from *active* to *passive* to *expired*.
2) A certificate in state *active* is used for issuing certificates to subordinate CAs or IRS gateways.
   - Assume that an IRS-E-RCA root key pair (secret key: ${}^{RCA}E_{SK\_1}$, public key: ${}^{RCA}E_{PK\_1}$) is generated at time 0 of Figure 6. The secret key ${}^{RCA}E_{SK\_1}$ is used to sign and issue a self-certified E-RCA certificate ${}^{RCA}E_{cert\_1}$, first. The certificate ${}^{RCA}E_{cert\_1}$ is in state *active*.
   - The secret key ${}^{RCA}E_{SK\_1}$ is used to sign EA certificates: ${}^{EA}E_{cert\_1}$ and ${}^{EA}E_{cert\_2}$.
   - The certificate ${}^{RCA}E_{cert\_1}$ switches to state *passive* at time point *I* when the next root key pair (secret key: ${}^{RCA}E_{SK\_2}$, public key: ${}^{RCA}E_{PK\_2}$) and according certificate ${}^{RCA}E_{cert\_2}$ are issued. Now, the certificate ${}^{RCA}E_{cert\_2}$ is in state *active*. A certificate in state *passive* is not used to issue certificates any longer. However, it is still needed to verify already issued subordinate certificates. At time point *II* certificate ${}^{RCA}E_{cert\_1}$ expires.
3) Certificate ${}^{RCA}E_{cert\_2}$ is termed *Link Certificate* because it is signed with the former IRS-E-RCA secret key ${}^{RCA}E_{SK\_1}$.

Over long lifetimes the requirements for cryptographic mechanisms are changing. This has implications for the cryptographic mechanisms applied within the PKI domain, too. The cryptographic setting of the PKI has to be adapted according to current cryptographic requirements. All CAs in an ITS PKI have to follow the common PKI policy and the specific certificate practise statement of the root CA. Therefore, changes of a cryptographic setting for a whole IRS PKI are prescribed by the root certification authority E-RCA or A-RCA.

Changes to the following components due to newly discovered weaknesses are conceivable:

1) Elliptic curve domain parameters,
2) Hash algorithm,
3) Signature algorithm.

We suggest to implement a new PKI crypto setting by means of a link certificate, assuming that the certificate format allows the specification of cryptographic parameters. Obviously, modifications can only be applied if the infrastructure components are technically able to run the new algorithms.

The validity period of an E_{cert} and an A_{cert} differ a lot. An E_{cert} has a validity period of several years, whereas an A_{cert} has a validity period of few days at most. If the issuing certification authorities AA and IRS-A-RCA have similar short validity periods with respect to the shell model, the cryptographic settings between E_{cert} and A_{cert} can differ. In particular, shorter keys can be used for signing A_{cert}

towards signing an E_{cert}. Today, the ETSI certificate format only provides the NIST Elliptic Curve Domain Parameter P-256 with 256 bits long secret keys, see [28]. This key length is sufficient for the very near future but other ECC domain parameter should be used due to [29]. However, it is highly probable that longer key length have to be used for long term certificates E_{cert} in future.

D. Trust Establishment between PKI domains

An examplary architecture of a multi-domain PKI with three PKI domains (IRS_I, IVS and IRS_II) is shown in Figure 7. In our example there is only one IVS domain with the IVS-RCA to issue certificates for vehicles managed by the vehicle manufacturers and two separate IRS domains IRS_I and IRS_II with the root CAs A-RCA_I and A-RCA_II managed by different infrastructure authorities. These two IRS domains issue authorization certificates to IRS gateways in their respective domain. Now trust relations between the different PKI domains have to be established somehow. This can be accomplished by securely exchanging self-signed certificates of the respective root CAs of the PKI domains. Each root CA maintains a LTL containing the certificates of root CAs of other PKI domains it trusts. The LTL of a PKI domain is signed (for authentication reasons) and issued to all members of the domain by the root CA, e.g., A-RCA_I manages the LTL for the IRS_I domain. Each PKI domain can individually define the needed rules that are sufficient to trust a separate PKI domain.

To verify the authenticity of IRS gateway DENM messages in our examplary architecture, the vehicles have to know the root PKI certificates of the PKI domains IRS_I and IRS_II: ${}^{A-RCA\_I}A_{cert\_1}$ and ${}^{A-RCA\_II}A_{cert\_1}$. If the IVS PKI domain trusts in the IRS_I and IRS_II PKI domains the certificates ${}^{A-RCA\_I}A_{cert\_1}$ and ${}^{A-RCA\_II}A_{cert\_1}$ are elements of the LTL of the IVS PKI domain. Just after issuing of a new certificate, e.g., ${}^{A-RCA\_I}A_{cert\_2}$ for the infrastructure PKI domain IRS_I this certificate has to be appended to the LTL of the IVS PKI domain. Dependent on the validity period of the certificates ${}^{A-RCA\_I}A_{cert\_1}$ and ${}^{A-RCA\_I}A_{cert\_2}$ and due to the chosen shell model both certificates are valid for a defined time frame, see Figure 6. If a LTL of a PKI domain is changed all entities of the PKI domain (subordinate CAs and EEs) have to know this information. A time-critical situation arises when one specific PKI domain, e.g., the IRS_I PKI domain loses trust and has to be removed from the LTL of the IVS PKI domain. In this case all affected entities in the IVS PKI domain have to update their LTL as soon as possible.

Based on the currently discussed ITS applications, trust relations between the different ITS domains, here IRS_I and IRS_II, are not really required since no messages are exchanged between these domains. In our example the LTL of the two IRS domains just contain the current root certificate of the IVS PKI domain ${}^{RCA}E_{cert\_1}$.

E. Necessary ETSI Certificate Format Adaptations

In our paper, a multi-domain PKI based on LTLs and an according crypto agility concept is presented. The described mechanisms require some adaptation of the current ETSI certificate format.

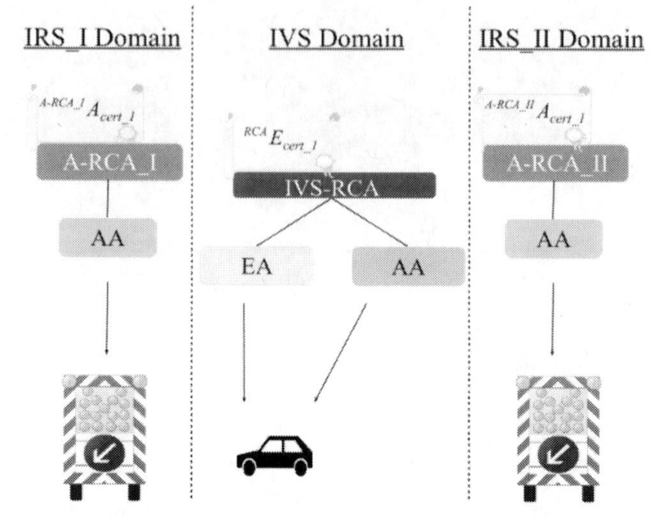

Figure 7. Examplary multi-domain PKI architecture with one IVS domain and two IRS domains: IRS_I and IRS_II.

a) Elliptic curve cryptography: The ETSI certificate format regards only Elliptic Curve Cryptography (ECC) performed on NIST domain parameters P-256. These domain parameters have a specific structure to perform ECC calculations very fast. But this structure opens specific side channel attacks. For example, even effective countermeasurements like point blinding and scalar blinding of ECC implementations are not sufficient to resist side channel attacks on NIST ECC implementations, see [34]. Therefore, further cryptographic ECC domain parameters (e.g., brainpool curves) should be added [35].

b) Rights management: Fire trucks and police vehicles need specific rights during action. These rights have to be coded within certificates, too. But only qualified CAs may issue these kind of certificates. The ETSI rights management concept should be enhanced in a sense that a subordinate CA can only assign restricted rights to issued certificates.

c) Link certificate: The ETSI certificate has to support link certificates to allow change of the root CA key and crypto agility as suggested in Section V-C.

VI. Conclusion

In this paper, a secure vehicle-to-infrastructure communication is discussed based on the existing ETSI standards. We constitute that the existing ETSI security specifications have some limitations. Especially, the missing crypto agility concept and adaptations on the ETSI certificate format are needed. Moreover, the proposed PKI of the Car2Car Communication Consortium for ITS vehicle stations (IVS PKI) does not regard all needs of ITS roadside stations. For this reason, we suggest a multi-domain PKI to adequately address the requirements of vehicle manufacturers and infrastructure authorities. The different PKI domains are cryptographically linked based on LTLs. In addition, a brief vulnerability analysis of ITS roadside stations is given.

As a next step, the IRS PKI architecture will be substantiated und implemented as a pilot system in the C-ITS corridor project to gather experiences. Beside that a common PKI policy is prepared within the security working group of the C-ITS platform of the EC DG MOVE for intelligent transportation systems in Europe. Important is that these common PKI policy enables specific requirement distinctions of PKI domains based on certificate practise statements to consider necessary differences between ITS vehicle stations and ITS roadside stations as shown in this paper.

VII. Acknowledgement

The authors would like to thank Sandro Berndt and Arno Spinner from the Federal Highway Research Institute (BASt), our colleagues Nicolas Thenée and Hans-Peter Wagner and the anonymous referees for valuable remarks. Moreover, thanks to Hessen Mobile and the C-ITS Corridor project office for providing us with photo material.

References

[1] M. Ullmann, C. Wieschebrink, and D. Kügler, "Public key infrastructure and crypto agility concept for intelligent transport systems," in Proceedings VEHICULAR 2015: The Fourth International Conference on Advances in Vehicular Systems, Technologies and Applications. IARIA, 2015, pp. 14–19.

[2] SimTD, "Secure intelligent mobility," 2008-2013, http://www.simtd.de/index.dhtml/deDE/index.html.

[3] European Commission, "SCOOP@F," 2013, http://inea.ec.europa.eu/en/ten-t.

[4] BMVI, "Cooperative its corridor rotterdam-franfurt-vienna joint deployment," 2014, http://www.bmvi.de.

[5] N. Bissmeyer, H. Stubing, E. Schoch, S. Gotz, J. P. Stotz, and B. Lonc, "A generic public key infrastructure for securing car-to-x communication," in 18th ITS World Congress, 2011.

[6] ETSI, "Intelligent Transport Systems (ITS);Security; Security header and certificate formats, ETSI TS 103 097 V1.2.1," 2015, http://www.etsi.org/.

[7] G. Samara, W. A. Al-Salihy, and R. Sures, "Security analysis of vehicular ad hoc nerworks (vanet)," in Network Applications Protocols and Services (NETAPPS), 2010 Second International Conference on. IEEE, 2010, pp. 55–60.

[8] P. Papadimitratos, L. Buttyan, J.-P. Hubaux, F. Kargl, A. Kung, and M. Raya, "Architecture for secure and private vehicular communications," in Telecommunications, 2007. ITST'07. 7th International Conference on ITS. IEEE, 2007, pp. 1–6.

[9] J. Freudiger, M. Raya, M. Félegyházi, P. Papadimitratos et al., "Mix-zones for location privacy in vehicular networks," in Proceedings of the first international workshop on wireless networking for intelligent transportation systems (Win-ITS), 2007.

[10] P. Papadimitratos and J.-P. Hubaux, "Report on the secure vehicular communications: results and challenges ahead workshop," ACM SIGMOBILE Mobile Computing and Communications Review, vol. 12, no. 2, 2008, pp. 53–64.

[11] M. DI and G. Tsudik, "Security and privacy in emerging wireless networks," IEEE Wireless Communications, 2010, p. 13.

[12] Hagen Stübing, Multilayered Security and Privacy Protection in Car-to-X Networks - Solutions from Application down to Physical Layer. Springer Vieweg, 2013.

[13] E-safety Vehicle Intrusion proTection Applications, "Scientific publications," 2009-2011, http://www.evita-project.org/publications.html/.

[14] Open Vehicular Secure Platform, "Scientific publications," 2010-2012, https://www.oversee-project.com/.

[15] F. Schaub, Z. Ma, and F. Kargl, "Privacy requirements in vehicular communication systems," in Computational Science and Engineering, 2009. CSE'09. International Conference on, vol. 3. IEEE, 2009, pp. 139–145.

[16] M. Raya and J.-P. Hubaux, "Securing vehicular ad hoc networks," Journal of Computer Security, vol. 15, no. 1, 2007, pp. 39–68.

[17] J. Camenisch, S. Hohenberger, and M. Ø. Pedersen, "Batch verification of short signatures," in Advances in Cryptology-EUROCRYPT 2007. Springer, 2007, pp. 246–263.

[18] R. Lu, X. Lin, H. Zhu, P.-H. Ho, and X. Shen, "Ecpp: Efficient conditional privacy preservation protocol for secure vehicular communications," in INFOCOM 2008. The 27th Conference on Computer Communications. IEEE, 2008.

[19] F. Armknecht, A. Festag, D. Westhoff, and K. Zeng, "Cross-layer privacy enhancement and non-repudiation in vehicular communication," in Communication in Distributed Systems (KiVS), 2007 ITG-GI Conference. VDE, 2007, pp. 1–12.

[20] K. Plößl and H. Federrath, "A privacy aware and efficient security infrastructure for vehicular ad hoc networks," Computer Standards & Interfaces, vol. 30, no. 6, 2008, pp. 390–397.

[21] B. Wiedersheim, Z. Ma, F. Kargl, and P. Papadimitratos, "Privacy in inter-vehicular networks: Why simple pseudonym change is not enough," in Wireless On-demand Network Systems and Services (WONS), 2010 Seventh International Conference on. IEEE, 2010, pp. 176–183.

[22] C-ITS Platform of the EC DG MOVE, "Final Report," 2016, http://ec.europa.eu/transport/themes/its/doc/c-its-platform-final-report-january-2016.pdf.

[23] J. Linn, "Trust models and management in public-key infrastructures," RSA laboratories, vol. 12, 2000.

[24] R. Nielsen, "Memorandum for multi-domain public key infrastructure interoperability, rfc 5217," Tech. Rep., 2008.

[25] ETSI, "ETSI EN 302 665 V1.1.1: Intelligent Transport Systems (ITS) - Communications Architecture," 2010, http://www.etsi.org/.

[26] ——, "ETSI EN 302 637-2 V1.3.2: Intelligent Transport Systems (ITS); Vehicular Communications; Basic Set of Applications; Part 2: Specification of Cooperative Awareness Basic Service," 2015, http://www.etsi.org/.

[27] ——, "ETSI TS 102 637-3 V1.2.1: Intelligent Transport Systems (ITS); Vehicular Communications; Basic Set of Applications; Part 3: Specifications of Decentralized Environmental Notification Basic Service," 2013, http://www.etsi.org/.

[28] Recommended Elliptic Curves For Federal Government Use, National Institute of Standards and Technology, July 1999. [Online]. Available: http://csrc.nist.gov/groups/ST/toolkit/documents/dss/NISTReCur.pdf

[29] National Security Agency, "Cryptography today," 2015, https://www.nsa.gov/ia/programs/suiteb_cryptography.

[30] N. Koblitz and A. Menezes, "A riddle wrapped in an enigma," Cryptology ePrint Archive, Report 2015/1018, 2015, http://eprint.iacr.org/.

[31] ETSI, "ETSI TR 102 893 V1.1.1: Intelligent Transport Systems (ITS); Security; Threat, Vulnerability and Risk Analysis (TVRA). Technical Report," 2010, http://www.etsi.org/.

[32] N. O. Tippenhauer, C. Pöpper, K. B. Rasmussen, and S. Capkun, "On the requirements for successful gps spoofing attacks," in Proceedings of the 18th ACM conference on Computer and communications security. ACM, 2011, pp. 75–86.

[33] B. Sklar, Digital Communications, Second Edition. Prentice Hall PTR, 2001.

[34] B. Feix, M. Roussellet, and A. Venelli, "Side-channel analysis on blinded regular scalar multiplications," in Progress in Cryptology–INDOCRYPT 2014. Springer, 2014, pp. 3–20.

[35] Brainpool, "ECC Brainpool Standard Curves and Curve Generation, Version 1.0, available online at http://www.ecc-brainpool.org/ecc-standard.htm," 2005.

International Academy, Research, and Industry Association (IARIA)
412 Derby Way
Wilmington, DE 19810

CURRAN ASSOCIATES INC.
proceedings.com

ISBN 978-1-5108-5625-7
9 781510 856257

6th International Symposium on Hydrogen Energy and Energy Technologies (HEET 2023)

Journal of Physics: Conference Series Volume 2723

Osaka, Japan
10-11 November 2023

Institute of Physics